The
Corporate
Communications
Bible

Also by Robert L. Dilenschneider

Power and Influence:
Mastering the Art of Persuasion

A Briefing for Leaders:
Communications as the Ultimate Exercise of Power

On Power

The Critical 14 Years of Your Professional Life

Moses: CEO: Lessons in Leadership

The Corporate Communications Bible

Everything You Need to Know
to Become a
Public Relations Expert

ROBERT L. DILENSCHNEIDER

New Millennium Press

Beverly Hills

Library of Congress Cataloging-in-Publication Data

Dilenschneider, Robert L.
  The corporate communications bible / Robert L. Dilenschneider
  p. cm.
  Includes index.
  ISBN 1-839224-08-2
  1. Business communications. 2. Public Relations. I. Title

HF5718.D58 2000
659.2--dc21   00-022262

Printed in the United States of America

New Millennium Press
A division of NM WorldMedia, Inc.
350 S. Beverly Drive, Suite 315
Beverly Hills, California 90212

www.newmillenniumpress.com

10 9 8 7 6 5 4 3 2 1

To my sister, Martha,
whose selfless contribution
has meant so much
to so many

Contents

Acknowledgments

A book of this nature, which laps into the experience, knowledge, insights, and talents of a broad range of acknowledged experts in their respective fields, owes a great deal to others. To complete this book, I received invaluable assistance from so many who have supported me throughout my career.

The Corporate Communications Bible would not have been possible without a gifted researcher like Mary Jane Genova. She worked closely with me from start to finish and I am deeply in her debt.

Of course, my wife, Jan, and our sons, Geoffrey and Peter, supplied unfailing support and encouragement throughout this project.

Reid Boates, my hardworking agent, deserves recognition for counseling me to undertake this effort.

I am likewise indebted to my friend, Michael Viner, co-president of New Millennium Press, who gave me the opportunity to present my views. And, without the tremendous toil of Shelly Kale, my senior editor, this work could not have come to fruition. Kurt Wahlner and Anita Keys provided their expertise in the design and production, respectively, of this book.

As for the book's substance, I wish to thank everyone on whose wisdom I relied, particularly: Harvey Mackay, a friend and supporter for countless years, whose keen insights have also been an inspiration to me; Chuck Rossie, one of the best in the field of crisis communications; James Hart, former public affairs chieftain with Duke Energy, who also provided numerous critical insights; and Roy Clason, one of the best public relations practitioners I know, and Kristin Ausanka, a young public relations manager with The William Carter Company, who both bring a unique perspective to their fields that I have always admired.

Karen Hendricks, who leads Baldwin Piano & Organ Company, is among the nation's top female CEOs. Her ideas and opinions about the smaller company's corporate communications and image are unfailingly on target. Carol Kinsey Goman, an employee communications consultant to many organizations, never fails to provide important guidelines for all to follow.

Finally, I would like to thank all my colleagues at The Dilenschneider Group, especially James Wieghart, Art Gormley, Ted Feurey, Bob Stone, Joel Pomerantz, Linda Smith, John Kasic, and Joan Avagliano.

Foreword

Media innovator Ted Turner certainly knows how to deliver a message. When he wanted to "put the rich on notice" that they should be giving more to good causes, he announced that he was donating one billion dollars to the United Nations. He changed TV news-viewing habits into a twenty-four-hour-a-day happening.

People like Ted Turner can shake up the status quo and make things happen because they know the basics of communication. They instinctively know when it's time for showmanship and when it's time to be wise and fatherly; when to give a longer-than-eighteen-minute speech and when to say just a few words; when to call Larry King with a hot news tip (they expect him to act on it, and he does).

Now, with Bob Dilenschneider's help, you can learn all these things communications giants do instinctively. In this book the father of big-impact public relations explains how to position and package all your messages. From his office on Park Avenue over Grand Central Station in New York City, he observes which people are winning and which are floundering when it comes to presenting themselves and their organizations in the best light. Then he turns that information into principles of public relations his clients can use. For example, if the mail clerk—the least-jaded reader in his company—laughs while reading a press release, Dilenschneider knows the press release won't work. He turned this test of whether the information is credible into the "Chuckles Test." Now he has clients apply the Chuckles Test to all their communications. So far, no one has come off sounding shifty.

There are plenty of other things Dilenschneider has observed: that leaders speak in headlines and followers speak in complex sentences; that people with a strong image fine-tune that image rather than discard it for a new one every few years; that those who run small businesses should ignore most of the marketing advice that comes their way. From these observations, he distills to us million-dollar lessons in public relations.

And it's all here. I especially found useful Chapter 11, Keeping Communications Young. When I was writing my book *Dig Your Well Before You're Thirsty,* I kept wondering if my writing was getting stale (usually when we're stale we're the last to know). So I applied Dilenschneider's Chuckles Test. I looked at the book through the least-jaded eyes and concluded (rightly) that the book had something to offer contemporary society—that I wasn't out of touch. *Business Week*'s listing of best-sellers agreed with my perception.

Another home run is Chapter 1, Media. Chuck Rossie is right on the money when he says that a news interview isn't a social conversation. Don't be led by the interviewer to feel like you're talking to your best friend on the golf course. And from Chapter 4, Oral Communications, I picked up how to ensure that there won't be one glazed-over look in the audience.

Whether you're a CEO or someone considering starting an organization to help those with bipolar disorder, this book is a gold mine. And it's a fast read. After you finish it, pass it on to those who have everything going for them—except a talent in communications. They can acquire that talent. Ability in public relations isn't necessarily genetically passed down.

Bob Dilenschneider is a generous man: He shares with you what it took him thirty years to figure out.

Harvey Mackay
January 2000

Introduction

Those seven days in September 1997—the days of mourning for Princess Diana—certainly showed the power of public relations. It was public relations that forced the royal family to abandon its aloof attitude about Diana's death into an acknowledgment of the British people's grief. Public relations also played a part in the speculation over whether Prince Charles could ever marry Camilla Parker-Bowles—the woman of his dreams. The family of Henri Paul, the driver of the car in which Princess Diana was riding at the time of the fatal car crash, used public relations to try to save his reputation. And public relations will ultimately decide how freelance photographers can make a living; how much privacy will be accorded Princes William and Harry; whether the monarchy itself will survive; and whether Britain will adopt a new image as a country of emotionally expressive people.

The power of public relations is nothing new. From the earliest times, leaders recognized that they could influence perception, which is what public relations is all about. You might say that the Old and New Testaments of the Bible are intended to create images of God and Jesus. The image of the God of the Old Testament is one of fire and brimstone; He is no one to fool around with. The image of Jesus of the New Testament is one of love and accessibility. When Queen Isabella of Spain sponsored Columbus's trip to sail to India, she was probably interested in being perceived as a "cutting-edge monarch." And some people could argue that former president George Bush really didn't want to serve another term as president of the United States—otherwise, why did he look at his watch during a nationally televised debate in the 1992 campaign? Public relations can help us achieve our goals, or it can undo us.

What *is* new about public relations is our growing awareness of its strategies and tactics. This interest has become so acute that even those

1

who never before were interested in politics now monitor how our presidents handle their many challenges; now wonder if a leader's extramarital affairs will hurt his or her chances of reelection; now devour books such as Joe McGinniss's *The Selling of the President*, Hedrick Smith's *The Power Game,* and Kathleen Hall Jamieson's *Packaging the Presidency.*

Similarly, even people with little interest in business have become fascinated with how major corporations handle problems ranging from unfriendly takeovers to tainted meat. The media coverage of the United Parcel Service workers' strike in 1997 and the ensuing "spin doctoring" and offensives conducted by both union leaders and management constituted a national pastime as popular as some sports. In *Fortune* magazine Linda Grant discussed all the public relations mistakes the UPS management made before and during the strike.[1] The Teamsters, on the other hand, were PR masters. Even though the strike inconvenienced millions of Americans, the public remained sympathetic with the strikers. The union brilliantly positioned the issue as "contract" vs. full-time work. In the wake of the union's perceived victory, executives in business and nonprofit organizations alike carefully analyzed the lessons of that strike.

In this book I discuss how any person can handle public relations for any organization or for his or her own image-building. I reveal the strategies and secrets we pros use. Much of it may sound strange to you. You may think, for example, that in getting your message across you should be creative, have numerous variations of a theme, and continually keep the audience stimulated by new and imaginative approaches. Wrong. The most successful corporations in the country— Ford Motor Co., General Electric, Coca-Cola—keep their message simple, keep it the same, and keep repeating it.

Here are some other unusual surprises you will learn in this book:

- The media are not only out for themselves. You *can* get the media on your side. And I mean *really* on your side. I know media relations representatives whose relationships are so good with reporters and producers that the media brings *them* information.

- Wall Street will never let you get away with hype—at least not for long—so don't even *think* about saying that things are much better until they really are. As we learned from Watergate, a bad situation isn't the worst sin. Trying to cover up *is*. When he spoke with security analysts during his company's comeback attempt in the late seventies, Chrysler's Lee Iacocca was very open about what was wrong with the company. And the stock kept going up.

- Employees are waiting for you to *do* something. They're probably not listening to what you *say*. Words reinforce actions—not the other way around.

- What comes out when you open your mouth, even on the elevator, is what determines whether you'll do well in the organization or get sidelined. Talking is a strategic act. If you're a blurter in these verbally buttoned-down times, you belong in nursery school with a teddy bear.

- You don't have to know a killer, be a killer, or kill a killer to break into the publishing industry. Average Joes are publishing best-sellers—and galloping past their colleagues in the profession. Print is far from dead. It's still a good ticket to success. When you feel stuck in your career, think book.

- There are no longer right answers about community and government relations. There's no longer any consensus as to whether it's a good or bad thing to support Pittsburgh's symphony orchestra or aggressively lobby Congress for fewer over-the-counter drug regulations.

- A crisis could be the best thing to happen to your organization or your career. When General Electric's CEO Jack Welch was a young manager, his plant blew up. He certainly came to the notice of the powers-that-be at the company. The rest is history. Always look upon a crisis as something you can use to advance.

- Just because you represent a noble cause like diabetes or unemployed heads-of-household, don't expect people to help you out. The "favor bank" governs good works just as it does political and corporate life. If you want to do good, figure out what to trade with—or give to—the people who assist you.

- The Oprah Winfreys of this world survive and thrive, while the Phil Donahues fall by the wayside. Why? The Oprahs know how to position and reposition themselves. Had Madonna not repositioned herself, she would have been a has-been years ago. Phil Donahue wasn't smart about how to update his act; wearing a dress just didn't do it. Positioning and repositioning are critical to all types of success.

- Your small business can get millions of dollars of free publicity if you know what you're doing and stop listening to the advice of all your friends. Small-business self-marketing has got to run on instinct.

- If you—or your communications—are getting stale, it's probably because you haven't been involved enough with the media. Turn on the tube or get on the Internet, read *Wired* or watch a video. Analyze how the media are keeping you interested. Then apply that to yourself and your own communications. There are no "old farts"; there are just human beings who've lost touch with the media.

After you read this book you'll have solid skills in media relations, investor relations, employee communications, dealing with the community and legislators, speaking on your feet, managing a crisis, getting published, orchestrating the right image, getting new (and repeat) business through shrewd public relations, and keeping yourself from being fired because you're coming across as "old."

But you'll make progress on the learning curve only if you *apply* what you learn. Suppose you own a small business. For ten years you have been the sole proprietor, grossing about ninety thousand dollars per year. Then you get a partner. The partnership starts grossing six hundred thousand dollars a year and hooks prestigious clients in the Fortune 50. After you read this book, you'll realize you have a story. And if you package that story well, you can get a lot of public relations mileage.

The first step in the process is to analyze what aspect of your story will sell. You may come up with the hook that partnership, despite all its interpersonal problems, is more lucrative than going solo; or that partnership can actually impede entrepreneurial activity; or that you know what kind of person you need to be in order to succeed as a partner. After you decide on your positioning for a story, you can:

- Call the business editor of a paper you want to influence to pitch your story—and the particular angle you're taking.

- Let the chamber of commerce know that you'd like to give a speech on this issue.

- Do some research on partnerships and write an op-ed (opinion-editorial) piece about it for a newspaper or magazine that you want to influence.

- Create a client brochure in which you explain how *your* partnership adds value to the client's business.

- Approach an agent about doing a book on the subject.

- Pull out all stops in promoting your book.

- Create audiotapes and videos about how to make a partnership work.

If you understand public relations, the world is yours. If you don't, you can end up in serious trouble. Two third-generation Kennedys ignored public relations and became poster boys for bad behavior. Former presidential adviser Dick Morris bungled his own public relations when he was discovered consorting with a prostitute.

Public relations has become the new genetic code for obtaining initial success, gaining momentum in your current career, and resurrecting a career. The unaware bumbler (like the character in an old Frank Capra movie) wouldn't last in a job or business for a month today. Now, just to survive you have to have the fundamentals of public relations—and you have to have them down cold.

Note

1. Linda Grant, "How UPS Blew It," *Fortune*, September 29, 1997, 29.

Chapter 1

Media

Normally the press is neither friendly nor hostile. They're just after the news.

—James G. Wieghart,
veteran of three decades
of work in the media and
in media relations

When I was a young man I was really struck by the idea that President Kennedy read about five or six papers a day. Naively, I assumed he did that only because he wanted to stay on top of world events. Actually, Kennedy was ahead of the curve in recognizing the importance of the media. He really understood that the media could make or break an administration. So he closely monitored reporters' interests and points of view. His press secretary, Pierre Salinger, approached just the right reporter with just the right story.

In Kennedy's case, the media helped create and sustain the image of Camelot—one of the most powerful political metaphors in history. Since then, the influence of the media has multiplied exponentially. Those who know how to work well with the media, such as media relations representative Richard Kosmicki, can get their clients billions of dollars of free publicity. And those who are inept with the media, such as President Clinton's former chief strategist Dick Morris, can get destroyed.

In this chapter you'll learn the fundamentals of working with the media—everything from announcing a new product and introducing a new CEO to correcting an error in a media article to avoiding making enemies in the media.

Point of View

Chuck Rossie, principal of the CMR Group in Woodland Hills, California, trains executives how to speak with the media. The success of an interview, Rossie says, depends on how the executive-interviewee views the media. Rossie tells his clients over and over again, "There are no hostile questions. There are questions that are presented with a hostile attitude, skepticism, or even loathing, but the question itself is just a prompt for you to say what you want to say on the topic."

If executives handle questions strategically rather than emotionally and give full, accurate answers, the interview usually goes well. The executives get the story out. But if they take the attitude that the media is out to get them, then their tone of voice, body language, and the sweat on their upper lip will convey to the media the message, "We are uneasy about being scrutinized. And we probably have something to hide."

Not the Villains

It has become fashionable to analyze the alleged flaws of the media, as James Fallows does in his muckraking book *Breaking the News: How the Media Undermine American Democracy*. But, says Lou Colasuonno, former editor with *The Daily News* and *New York Post* and now in public relations, crying "bias" doesn't get you better coverage.

Rather than trying to reform the media, you will have a better chance of positioning your company, your CEO, or your product in a positive light simply by being prepared. Have the subject you're discussing down cold. Be ready to educate the media about it in terms they can understand. Know the philosophical-political bent of particular reporters and producers. Anticipate how your audiences, from the financial community to employees, might react to your comments. Rossie helps executives prepare both what they're going to say and the manner in which they should say it.

Interview with James G. Wieghart:
An Overview of Media Relations

James G. Wieghart is a member of the media who has handled media relations for Fortune 500 executives, Senators William Proxmire and Ted Kennedy, and the Office of the Iran/Contra Independent Counsel. He has also been on the other side of the desk, handling news for *The Daily News, Scripps Howard News Service,* and the *Milwaukee Sentinel.* He now teaches at Central Michigan University. In the following interview, he shares his insights about media relations.

RLD: Why is media relations such a difficult subject to "get your arms around"? I know many professionals in public relations who steer clear of media relations.

JGW: Media relations is probably the most important and yet most complex aspect of public relations. That's because there are a lot of publics that our clients have to reach. Some of those publics, such as employees, can be reached easily. You might say they're a captive audience. Other publics, such as customers and suppliers, are harder to reach. That's one part of the complexity. The other part is the media itself. The media is not a simple, uniform tool. There are all types of media. And many of them are very different from one another.

In many ways each publication or program in the media requires different approaches. You would, of course, approach *The New York Times* differently than you would the *New York Post.* You would approach the *Today* show differently than you would the *Tonight* show. And as the media change or circumstances change, our approach may have to change. For example, you might have read in *The Wall Street Journal* that the "Chinese Wall" between the editorial and business side of newspapers and magazines is coming down. As a result, the business side can now exercise more influence over the editorial side. That means we should investigate how we can shape editorial content through the business side. For most of us, that's fairly new.

Given all these changes, all of us must be—like President Kennedy—lifelong students of the media. I've been involved either in the media or in handling media relations for a long time, and I still analyze what's going on in the print and electronic media every day. To this job has been added, of course, investigating what's happening in cyberspace. To help us over-forty folks understand cyberspace, we should get on the Internet, regularly read publications like *Wired*, and speak with younger people.

RLD: What do you think is the essence of the media? What is the so-called genetic code that determines what kind of coverage you will get?

JGW: I'm convinced that the essence of media relations is the relationship between practitioners in public relations and those in the media. If over the years you've built up trust, the likelihood is that you'll have the media's attention. With that trust you won't need gimmicks to attract the interest of the media. A big part of this relationship is the simple recognition that you have a job to do and so do they. You've got to ask yourself: What can I do to make the media's job easier? Maybe it's "translating" technical material into concepts and language the media can easily understand. Maybe it's making the experts in the company, such as the chief financial officer, available for interviews for stories that do not concern your company. Maybe it's presenting interesting ideas for stories. One of the best people in the business, Richard Kosmicki, is a genius at accommodating the media. The media like doing business with him and contact him on issues that have nothing to do with his clients.

RLD: Some public relations people talk about the "good old days," when all you had to do to get publicity was take reporters out to a nice restaurant. Did those good old days really exist? Was media relations ever "easy"?

JGW: I've heard my share of stories about how a public relations person took a reporter to lunch and got that reporter to write an article on some nonevent, such as the CEO's wife's art exhibit. I've always been skeptical about the truth of those stories. Sure, we often have breakfast or lunch with a reporter or producer. An article or thirty minutes on the *Larry King Live* show may come from those meetings. But there's no guarantee. If what you're offering to media professionals isn't of use to them, no lunch will move them into your corner. You have to have substance.

Also, there are now ethical issues about those so-called lunches. Many people in the media have been sensitized to the idea that a free lunch might compromise their position. So if they *do* join you for lunch, frequently they'll pay their own way. There's nothing wrong with asking media people to lunch, but don't expect any special treatment. What breakfasts and lunches do is establish a framework in which you can really talk and establish a relationship. The objective here is to try to get them to understand what you're attempting to do and then help them figure out how they can make news out of that.

As for the second question—has media relations ever been easy?—the answer is no. Oh, some people have been lucky and have "sold" their story to the media without too much trouble. But, in general, it's hard work. That's because the challenge is how to get your message into the media in a way that's acceptable to your client. In media relations, you serve a number of masters—the media, the clients, and the publics who are your audience.

RLD: In terms of the big picture, what institution today is as powerful as the media?

JGW: One of the great paradoxes today is that the media, particularly the electronic media, has never been less respected, yet it has never been so powerful. In terms of an analogy I would say that the media has become as powerful as the government. Just look at the front page of a daily newspaper and think about what kind of influence it has. What about something that appears on CNN? The media has the power to destroy a person such as Dick Morris, or elevate a person like Tiger Woods to celebrity status. Is that power a bad thing? Not necessarily. But you have to understand that it exists.

RLD: What do you think a client wants from the media, and what does the media want from you, a public relations person?

JGW: Often clients have no understanding about the media or how it works. Therefore, they probably don't know what they can realistically expect. You have to educate them. For instance, you have to explain that dealing with the media doesn't ensure that all the news about them will be good. So, you must also educate your clients about the risks involved and their options in the event a negative story comes out.

As for reporters and producers, they're neither your enemy nor your friend. They're interested in developing a story. As they pursue that goal, you may get helped—or hurt—in the process.

RLD: What happens if your client *does* get negative coverage?

JGW: Assuming you have first educated your clients about the risks involved, you have to work out a strategy for what we call "damage control." There are different ways to approach this. If clients are in the wrong, they may just say, "We were in the wrong. We are sorry. And we have a ten-point program to correct this situation." In other words, stop the bleeding and go on from there. Sometimes, though, this is not possible. Often there are ongoing problems in which the facts have become irrelevant and the situation is a hot spot in the public consciousness; asbestos poisoning is an example of that. Also, there are certain problems that can't be solved. And if you attempt to present your side of the story, either no one is listening or you can make the situation worse. In that type of case, maybe you should be silent.

RLD: Going back to the relationship you develop with the media, how do you know what particular reporters and producers want?

JGW: Knowing what reporters and producers want involves experience. And that experience is continuous. You must keep up with who's who in the media—print and electronic—and figure out what turns them on, what seems to bore them, and how they're getting ahead. This requires analysis on your part. Next, you have to reach out to the media, first in an informal way. If you represent a utility, you know that you'll need the energy reporter on the newspaper and the business reporter on the evening news. Explain to them how you share mutual interests, and set up a time you can get together so that when you *do* have a story, some type of relationship is already in place.

RLD: A big problem in our business is determining what's really a story that the media will be interested in and what's a non-event, or fluff.

JGW: That's the eternal question: What is news? There are probably hundreds of definitions of news. But it really comes down to that old cliché: I really can't define what news is, but I know it when I see it.

When we're trying to decide what's news, we have to stand back and consider why the media would be interested in developing a story about *this* person or *this* product. What are the elements of news? Maybe the news aspect isn't its timeliness but its history; maybe it's the fiftieth anniversary of the invention of the widget.

There are also different kinds of news. There's human-interest news; i.e., stories about the survivors from the Oklahoma City bombing. Another type of story is the bizarre or the novel; i.e., the twenty-six-year-old who becomes CEO of an old-line financial services firm.

Still another type is what affects people. Here, media

relations representatives might not be alert enough. There's so much in our client's operations that affects people; we should be trying to sell more of that. Maybe we won't sell it to a general-interest publication like *Life*, but perhaps we can pitch a story on longevity to *Modern Maturity*.

RLD: There's a lot of confusion out there about selling a story as an exclusive: Should I go to *The Wall Street Journal* and offer them a story about our new product as an "exclusive," or will that make me enemies at *The New York Times* and other print media?

JGW: Well, there *are* times for an exclusive. For example, you may want a story in *Fortune* on your company's new strategic plan and you know that if it's in *Fortune*, other publications will pick it up. For you, this seems the most efficient way to go— and you may be right.

However, exclusives *can* get you enemies. The media is very competitive. If you give Joe the story and leave out Rita and Bob, you might create long-term enemies. Basically, we should be treating everyone in the media equally. One way to do that is to give the same story to everyone, but with different angles.

RLD: How do you decide *where* to place a story?

JGW: That's an art. Some stories should have large general distribution—the more people you reach with this story, the better. It doesn't have to be a big story; maybe it's about a new development in your client's ongoing business. So you go to the general media with a press release.

In other cases, there might be specific audiences you want to reach. That's where you use the "rifle-shot" approach and contact only certain members of the media. Perhaps if you want to reach your customers, you would contact the trade magazines. If it's a technology story for people under thirty years of age, you might go to *Wired*.

RLD: When do you use the wire services such as The Associated Press, Reuters News Agency, Dow Jones Service, and Bloomberg Business News?

JGW: If you have a local story about a new wing for a hospital, you're not going to put that on the wire services. Wire services are appropriate if you have a story you want to get out *now* and you want to have regional, national, or global reach. The impact of wire services can be enormous. The story doesn't have to be a major one; what's essential is that it have large general interest. You can put it out as a news release or as an interview with a wire service correspondent who covers the industry or business your client is involved in. And you can ensure even wider distribution of your release by placing it on a paid wire service like the PR Newswire.

RLD: What are your options if the media seems to be hostile?

JGW: Most of the time media people aren't really being hostile; they're just after the news. But, of course, there's always a bad apple; for some reason a reporter or talk show host is actually hostile.

Also, it sometimes happens that the relationship between the client and media gets very touchy because the client complains about coverage while the media complains it can't get the information it needs to do the story. In this case, you have to figure out what's really impeding the relationship and neutralize the negative feelings. It frequently happens that the story is a difficult or controversial one, and the client would like to shut off coverage. Well, that's not a good option. You can't tell the *Chicago Tribune* that you're not going to talk with them. Actually, you *could* tell them that, but it's a bad start. What I do in this case is analyze the dynamics of what's going on between the media and the client and try to reestablish communications. The bottom line is that you really *can't* shut out the media.

RLD: When the media is interviewing the client, do you sit in?

JGW: It's usually advisable that someone sits in; it's a wise thing to do. Sometimes I tape the interview. Of course, you don't want to be too visible or intrusive. But agree on the ground rules with the reporter beforehand and make sure that these rules are being observed during the interview. Sometimes it happens that the interview seems to be running downhill—the client and the interviewer start shouting at each other, or the client seems to be at a disadvantage. It's your job to get things back on track. So you might try to clarify what you think the client is saying.

RLD: We covered this a little before, but let's reframe it: A negative story comes out about your client. What do you do?

JGW: You have to figure out *why* the story is negative. Maybe it's accurate; your client might have gotten snagged. But suppose there are errors in the story. You want to correct those, but it's often counterproductive to demand that the correction run the next day. Also, there's no payoff in beating up on the reporter. The most effective way to correct an error is to ask for a correction in the database. You can get the media to do that; they don't *like* to do that, but it's necessary for your client. Let's say the *Advocate* calls up the *Detroit Free Press* for their last three stories on General Dynamics. Well, if your correction is in that database, then the *Advocate* will receive that correction along with the last three stories.

RLD: So many clients request a press conference. Are press conferences being overdone, and when is it appropriate to call one?

JGW: Yes, too many press conferences are being called. What usually happens is that too few media show up, and those who do are annoyed because there really wasn't a need for a press conference; you could have delivered this information in the form of a press release. Ideally you call a press conference when you have something very important to say and it's both positive and newsworthy. And the reason for a press conference vs. a press release is that you need an actuality—video clip or audiotape—for the electronic media. Also, a press conference gives you an orderly environment for questions.

But you have to prepare the client for the possibility of all kinds of questions from the media. Suppose the press conference is held in the middle of a big, long-running negative story. You can't really control what the media will ask. If your client doesn't want to deal with those questions, then don't call a press conference.

RLD: What goes into a press kit?

JGW: A press kit should contain whatever is relevant. That would include the announcement; for example, the appointment of a new CEO. The announcement should have the proper quotes from the proper people within and outside the corporation. You want a biography of the new executive and probably a picture. Also a fact sheet on the company, what its products are, that sort of thing—whatever tells the story. You don't want to obscure your story with *too much* information. Too much material in the press kit makes you appear like an amateur. But there are cases—for example, an acquisition—in which you'll need plenty of material. You need background information explaining why the company paid the price it did for the acquisition; how the acquisition will fit into the company's strategic plan; whether the acquisition will result in layoffs; and so on.

Sometimes the media requests that you e-mail the material in the press kit to them. With all the new technology, you now have to find out how the media likes to receive its material. One advantage of e-mail is that it isn't intrusive. Often, to avoid telephone calls around deadline, editors will request you contact them only by e-mail.

RLD: What do you think about theatrics at a press conference? Some companies use them when they're rolling out a "gee-whiz" product.

JGW: I remember when a company first introduced a two-way pager. They demonstrated it at a press conference and that went over very well. But you have to consider how gee-whiz your product really is. A demonstration can be especially useful in high-tech. Your verbal description of your new product may make it seem a "me-too," but when you demonstrate the product it becomes apparent how unique it is. The electronics industry likes visuals. But be sure that the demonstration is glitch free. It can be very embarrassing if the CEO presses a button and nothing happens.

RLD: Are video releases useful?

JGW: Yes. The electronic media frequently uses them. The trick is to make them *right*. For example, they have to fit the time frame that the station allots for a single story. They have to look and sound natural. They have to be of good quality—right up there with the videos the station makes. When I worked for Senator Ted Kennedy, we put out an actuality for radio every day. We targeted it to the morning and afternoon rush hour. It was about thirty to forty-five seconds of Ted Kennedy on the subject of the day. That tactic was very successful.

RLD: What about the Internet?

JGW: Many of our clients have Web pages on which they display their products and philosophies. Some post their annual reports on the Websites. They can track how many people visit the site. At this point it seems that if you don't have a Web page you're at a competitive disadvantage, at least in terms of your image. The Internet is still in its embryonic stages, but we will see rapid developments. What do reporters think of the Internet? It depends. Some older reporters prefer the piece of paper and don't go on the Internet often. Some younger ones expect *all* the background information about the company to be easily accessible on the Internet.

The problem here, already, is information overload. There is so much information on the Internet—so much to monitor and so many errors to correct. [Craig Jolley, head of OASIS (Online and Strategic Information Solutions) Consulting and an expert in both technology and public relations, gives further information below in the section on technology.]

RLD: What about the trade press—newspapers and magazines devoted to a special subject like personal computers or advertising?

JGW: The trade press is becoming more important and more sophisticated. If you want to find out the latest information about business in New York, it'd be most productive to see *Crain's New York Business*. If you want to get information about your PR department to public relations professionals, contact one of the publications devoted to the public relations industry. You might be more successful getting your story out to the right audience in the trade press rather than in the general press. The trade press relies on people in the industry to feed them information. If you have information they will be eager to receive it. Study the trade press that you're interested in, such as *American Banker* or *CFO Magazine*. How do they present information? Use the same format. That may mean attaching charts. Perhaps they use case studies; if so, you would be expected to submit a case study. As soon as you enter a new industry, analyze the trades in your business and build relationships with the people on staff.

RLD: OK, suppose you've just hit a home run. *Fortune* printed a very positive article about how successfully your company restructured its operations. How do you "milk" this?

JGW: Get permission from the magazine to have reprints made. Often the magazine will print those up for a fee. Send them to clients and prospective clients. If it's appropriate, you might also send them to others you are trying to influence, such as the mayor of Akron, Ohio, or a group of environmentalists. In addition, you might send them to certain selected media. You would do this with a very short cover letter that reads something like: "Dear Tom, since you're interested in our industry I thought you might find this useful reading." Be prepared to suggest other story ideas when the media calls. The media is very busy but reporters are always looking for good news stories and frequently they will follow up on story ideas or good angles for a news story.

Now that we have the big picture, let's look at the nuts and bolts of media relations, everything from the technology to what directories to use.

Technology

Media relations is being revolutionized by technology. The editor at *BridgeNews* wanted us to e-mail him an op-ed piece our office had prepared. It wouldn't have satisfied him had we sent the op-ed by messenger or fax. Also, e-mail is a great way to make a spokesperson available to reporters. You can do this through CompuServe, which administers MediaNet.

Craig Jolley, a technology and public relations expert who heads up Online and Strategic Information Solutions (OASIS), a firm specializing in information technology and public relations, points out that the growth of databases may have changed how much reporters might know about the subject before they meet with you. Databases such as Lexis-Nexis have existed for years, says Jolley, but recently they've increased in number and have become more accessible and affordable. If reporters or producers are working on a story about your company today, they probably are using databases—such as Dow Jones and Bloomberg—to get information about your industry; developments in businesses that affect your industry; what security analysts are saying about your company; and what other media have written or said about you. Therefore, when they come to interview you, expect them to be thoroughly briefed.

This also means that if there are mistakes in the database about your company, it's really important to correct those mistakes before someone does a database search that involves your company. If you don't, the erroneous material will continue to be distributed.

It's worth the investment to have staff or hire an outside service to scan all databases for what's being said about both you and your competition. Electronic clipping services are available through Burrelle's Information Services, 75 East Northfield Road, Livingston, New Jersey 07039. By monitoring databases, you can also identify emerging issues. A U.S.-based company tracked database information about environmentalism in Europe. It spotted a new trend: Environmental activists were concerned about the excess packaging for compact discs. The company was able to prepare for this trend as it worked its way to the United States. Its leaders were ahead of the curve.

According to Jolley, more and more companies are allotting space on their Web page to media relations. This is where they post their press releases. Sometimes they require reporters to use a password in order to access the material. Information about the company, its executives, products, and strategy is also posted on the Website. But media relations representatives should approach e-mail opportunities with caution. Recently, Toronto publishers were bombarded with press kits and animated videos from a number of companies. This unsolicited material tied up their inbound server for eight hours, and the publishers were furious. They probably formed a "drop dead" list of media reps they didn't want to hear from again. Before sending any briefing material via e-mail, think about how long it would tie up the line. You might want to downsize what you're sending.

Right now the Internet is very much like the Wild West. Just about anything can be said about you and your company. That means you or your public relations agency should monitor the online services, including bulletin boards and the news groups that exist. There may be errors. Some parties may even be trying to undermine you. It's imperative to post the accurate information quickly.

Another ramification of life online is that research has become a commodity. Anyone can get on CompuServe and find out a great deal about, say, the work vs. family balance issue. Whereas previously a well-researched press release would usually get picked up, media representatives now have to be more creative in how they attempt to "add value" to their releases or the stories they pitch. Sometimes what it takes to get noticed is a provocative analogy or soundbite.

A slightly dated but still very good discussion of technology in public relations is available in the September 22, 1995, issue of *Public Relations Quarterly*. The article, "An Internet Primer for Public Relations," by Randy Bobbitt, contains an excellent bibliography, including the monthly publication *Technology for Communicators'* "Ideas for Communicating in a Wired World," published by Lawrence Ragan Communications, Inc., 212 West Superior Street, Chicago, Illinois 60610.

The Media Interview

Media relations consultant Chuck Rossie prepares clients to appear on programs such as *60 Minutes* as well as routine encounters with reporters and producers. He's coached more than six thousand executives.

Earlier I explained Rossie's concept of point of view. He advises executives to see the media as an efficient delivery system of news and information rather than a threat. Another concept Rossie advises executives to embrace is preparation. "Go into the media interview with an agenda," he counsels them. "Don't be lulled into thinking that the interview is a nice conversation with the reporter. Reporters are trained to interview as if it were a conversation. But if the executives do proceed in the interview as if it were a conversation, they will either not get their message communicated and/or simply say too much, some of which can be damaging."

Executives are used to having a complete support system at work, observes Rossie. When they go to a media interview, they're almost fish out of water. The reporter or the talk show host may *seem* supportive, but he or she is there strictly to get a job done, not to help executives come across in the best light. Therefore, executives must be prepared for even the most routine interview and not be seduced into thinking they're simply having a friendly chat. How? According to Rossie, executives should:

Understand how the media works

The media relations representative can explain to them how the media works and provide examples of interviews that went well for executives, as well as those that went out of control. It's the media relations representative's responsibility to flag clients about all possible pitfalls.

Know what message they want to communicate

As they say in politics, executives should stay "on message." If the interview meanders to other topics, executives have to take the initiative to get it back on track. In short, *get control over the interview.* Executives should practice this with a staff member who acts the role of the shrewd reporter.

Anticipate the questions the media will ask

It often happens that a corporation's staff members will create a list of questions that the executives could be asked. Then they'll "censor" some questions as inappropriate for the media to ask and cross them off the list, so the executives never see them. The reality is that it's the media's job to ask all kinds of questions. If staff members refuse to pose some questions, they're putting their company's own executives at a disadvantage once the interview begins.

Monitor themselves constantly throughout the interview

Executives should make sure they're not talking too much. Reporters and talk show hosts frequently allow executives to ramble. Executives shouldn't wait for the interviewer to say, "Enough." That won't happen. Any smart reporter will allow the person being interviewed to hang himself.

Show genuine empathy about the situation

If their plant explodes, executives should express the same type of public outrage that the community feels. They should make it clear they are working on ways to prevent that kind of accident from ever happening again.

Rehearse in front of a video camera

During rehearsals executives should practice giving answers to difficult questions. They will discover that they can put their cards on the table face up as long as they are careful about what they say. They also have to practice saying that they don't have the answer. Instead of responding "No comment," they can say they don't have the answer at this time or will get it as soon as possible. Executives can also hone their media skills by watching how political figures handle themselves, particularly politicians with whom they disagree.

Print vs. Electronic

It used to be said that the print media offers depth and the electronic media basically functions with a "headline" mind-set—FLOOD KILLS 200 IN MIDWEST. ONE-HUNDRED THOUSAND HOMELESS. PRESSURE ON WASHINGTON FOR FEDERAL AID. However, the line between print and electronic has blurred. Even *The New York Times* has made its copy more accessible to readers. There aren't as many complex sentences with subordinate clauses as there used to be.

To prepare executives for interviews you have to study that particular media. Don't assume that because *Charlie Rose* is part of the electronic media it's just a lightweight show. You might also talk with other executives who were interviewed by this host or that reporter. Doing this will help you understand the strategies used by different interviewers. Not surprisingly, some of the best interviewees, people like former president Ronald Reagan, intuitively know how to function brilliantly in all sorts of media environments. The lesson we can learn from Reagan is that experience with the media pays off. Expose your clients to as many media opportunities, environments, and venues as possible. With experience, they usually improve greatly.

Media Directories

Your best media directory is actually to read, listen to, or view the media you're interested in. *The Writer's Market*, which is available at libraries and bookstores, will also give you a good idea as to the nature of certain print media. Also monitor the newsracks for new publications and *TV Guide* for new programs, including local publications and local television. Much of the news you will want to get out there will be through local media.

Let's look at particular kinds of media.

Newspapers

Libraries carry many newspapers. Spend time there studying the content and tone of different newspapers. You can also get a feel for newspapers by retrieving them online. One of the best directories is *Bacon's Newspaper Directory*, 332 South Michigan Avenue, Chicago, Illinois 60604. For information about regional newspaper outlets, you can contact Burrelle's Information Services, 75 East Northfield Road, Livingston, New Jersey 07039. Or, you can go straight to the horse's mouth; if, for example, you're interested in getting an article in the *Cleveland Plain Dealer* and you have public relations contacts in Ohio, ask them directly for the real scoop about the newspaper.

Magazines

There are more than twelve thousand consumer and trade magazines. Many of them are online. *Bacon's Magazine Directory* will help you find out what's available. You can also find out who are the local stringers of the magazines in your area. They are probably the best ones to pitch a story to. A media rep at the University of Pittsburgh was able to get a full-page story in *Business Week* about the School of Engineering's new program by contacting the local stringer.

Wire services

The wire services are a gold mine. They operate around the clock and their reach is global. Most comprehensive directories, such as *Burrelle's Media Directory*, include the names, addresses, and phone numbers of all the right people to contact at the wire services. In addition, there are private wire services that will carry your press release or story for a fee. Write PR Newswire, 810 Seventh Avenue, New York, New York 10019 and Business Wire, 1185 Avenue of the Americas, New York, New York 10036.

Radio

Radio has come back. It's a good vehicle for communicating your client's message. Listen to radio stations, especially during drive time. You can find out more about radio stations through *Bacon's Information Inc.* and *New York Publicity Outlets*.

Television

In the United States there are nearly fifteen hundred TV stations and seven hundred cable systems. You want to watch as many of these as possible. You can consult *Bacon's Information Inc.* and *New York Publicity Outlets*.

Press Releases

Some public relations people claim that press releases are dead, particularly the traditional paper release. Actually, as Richard Kosmicki points out, many people in the media still feel comfortable with the information format of the release and like having a piece of paper on their desk.

The best way to learn about press releases is to analyze releases issued by your organization that have gotten good pickup by the media in the past. While it's true that your press release should break through the clutter and catch the media's interest, it's just as important that it contain all the appropriate information, efficiently packaged. A poorly done press release, no matter how provocative, will hurt your reputation and the reputation of your organization. Once the media is aware that you are not doing your job properly, they will probably cease to open releases from you.

There's no one way to do a press release. But, in my experience, there are ways to optimize your chances of interesting the media in your press release:

Package an idea for the media

To publicize my book *The Critical 14 Years of Your Professional Life,* media relations staff at The Dilenschneider Group wrote one general media release focusing on the idea that young people—the so-called Generation X—have been left high and dry in the workplace with no mentoring from the pros. But in addition to the general release, we issued other releases that focused on specific topics in the book, such as benefits, pitfalls of having a mentor, and how to handle the boss. All these releases received excellent pickup.

The idea you provide should be simple, not overly complex. It should be clearly stated. And it should be of interest to the target audiences you're trying to reach.

Provide all the pertinent information

The most critical information—who, where, how much, how long—should be presented early in the release. The less-important information should be presented later.

Include a quote or quotes from the appropriate people

If an auto company is announcing a reorganization of its parts division, the president of that division should be quoted. Sometimes it's also useful to quote the CEO of the company.

Supply background information

For example, your auto company reorganization release may contain statistics on how many U.S. companies reorganized in 1999, or brief background information about global trends in parts manufacturing in the auto industry. As I said earlier, research is a commodity, but it still can be very useful to a reporter on deadline.

Provide attachments

As long as they're relevant, it's sometimes useful to have attachments—a photo of a plant or an executive, a speech by the executive, a white paper on the changing global auto industry.

News Conferences

If you have real news to present, a news or press conference may be the best way to release it. Earnings reports, large reorganizations, top-level executive changes, and responses to negative news are frequently presented at news conferences. If you want your news conference to be successful—that is, attended by many reporters—here are some guidelines you should follow:

Make sure your topic is really news

Your boss or client might want a news conference about something that is *not* news. It's your job to educate him or her that this isn't the way to go.

Locate the conference in a place accessible to the media

Your car division may be located in Tennessee, but it might be best to hold the conference in a hotel in New York. If you want to give a media tour of the car division, you have to decide how many reporters would travel to Tennessee. To find that out, consider asking them.

Allow time for both a presentation and a Q&A

Block out about twenty minutes for the executive presentation and about twenty more minutes for questions and answers. During rehearsal with the executives, make sure they stick to the message. And throw tough questions at them during rehearsal.

Prepare press kits

Press kits that are helpful to the media could include everything from a press release to a white paper on a topic of vital interest to the media. Err on the side of having *less* paper rather than more.

Provide advance notice

Alert the press ahead of time that there will be a conference. Send a few paragraphs in a pre-event media advisory that will whet their interest. But if the issue is really news, you don't want to give them *too much* lead time, or else the story could break before the conference.

Leaks

Richard Kosmicki is an expert on "leaks," or information becoming public in unorthodox ways. Kosmicki has counseled hundreds of organizations about leaks, including ways to prevent them. There are two kinds of leaks, observes Kosmicki. One of them is the leak you didn't want: Someone in the organization tells the media that there is going to be a 25 percent reduction in staff before you want that news to get out. The other kind is the leak you *want* to reach the media: You anonymously leak the information that you're considering the idea of moving your headquarters to California to see how the public will react. The leak is a so-called trial balloon.

Leaks you didn't engineer are usually a symptom of a problem in the organization. Frequently it's a hiring problem. In Kosmicki's estimation, "You hired people who didn't share your mission and values." Another reason for the leak may be that you're talking to too wide a circle. This will necessitate reducing the number of people in your inner circle, figuring out whom you can trust, and then finding out if you're right.

If you *want* to leak, it's best to meet with reporteres away from either your office or their place of business, preferably in person. However, you should have an already established relationship with the reporter so that you feel reasonably secure he or she will protect your identity.

Not Maxing Out

Media coverage can be intoxicating, and our clients want more and more of it. As any Hollywood star knows, though, there's a downside of publicity: overexposure. It's your responsibility to warn clients that they may be becoming *too* prominent in the news; the public may get sick of them or decide they are preoccupied with publicity instead of minding the store. Shareholders and employees might begin grumbling that the executives should spend more time solving the company's critical problems and less time hobnobbing with the media. Customers might be turned off by an executive's high profile. In addition, the media is a lot like a borderline personality: It loves deeply, but without warning it can turn on a person. During the early days of John Akers's tenure as CEO at IBM there were many glowing articles about him and his company. But the media attacked him savagely during his last years at the helm.

I advise my clients: Don't give the media a reason to turn on you. Monitor how high a profile you and your publics can handle.

Things to Remember

- There's no payoff in being critical of the media. Leave analysis of the media's shortcomings to the researchers at think tanks.

- The media is just a bunch of human beings doing their job. The more you help them do that job, the greater your odds for good coverage.

- Never overpromise and underdeliver to the media. If you say you have news, you'd better have news.

- Let the media know who you are *before* you need them.

- Educate your clients about how the media works, especially regarding the risks they might be taking.

- Help your clients with leaks. Here's where you don't want anyone doing an amateur job.

Chapter 2

Investor Relations

One of the biggest changes in investment relations is how competitive it's become to market yourself as a company. The ten thousand or so publicly listed companies that are U.S.-owned are now competing for capital with companies around the world. Latin America, Eastern Europe, Western Europe, and the Far East, including Japan, all have stock exchanges. We're seeing especially high growth in the number of companies going public in the emerging markets, such as in Latin America. That means that it's increasingly difficult to get the attention of the financial community, including security analysts.

—Russell K. Mason, president and founder
of the Investment Management Institute
and former director of Education and Programs
with the Financial Analysts Federation

If you walk into a hotel in New York, Chicago, Los Angeles, Hong Kong, or London, you might find representatives from five different publicly traded companies in five different ballrooms presenting their investment story to members of the financial community. Based on how well they tell their stories, these companies' stocks may go up or down; the financial community may continue to follow or ignore them; and their image may be enhanced or ruined.

Before beginning these presentations, or "road shows," investor relations experts give advice on every aspect of their story, ranging from who should be the major spokesperson to what the key messages should be to how to explain away disappointments and shift investor focus to the positive aspects of the story. Investor relations has become one of the most important and influential functions in a public company.

According to Lois Brown, vice president and group director of Ruder-Finn Corporate/Investor Relations, "Investor relations is a strategic corporate marketing activity, combining the disciplines of finance and communication."[1] Investor relations is no longer an invisible function that primarily distributes earnings releases and ensures that the annual report gets out on time. CEOs and other senior operating executives are spending more and more time working with security analysts and money managers to raise investors' comfort levels and articulate big-picture issues like corporate strategy. According to a 1995 survey by the National Investor Relations Institute (NIRI), 35 percent of investor relations staff members report to CEOs and 52 percent report to CFOs.[2] However, because the primary mission of investor relations is communications, it's usually still considered part of a corporation's overall public relations.

In this chapter I explain how investor relations, whether part of a corporation or a competent agency, can help a company present its story in a way that builds credibility and attracts investors to the stock. A company like Coca-Cola might have a wonderful story to tell, or it may have to instill confidence in a turnaround strategy, or it may have to deal with criticism. In the late eighties, when Wall Street complained it wasn't getting the whole story from Texaco, CEO James Kinnear personally spoke to every investor with more than twenty thousand shares and asked them what kind of information they needed.[3]

The particular situation a company is in, good or bad, is basically irrelevant. What matters is how investor relations positions the message and how the corporate spokesperson—usually but not always the CEO—delivers it. I have watched CEOs whose companies are in deep trouble, such as Chrysler's former CEO Lee Iacocca, charm the pants off the financial community, moving up the company's stock almost entirely on the strength of the confidence they project. I've also witnessed CEOs with solid companies misspeak or appear less than forthright in such presentations, damaging their credibility and the underlying price of their stock. These leaders often fail to convince investors they have a viable strategy for their company or refuse to provide adequate financial information. Without such information, the financial community may decide it does not have what it needs to reliably predict performance, and without guidance and recommendations the investors lose interest and the stock suffers.

Interview with Art Gormley: An Overview of Investor Relations

Art Gormley is a certified public accountant who started his career with Arthur Andersen & Company. In the mid-seventies he was a senior member of the financial staff of Weeden & Company, a securities house. Later he worked in senior executive positions in investor relations at the public relations firms Doremus & Company, Hill & Knowlton, and most recently The Dilenschneider Group. Earlier in his career he was a financial analyst for the Italian steel industry.

RLD: What is the essence of investor relations?

AG: The essence of investor relations is to provide the financial community with a sense of where the company is headed and what to expect in terms of future performance.

RLD: What major changes do you see in the field of investor relations?

AG: There are a number of them. One is the increased competition for capital from companies around the world. Another is competition for research coverage. The pension funds, insurance companies, and other institutions that dominate today's securities markets rely heavily on sell-side research in making their buy-and-sell decisions. Today there are many more companies seeking research coverage from fewer and fewer security analysts. Bob, you always talk about "breaking through the clutter." Well, in the face of stiff competition for attention, a company has to be far more creative, resourceful, and persistent in getting its IR message heard and understood.

The impact and importance of securities analysts' earnings forecasts cannot be understated. Securities analysts stake their reputations on their ability to readily predict quarterly earnings per share right down to the penny. In fact, the consensus of analyst earnings estimates [as compiled by such services as First Call, Zack's IBIS, and others] has become Wall Street's most unforgiving yardstick. It doesn't matter if earnings are up 18 percent; if Wall Street is expecting 20 percent, that is a negative earnings surprise and the stock price invariably suffers. Just about every day *The Wall Street Journal* carries at least one story noting that Company A missed the consensus by X and its stock price dropped by Y. The stock price impact of a negative earnings surprise has become nearly as predictable as Newton's law of gravity.

A consistent history of missed estimates damages management's credibility and may prompt analysts to drop coverage. Remember, their reputations are on the line here, too. If they feel management doesn't have a handle on the business, or worse, believe they have been misled, they will urge their institutional customers to take a wait-and-see approach to every company announcement.

The financial community does not like surprises. Companies that have good investor relations functions track analysts' estimates closely. If a gap develops, they skillfully provide guidance to get estimates back in line, or if the gap is dramatic, they publicly issue a prompt warning in advance of the company's earnings announcement. If it's an earnings shortfall, the stock may still suffer but management can preserve its credibility—a priceless commodity—by acting swiftly to close the gap. Again, let me say, *the financial community does not like surprises.*

Another major change that is still taking shape is the impact of the Internet on investor relations. Now that the Internet has made sophisticated and detailed financial information available to both large and small investors, management has yet another channel and another opportunity to share the company's message.

RLD: About the Internet, when *Barron's Online* announced that it had joined the Investor Relations Information Network on the World Wide Web, it listed the investment information that the site provided: comprehensive dossiers for fifteen thousand stocks, seven thousand mutual funds, and one thousand ADRs, in addition to company news and access to archives.

AG: We'll be seeing a lot of that kind of online access to comprehensive investment information. The Internet is probably the fastest-growing influence on investor relations and it will continue to grow. Even now all kinds of current corporate and financial information is readily available from a number of sites. For example, many company Websites contain full-text annual reports, SEC filings, and new releases. It has even become possible to participate in a financial analyst meeting via the Web.

This ability to immediately access information will affect many aspects of investor relations. For example, take quarterly reports. As you know, quarterly reports to shareholders aren't required by the Securities and Exchange Commission. A survey by the National Investor Relations Institute found that although 90 percent of the companies surveyed believed they would send quarterly reports—which isn't legally required—many are backing away from mailing out the traditional quarterly report. Eventually, we'll probably see what used to be the "paper and ink" version of the quarterly report completely online. Shareholders will have access to information without waiting for snail mail or, even worse, their broker to send it to them. The report may be in the form of a press release or letter from the CEO with financial highlights. Right now, for a number of companies, you can be briefed on their quarterly results by dialing an 800 number.

Another change we're seeing in investor relations is the increasing sophistication of the practitioners. At one time, just about any seasoned public relations pro conversant with a company's financial statements and reasonably knowledgeable about the company could handle investor relations. For all but the smallest microcap companies, that's no longer advisable. Investor relations has evolved into a highly focused specialty. Now the investor relations person is expected to know as much about the financials as the CFO and to be able to work one-on-one with members of the financial community. That includes all the complexities of the financial models analysts use to forecast earnings.

RLD: How should a company deliver bad news?

AG: There's all kinds of bad news, ranging from disappointing earnings to the sudden departure of a respected executive. The best way to deal with bad news is to release it all at once. It's a big mistake to let it come out piece by piece. Whatever the news is, get it out, along with a thoughtful plan for how management will deal with the problem. In that way you can put it all behind you and move on.

RLD: What constitutes an effective investor relations press release? Should it be just the facts?

AG: The numbers have to be there, but they do not speak for themselves. There has to be more. You have to put the news in the context of the key events. If at all possible, quantify the impact of the news on future performance. If you don't bracket the financial impact in some way, Wall Street will create its own number, which invariably will be wrong. Perhaps the most important part of this communication, however, is to let the financial community know how a particular development fits into management's overriding strategy. For example, the company's overriding strategy may be to reduce cyclical earnings by diversifying globally. That would be the theme of the release, which would go on to explain how the news announcement enhances the implementation of that strategy.

RLD: To protect and attract investors, the capital markets are highly regulated. Does that mean that investor relations executives have to be knowledgeable about federal and state securities laws and the rulings of regulatory bodies, such as the Securities and Exchange Commission?

AG: Securities laws governing such matters as timely financial disclosure, tender offers, and conditioning the market are stringent and the penalties are severe. In investor relations you're expected to know the applicable regulations and legal requirements governing material disclosures, be it in connection with an Initial Public Offering [IPO], a proxy contest, or a tender offer for the stock of another company. Ordinarily securities lawyers and investment bankers will give you some guidance on this. The business and financial media are very sophisticated in this regard and will respect that you must rigorously comply with these rules. For instance, you might not be able to disclose certain information to the media before a particular date and time prescribed by law or regulation. The media know why, but that will not prevent them from asking for it. It's their job to ask.

RLD: Whether it's an IPO or other securities offering, we hear a lot about road shows—even "virtual road shows."[4] How can they be made effective?

AG: The road show may take place at a Holiday Inn, in an investment banker's conference room, or in cyberspace. What makes it effective is the level of excitement it creates. Those making the road show presentation must be able to fire the imagination of the financial community without artificially raising future expectations. This is not just a presentation of financial information, although required disclosures are certainly part of the presentation. It is a matter of conveying how the proceeds of an offering will further the business strategy and produce value for stockholders.

Securities offerings are the most common reason for a

road show, but certainly not the only one. I've seen the same kind of multicity tour used quite successfully to explain a complex merger or acquisition or to introduce a new CEO's turnaround strategy. For the sophisticated IR profession-al, circumstances, not precedent, dictate the most effective method of communications.

RLD: What makes for an effective securities analyst meeting?

AG: For the CEO the key is to communicate where the company is going and how it intends to get there. And the CEOs, CFOs, or other top executives who are hosting the meeting must put the company's progress in context of its business strategy. The message is: Here's our strategy; here's how we're achieving it; and here are the proof statements or how we're overcoming the obstacles that stand in our way.

RLD: What about those one-on-one meetings with the CEO? More and more pension funds and large and small mutual funds are asking for private meetings with CEOs. How should CEOs conduct themselves during those meetings?

AG: Obviously, a one-on-one meeting may actually involve a sin-gle individual, but more often than not it's a small group of buy-side analysts or portfolio managers or even the fund's chief investment strategist.

In addition to conveying a firm grasp of all the financial and operating data, CEOs should present themselves as sin-cere and dedicated, with a clear vision of where they are tak-ing the company. Perhaps equally important is the chemistry between the CEO and his or her immediate audience. Major investors want to see the CEO on his or her home turf, not only to assess the company's prospects, but as a means of taking the measure of who the CEO is and judging for themselves whether or not he or she is up to the challenge.

Despite the small audience and cordial atmosphere, CEOs must be mindful that this is not just a friendly chat; he or she is there to communicate a strategic message about creating shareholder value.

RLD: In terms of the big picture, how do you view the annual report?

AG: In thinking about the annual report, about 40 percent of the CEO's letter and the review of operations should be about what has been accomplished, with the balance focused on the future.

RLD: What is going to influence investor relations in the future?

AG: You'll continue to see many changes coming from technology. Everything from the Internet to 800 numbers to interactive media will be available to tell the company's story. In addition, investor relations people will have to begin to prepare now to deal with a bear market. Inevitably the bull market will change. Many people in investor relations have never had to tell their company's story in bad times, and many analysts and investors have never had to make investment decisions in a bear market. That will be a major challenge.

What Influences the Stock Price?

There are almost an infinite number of variables that can influence the price of the stock and therefore create challenges for investor relations.

Historically, one of these variables, especially for non-U.S. stock, has been a lack of information. Charles Abrams, of the International Business Network for World Commerce & Industry (IBNET), points out that modern technology—i.e., the Internet—makes it much easier to find out about non-U.S. stocks, such as those in China. I would add, as Gormley stated, that it's also easier to obtain information about U.S. stocks.

This easier access to information could be a mixed blessing, depending on what investors find out. Having more up-to-date, detailed information about a specific company can often generate more questions in the investors' minds, which might lead to reservations about buying the stock. So the current availability of information doesn't necessarily mean that investors will be more eager to purchase the stock. Those in investor relations have to be prepared to answer those questions and be accessible to shareholders and prospective buyers.

Another type of important information is what's on the minds of the financial community. Without this information, it's almost impossible to make the appropriate pitch to members of that community. I've been at numerous securities analyst presentations at which investor relations didn't aggressively research what analysts wanted to know about the company. Lack of relevant information can frustrate analysts, and the stock could go down.

To get information about particular analysts, investor relations people must operate like media reps. Media reps spend much of their days getting to know the producer of *Charlie Rose* or briefing the business editor of *The New York Times* on a general matter, not one related specifically to their company. The best investor relations professionals cultivate a number of contacts in the financial community. They give information to these contacts on just about anything that is legal to disclose. And, based on the feedback from these contacts, they can get a feel for how the financial community regards the company—its strengths and weaknesses. A company should be able to *anticipate* what analysts will say about it.

Then there is the issue of corporate governance. This too can affect the stock price. The board of directors may contain too many "insiders" for the investors' liking. Or the CEO might be perceived as receiving an overinflated salary, or (as was the case at IBM and General Motors) as an obstacle to the stock price, and he or she has to go. As both institutional and individual shareholders become activists, corporate governance issues will become more and more important in determining the stock price. This is another area in which investor relations people have to be in the know and give the financial community credible answers.

There are also myriad variables to consider involving how particular analysts view the company. Perhaps investor relations overpromised what the performance will be. When the performance turns out lower than expected, once-burnt analysts might not review that company again. Investor relations is accountable for *every* number that falls from its lips.

Or, as James Roop, founder of the Public Relations Society of America's Investor Relations Hall of Fame, points out in *Public Relations Quarterly*, investor relations may send out a very positive message in the midst of a turnaround.[5] If the once-friendly analysts find out that the turnaround is still in its embryonic phases, they can become alienated and might then avoid following the stock. During the Iacocca-led turnaround at Chrysler, the company's top executives were always addressing the financial community, explaining to them in detail where the turnaround was and where problems remained. Chrysler was a heavily followed company, and when securities analysts were invited to tour a high-tech plant in Detroit, they were willing to make the trip from New York. Good investor relations departments let analysts know where the problems still exist and what the company is doing to solve them.

Also, as Charles Abrams warns, there could be a bear market. And, boy, can that affect the price of your stock! "In a bull market," observes Abrams, "it doesn't take a genius to have a hot IPO." When the market cools down, though, your IPO might not catch fire. Or there could be a downturn in your industry. How many times has Detroit seen sales—and the stock prices of the Big Three—go south? It helps when management makes a statement about what it plans to do during the downturn. Frequently the financial community is willing to give a company the benefit of the doubt if it has a clearly articulated plan about how it is going to navigate through hard times. But the financial community *hates* uncertainty.

If there's a scandal or the rumor of a scandal, it's the job of investor relations to ferret out what is being said about the company in business grapevines and address the rumors. If the rumors are true, the CEO should admit it; apologize if that is appropriate; provide a plan for correcting the problem; and promise to keep monitoring the situation. If damage control is done in time, it can prevent the stock from taking a beating. The cardinal rule in damage control is to take the most human approach. Most of the time that's the path of empathy. When TWA

Flight 800 crashed, the company's leaders did not make enough of a human response. If the representatives of TWA had put themselves in the shoes of the survivors' families and presented themselves more humanely, the company would have emerged from the crisis with a much more positive image.

A charismatic CEO could die, or a key executive can abruptly leave the company. A competitor can announce a new product that makes your company's technology appear a little long in the tooth. A fringe group, or even a mainstream group like Mothers Against Drunk Driving (MADD), can express reservations about your products. All these things can have an impact on the price of the stock. In all these cases, the ball is in investor relations' court. Investor relations must respond.

The Functions and Goals of Investor Relations

Not too long ago investor relations had, in many large corporations, a fairly low-profile, passive role. Barring acts of God and management, earnings were often made out to be predictable. If "too much" was earned that year, the company might funnel the excess into buying additional advertising. That siphoned off the extra money. Much of the job of investor relations personnel was to make sure that the right numbers got out to the right people in the right time frame so that the company would be in compliance with all federal and state laws. They also saw to it that the right decision makers would show up for road shows if the company wanted to sell more stocks or bonds. And they wrote annual reports that might have won awards but were not taken very seriously. Since most business was fairly predictable, what new insights could the annual report provide?

Today, investor relations is part of a company's strategic management reporting to key executive functions, including the CEO. Investor relations is as accountable for results as manufacturing or marketing. In its case study of Texaco, Harvard Business School emphasized the importance of good investor relations to the success of a company. A company preoccupied with results, like Microsoft or Netscape, would never tolerate a weak investor relations department.

Some companies put a higher priority on some of the central functions of investor relations than on others. For example, one investor relations department might declare that it has one and only one mission: to enhance shareholder value. Another's mission might include serving employees, customers, and the community. The question of what constitutes the proper mission for investor relations has become controversial. Some companies perceive enhancing shareholder value as too narrow a pursuit.

During a takeover fight, the investor relations mission will frequently determine what strategies a company uses. Chevron was able to take over the former Gulf Oil Company in part because it took the stance that its number-one responsibility was to shareholders.

Your investor relations department may or may not include all these functions and goals:

Raise capital

Raise capital in the most inexpensive, efficient way possible in both the United States and abroad. As former Texaco CEO Kinnear remarked, "We compete for investors just as we compete for customers at the pump."[6] Every year there are more and more emerging companies competing for the best terms on capital. And there is increased competition from non-U.S. public companies.

There are myriad ways to get capital. Sometimes getting capital means applying sophisticated computer models to the data about institutional investors. This electronic approach may help investor relations zero in on just the right money manager to invest in the firm. Or a company may decide to deal with only a handful of analysts and cultivate those few, or use the "shotgun" approach and tell its story to anything in the financial world that breathes.

Protect the interests of shareholders

Although this has always been important, both institutional and individual shareholders have become more sophisticated and activist about their interests and rights. They are using a variety of tools to make their voices heard, from personal visits to the CEO and media coverage to proxies and lawsuits.

Investor relations must anticipate investors' concerns, bring them to the attention of management, and help shape a response.

Explain the results of the business and the strategic plan underlying those results

Full-blown, comprehensive strategic planning has had its heyday and has fallen by the wayside with other fads. But the financial community still wants to know where the company is going, how it intends to get there, and what the obstacles and opportunities will be along the way.

As Art Gormley pointed out, the financial community wants to look at the company from thirty thousand feet and see the big picture. If analysts sense that the company lacks a coherent, viable strategy, they probably will withhold a "buy" recommendation.

Ensure compliance with the laws

Everyone in the organization, including members of the board of directors, must comply with relevant federal and state laws. That includes educating them about what constitutes insider trading. As shareholders become more active, board members are demanding to be briefed on their legal responsibilities with regard to investors. The coup by the board of directors at General Motors in ousting CEO Roger Smith changed forever what is expected of boards.

Keep the workforce motivated and loyal

In our time, when the old employer-employee contract based on job security is dead, investor relations can keep the workforce motivated and loyal. Microsoft, whose stock price is high and whose employees own stock options, has a model workforce.

Create an image or brand identity

Investor relations helped ensure that Xerox would become the "document company." In turn, this helped the company make the transition from being an old-line copier firm to a leading-edge company with an integrated, high-tech approach to data transmission. When the former Singer Company diversified, its investor relations department advertised to the investment community and the public that the company no longer dealt only in sewing machines but had also become a high-tech company.

Establishing an Investor Relations Program That Gets Results

Perhaps your investor relations function has been operating effectively for a number of years. Your stock price reflects your company's achievements, and you have good relationships with the financial community. This section might still be useful to you as a way of taking inventory of your resources and methods.

On the other hand, maybe your company has just merged and you're reshuffling the deck. The following information can help you take inventory. Or maybe your company has just gone public and you have to commence "investor relations as usual." These guidelines on how to establish the investor relations function in your organization can help, whether your company is a Fortune 500 or a newly public company with one thousand employees.

Analyze continually what you have—or think you have—in place via a mission statement, a written investor relations plan, a link between the corporate strategy and investor relations goals, counsel regarding law and ethics, knowledge of the financial market, entrees to the network in the financial community, communications vehicles, links between other communications functions (such as advertising and media and samples of previous annual reports), road shows, and securities analysts presentations.

Here are some of the items for your checklist:

- Do you have a written mission statement? Maybe your mission is "to enhance shareholder value." Whatever the mission, it should be in sync with the overall strategy of the corporation. If the prime objective of your company is to improve the environment, maybe your number one mission shouldn't be about shareholder value, at least not exclusively.

- Does your investor relations plan outline what you should be doing, at least for the next year? If you're an established company, your plan could be longer term. The contents of that plan may be basic: to comply with the appropriate laws. Or it may be complex: to have a stock repurchase plan. But you have to know what you are seeking to accomplish during a certain time frame.

- Do you have a definite theme to use, in an integrated way, in *all* your investor relations communications? Whirlpool distinguished itself from its competitors for a number of years by emphasizing its global reach, particularly its penetration of the Far East. One of its annual reports featured a foldout section that graphically showed its operations around the world. That theme was reinforced in other communications. Your theme can change annually, as IBM's did during the eighties. Or it can be constant, such as GE's former theme, "Progress is our most important product" and its current "We bring good things to life." Naturally, this theme must be connected to your brand identity.

- Do you have a disclosure philosophy? In other words, what kind of information will be released? Some companies, even public ones, provide only minimum information. There could be a conflict. Investor relations may be called upon to establish a balance between what the company wants to tell and what investors want to know. If, when you interview to join an investor relations department, you discover that the corporate disclosure policy is not one you can live with, maybe you shouldn't accept the job. Art Gormley and Joseph Kopec offer a good discussion of disclosure policy in *Dartnell's Public Relations Handbook.*[7]

- Have you and the staff been thoroughly briefed in compliance issues—particularly what information you can and cannot release? Frequently, it will be your responsibility to educate the company about the laws and ethics. In terms of its image, the ethics of a company may not be as important as its compliance with existing laws.

Do you have down cold what the proxy system is all about and how you go about collecting proxies? There is also the important Rule 10(B)-5 of the Securities Act of 1934, which forbids any kind of insider trading based on information that has not been made public.

- Do you have research to support the wisdom of the transactions you're planning? If you're planning a stock buyback, for instance, is the market expected to be moderate or high? If you're planning to acquire Company X, is its stock price overvalued? If you're planning to take on more debt, what will interest rates be like?

- Does the department have solid contacts in the financial community? Are there a few in the financial community who are especially supportive? Many of the best investor relations reps I know cultivate "champions" in the financial community—analysts who are bullish on the company. Here location is important. As Theodore Pincus has pointed out, New York and Tokyo are no longer the only significant financial centers. Investor relations can also schedule meetings with groups of major potential investors in financial centers such as Toronto, Newark and North Jersey, Trenton and South Jersey, Houston, Baltimore, and Montreal.[8]

- Are you and senior management satisfied with the format of your communications vehicles? Can you ask your contacts in the financial community what they think about how you communicate—everything from phone calls to the annual report? How did the stock do after the CEO read his talk at the securities analysts presentation in Chicago?

Maybe he needs coaching on how to present himself. What do your customers think of your investor relations communications? What do your suppliers think? Your employees?

- Have you found out how much investors know about your company through focus groups or surveys? If it turns out there are gaps, you should mount an integrated communications campaign to tell the rest of the story. Here is where you'll need to work with other areas of corporate communications, especially the media department. As your executives go on road shows, for example, the media department can arrange general interviews for them in each city. This can have an enormous impact in telling the company's new story.

- Have you examined the archives of old investor speeches, annual reports, and shareholder letters? Find out what the company used to be and how it presented itself in past years. Compare that to what the company *wants* to be. In this research you may be able to identify a core identity or core strengths of the company that you can resurrect and highlight.

- Have you determined what kinds of resources you have and how you want to use those resources? You might find that you want to outsource some or all of your investor relations function. At Meridian Diagnostics, Corporate Secretary Jerry Ryan has handled about 90 percent of the contacts with the investment community. "It's very time consuming," Ryan has been quoted as saying, "and I'm not sure it's a cost-effective use of my time."[9] In this regard it's imperative to determine what you might *not* be doing because of lack of resources. For example, you might be better off spending your time contacting analysts, outsourcing the annual meeting, or conducting a search for appropriate underwriters. About eight billion dollars a year is spent on investor relations.[10] It's the job of the investor relations department to see to it that the money is well spent.

The Annual Report

By federal law, every public company must publish an annual report. Because the annual report is so important, it can strike fear and dread in the hearts of those responsible for it. However, producing the annual report—from the first concept meeting to when it rolls off the printing press—can be a satisfying experience. Honest. I've worked on plenty of them, for everything from high-tech to consumer-product companies, in good times for the company and bad. Two things are necessary for producing a successful annual report that doesn't burn out investor relations: ongoing planning and "buy-in" from all the relevant constituencies.

Why Is the Annual Report So Important?

Many members of the financial community take only a few minutes to scan a company's annual report. But the impression of the company they gain from doing so can have an impact on the stock. That doesn't mean, of course, that the annual report is the only piece of communication the company provides the financial community. But it's an important document, because the financial community looks for several things in the annual report (not necessarily in any special order):

> **Clear articulation of the strategy of the company**
> When the financial community scans annual reports, they want a snapshot from thirty thousand feet. Yes, the details are important, but so is the big picture and how it's communicated. This is often presented in the annual report as a theme. Coca-Cola's 1994 annual report, which won an award from *Institutional Investor*, had the theme "Coca-Cola—a great brand name and a great investment that is keeping its momentum." The graphics on the front and back cover, and the first sentence of the chairman's letter, spelled that out. Saks Fifth Avenue, in its first annual report, released in 1997, displayed "more of its fashion edge than its financials," as *Women's Wear*

Daily commented.[11] (That approach, however, could be appropriate right after an IPO.) The theme for Cognex Corporation's 1997 annual report was cost-effectiveness; the previous year *Forbes* had criticized Cognex for costly graphics that had little to do with the product.[12]

Clearly discussed financial information with easy-to-read graphics

This includes an explanation of how the company's strategy affected its performance, new developments, an explanation of disappointing numbers, and a discussion of any unusual circumstances.

Clearly discussed relevant issues

In 1994, Real Estate Investment Trusts (REITs) were controversial. *Institutional Investor* praised Post Properties, an Atlanta-based real estate investment trust, for its "evenhanded" discussion of REITs.[13] At that time, Post Properties was only a two-year-old public company. It simply could have avoided the controversy. Instead it labeled a section of the annual report "Why a REIT?" The financial community saluted the company's openness.

The annual report isn't just targeted at the financial community. Its audience extends well beyond the world of finance and investment. That's what also makes it so important. For a year, the annual report will be the key document distributed by the company. In many minds the company's image will be established by that document. An MBA may decide not to go work at a bank because its annual report depicts it as stodgy. Consumers may stop buying a product or a service because they think that too much money is spent producing the annual report. Since annual reports are frequently put into press kits, the media can easily get the impression from the annual report that a company is old-line. A committee in the U.S. Senate may review a company's annual report and conclude that the firm isn't adequately concerned about the environment. Members of a grassroots movement may analyze a series of annual reports and target certain companies for wasting money. On the other hand, the spirit of an annual report might make employees feel proud and make them more productive at work. The high-tech theme of a company may attract suppliers who want to be associated with a leading-edge company.

How Should the Annual Report Be Done?

There is no one way to do an annual report in print. Some companies choose to issue a summary report. In 1989, the SEC gave companies permission to issue annual reports whose front sections are in color and graphics and whose back sections present straight financial information in black and white. Although there are not many companies that have used this option, it has worked for some of those who did.

There is also no one way to put an annual report on the Web. Some companies use a lot of graphics. Some—among them, surprisingly, Microsoft—don't. GE includes photos of the heads of the business. Other companies do not.

How Should the Annual Report Be Approached?

As I said above, successful annual reports require ongoing planning and buy-in. And both of these have to proceed simultaneously, every step of the way. The direction the annual report takes will probably change a number of times. At each juncture, you may have to ask for management's agreement—and explain why their approach might not be the best way to represent the company. Investor relations staff members, if they're doing their jobs, ought to act like consultants.

A metals company in New Jersey decided to adopt the op-ed format for its annual report. The heads of the businesses were supposed to describe results, discuss strategy, explain the variables affecting the business, and make five-year predictions. The tone of each op-ed was supposed to represent the corporate officer's unique personality. By the time the report went to print, the majority of each op-ed was devoted to explaining current results; little attention was paid to the big picture or the future. The tone of each op-ed was the same. In this case, investor relations decided to go along completely with management's wishes. The result was an annual report that didn't tell the financial community very much. Investor relations wasn't doing its job.

The planning for the annual report starts with reviewing the company's past annual reports and the annual reports of other companies. Find out what worked and what didn't work in the company's previous reports. For example, if you are with investor relations at Post Properties, you would discover that its ten-page letter to the shareholders was a big success. You might decide to stick with that format.[14] But, if you work at Saks, you might decide that now is the time to emphasize financials as much as fashion.

The time for buy-in from your constituencies starts right here. You should be getting a feel for what management wants in an annual report. If you're going to ask management about their ideas, make sure you already have some ideas of your own—and are ready to explain why those ideas might be effective.

You can also learn a great deal from other companies' approaches. *The Wall Street Journal* frequently will make free mailings of a variety of annual reports to those who ask. You can also ask the "heavies" in the annual-report field (such as GE) for a copy of their report. The Internet is full of annual reports; study them for techniques, then do an online search to find out what the financial community and media are saying about the corporate annual reports. In addition, you can ask members of the financial community what they thought of certain reports.

At this point you also want to start searching for an appropriate designer. The best way to find a designer is through word of mouth. Ask your colleagues for some names. When you meet with those designers:

Request some recent samples of annual reports

The annual report is a special kind of project and the designer needs lots of experience. In addition, you want to know what the job will cost. Ask for a ballpark estimate for, say, a sixty-four-page report.

Request permission to talk with clients

You need to find out if the designer holds up well under the pressure of continual changes. Did she try to keep costs down? Did he add value to the project, such as providing worthwhile advice about the cover?

Discuss printers

Who does the designer work with? Why did he choose them?

Bounce off ideas

How might the designer depict your theme?

Check the chemistry

You and this designer are going to work closely together for several months. Sometimes he will have to meet with others in your company. Is the chemistry good? How will the chemistry work with senior management?

One of the most important parts of your planning is your selection of a theme, or a few themes. (I recommend sticking to one theme since that's an easier read for the financial community.) Sometimes there's no theme that characterizes the company at that time. One way to come up with a theme is to analyze executive speeches, quarterly reports, employee publications, strategy documents, philanthropic literature, company videos, e-mail, the corporate Website, media coverage, and customer complaints and commendations. From all this, it's possible to see a pattern. What you might discern is that the company has come a long way, on every level, in terms of its performance during the past few years. The theme could be these improvements. Or it could be the momentum going on in the company.

Planning also entails choosing a tone. If the company is on a roll, an exuberant tone might be OK. If the company is in transition, the tone should be different once the company gets on its feet.

As for format, as long as the annual report contains the necessary financial information required by the SEC, there is almost an infinite number of possibilities. The report can be as long or as short as necessary. The graphics can be flamboyant or subdued. The corporate offices can all be recognized or not. One word of caution: Do not closely imitate some other company's annual report. For several years GE produced an annual report that attracted a lot of attention. One year, for instance, the company candidly discussed its management philosophy. Those companies that tried to imitate the content and tone of GE's discussion looked foolish. *No* annual report should be a clone of another.

When scanning your report, the financial community is trying to determine exactly who *you* are.

No matter how well thought out, no matter how much buy-in there has been, there will be changes. Sometimes those changes come about due to developments in the marketplace, a sudden restructuring, or a realignment of the competition. On the average, producing an annual report requires about twenty weeks—roughly five months. I don't know many companies that *don't* get behind schedule. But federal law dictates that the annual report *must* be delivered to shareholders thirty days before the annual meeting. So expect to be rushed.

Things to Remember

- Obtaining capital on attractive terms is a highly competitive global business.

- The financial community is interested in seeing a company from thirty thousand feet—getting the big picture as well as the details.

- As with media relations, contacts are important. In the case of investor relations, the contacts that have to be cultivated and nurtured are in the financial community.

- Investor relations is a changing game. Global trading, analysts' earnings estimates, and technology have revolutionized how the game is played.

- To reinforce its message, investor relations has to link up with other communications functions in the corporation, including media and advertising.

- Don't imitate too closely a successful model of another company's annual report.

Notes

1. Lois F. Brown, "Getting a Grip on Investor Relations," *Directors & Boards,* winter 1995, 44.
2. Brown, 44–47.
3. James W. Kinnear, "The Role of IR in a Successful Company," *Directors & Boards,* summer 1994, 27.
4. Jerry Unseen, "The Virtual Road Show," *Inc.,* January 1997, 19.
5. James J. Roop, "Investor Relations for Turnarounds," *Public Relations Quarterly,* winter 1995, 15–18.
6. Kinnear, 27.
7. Joseph A. Kopec and Art Gormley, "Investor Relations," *Dartnell's Public Relations Handbook* (Chicago: Dartnell, 1996), 145.
8. Theodore H. Pincus, "16 Top Trends in Investor Relations," *Directors & Boards,* summer 1994, 44–47.
9. Dan Monk, "PR Firms See Investor Relations as Growth Biz," *Cincinnati Business Courier,* August 7, 1995, 1.
10. Pincus, 44.
11. Jennifer L. Brady, "Saks' Annual Report," *Women's Wear Daily,* May 13, 1997, 12.
12. Luisa Kroll, "Short, Sweet and Oh So Cheap," *Forbes,* June 2, 1997, 16.
13. Mary Lowengard, "The Best Annual Reports," *Institutional Investor,* September 1995, 124.
14. Lowengard, 124.

Chapter 3

Employee Communications

The social contract between employer and employee has changed. And, that, in turn, has changed just about everything in employee relations—and communications.

—Carol Kinsey Goman, Ph.D.,
an expert in organizational change,
culture, and business practices

In 1988, I had a computer company as a client. They wanted my agency to produce a video script to present to their employees in which senior management would explain why the company's return on investment—its ROI—had to be increased.

The writer I assigned to the project did what I judged was a terrific job. The pacing of the script, the simple concepts, the language used—all could have been taken straight from the evening news. But the client wasn't pleased. Why? Because the script included some negative implications of ROI. The client told me, "This is a happy computer company. We don't present any negatives." So the writer came back with a feel-good script, and the client was satisfied.

Today, few companies could get away with giving their employees only happy news. Employees are demanding communications that are credible, candid, and complete. Global competition, downsizing, re-engineering, and shareholder activism have changed the social contract between employer and employee. Few employers can provide their employees with lifetime job security, predictable promotions, automatic raises, ever-increasing benefits, and a feeling of family as they did in the past. As a result, employee relations has been reconfigured. Employees want reality from management—not just happy stories. They want to know where the company is going—and if they'll still have a job on Monday morning.

Technology has also revolutionized employee communications. With electronic networking, interactive intranets, and the Internet, access to information has become more democratic. Communications that used to be available only to senior management, shareholders, customers, or suppliers is now accessible to employees. They can e-mail their opinions to appropriate parties at the company. They may even hear back from the CEO.

In this chapter, you'll learn how to get your message across to employees in the most effective package. That might mean you'll discard some of the best practices you've learned since the 1980s, become passionate about technology, and rethink the role of paper in communications.

Communications—In All Sorts of Packaging

When it comes to employees, the term "communications" means many things. More and more employers are discovering that communications starts with the physical design of the workplace. If you want a "learning" organization—one in which ideas and knowledge are shared easily and conveniently—your employees need to be accessible to one another. As most business people know, more work gets accomplished around the coffeepot than at formal meetings.

Where Everybody Sits

Employers like entrepreneur Bill Gross, head of Idealab, have experimented with ways to reconfigure the physical space used by their employees. In an interview in *Internet World*, Gross explained that he has tried to "take some of the serendipity that one gets in chance meetings and discussions" and make that same dynamic available in the everyday workplace. By 1997, Gross configured Idealab in such a way that

the heads of all subsidiaries can communicate in person with one another as well as with the CEO.[1]

In your organization, perhaps your first job should be to look at the
current pattern of communications in the workplace. Do managers
"hide" in their offices, unavailable to staff? One of our clients, a manager of a Hartford, Connecticut, company, continually sent out mixed
messages. On the one hand, he sometimes managed by walking around
and communicating directly with people throughout the building. On
the other, he discouraged people from dropping into his office by erecting
various kinds of barricades. One such barricade was an excess of plants
that presented an obstacle to anyone who might approach him.
Another was always being busy on the phone in what appeared to be
personal conversations, making people hesitate to intrude. When he
worked on the computer in his office, his back was to the door. Most
off-putting of all, he was a bad fit in the organizational culture. His
body language, for one thing, was too loose for the conservative firm.
People saw him as a misfit and tended to steer clear of him.

How could you help this manager communicate more effectively
with his superiors, his colleagues, and his staff? One solution might be
to put the whole department in cubicles. Then there would be little
room for his plants, little privacy for his personal phone calls, and he'd
be more in touch with the rhythm of the corporate culture. An isolated
manager needs to be closer to the action.

You can also map communications patterns in your office. For
example, you can track who interacts with whom and then follow who
they speak with next. Who gets left out? Where is more interaction
needed? Between marketing and public affairs? Between manager and
subordinates? Between peers? Between the CEO and senior management? Anyone with eyes and common sense can track these dynamics
and come up with solutions. Maybe this manager (who has a good head
for finance) should be sitting closer to the finance department. That
interaction might make him more confident and feel more a part of the
organization.

If you want a consultant to help you with this, contact a public relations agency for some recommendations. Jack O'Dwyer has a directory
of public relations firms. You can reach him at J. R. O'Dwyer Company,
Inc., 271 Madison Avenue, 6th Floor, New York, New York 10016.

You can also contact companies that have tried out nontraditional configurations and see if they have written material on the plan they have implemented. In addition, you can research the topic online through CompuServe and other sites.

The Grapevine—In Person and Electronic

Another key factor in employee communications is the grapevine. Not so long ago, many organizations wrote off the grapevine as nothing more than a gossip mill. One writer I employed told me that at the end of the seventies her former boss at Gulf Oil told her that associating with the grapevine could damage her reputation. Now such corporate culture gurus as Terrence E. Deal and Allan A. Kennedy recognize the important role the grapevine plays in a company's daily operations. In *Corporate Cultures*, they point out that the cultural network or grapevine is "actually the primary means to communicate within the organization; it ties together all parts of the company without respect to positions or titles."[2]

In employee communications it's essential to be able to tap into the grapevine to retrieve and circulate information and get a sense of how people are feeling about things. In fact, working the grapevine should be part of the communications staff's responsibility—developing relationships with the biggest talkers, knowing how to move information, traveling, and being perceived as a trustworthy person who won't reveal sources.

In response to rumors about executive changes and layoffs at a Midwest utility, senior management called the organization's ten biggest talkers into a meeting and gave them the facts, indicating indirectly that they were vital links in the corporate communications chain. The rumors stopped abruptly.

There is also the electronic grapevine, increasingly called the intranets. Here is where e-mail has become perhaps most useful: CEOs can instantly find out what's on the minds of their staff, and management can get out its version of a story—fast. Employees can chat about a new announcement with coworkers around the world, finding out if marketing thinks the new corporate financial strategy will cut its funding for research. They can informally survey people, checking out if the new benefits package is viewed positively or negatively. And, since employees don't have to leave their desks and hunt down sources of information, the electronic grapevine is often more efficient than the in-person one.

Interactive intranets are also useful to employees with human resources issues, such as finding out more about their performance appraisals. They can pull up the information about the appraisals in the intranet, direct their questions to human resources experts, even ask how they can amend a negative review.

Companies are beginning to see that intranets are not just for large organizations. One Internet article described a firm in Ohio called Makino, whose four hundred employees not only shared information quickly, but also organized all the company's documents and purged outdated information on the company's intranet.

The pitfalls of e-mail, though, are also increasing. An obvious one is privacy. Many systems can be entered by management, sometimes making it difficult to send a note anonymously. Another drawback is the sheer volume. Etiquette and ground rules need to be established about which e-mail messages are appropriate to send and how quickly employees must answer their mail. At Makino, facilitators accepted and approved all material, then placed it on the intranet. There's also the problem of having to "always be in touch." Some organizations expect employees to check and respond to their e-mail almost around the clock, particularly if the company operates in several time zones.

Good Old-Fashioned Print

Another form of communications is print materials: newsletters, company magazines, brochures, benefits manuals. Many employees still enjoy having some paper in their hands. But what's expected from these materials has changed. They have to be a faster read and make important information accessible. An employee doesn't want to have to read through an entire newsletter to find out the company's new policy on mental health benefits; that should all be graphically flagged in the newsletter. *The New Yorker* magazine's formerly quiet, subtle style no longer plays in the workplace. Employee communications representatives must use all kinds of devices to highlight for employees the "must read" information.

In producing printed materials you must also keep in mind that you're not only competing for employees' attention with *The Wall Street Journal* and *Fortune*. You're also competing with electronic media such as *Wall Street Week in Review*. Your information has to be more candid and have more depth than its competition because employees now know where to go to get information about the company. They can call their broker to get the scoop on their company's performance on Wall Street; retrieve information about their company from a database, such as Lexis-Nexis; or contact a friend in the media to find out about the company's image.

Information about the company that comes through employee communications has to be as credible as the information that's available outside the company. Therefore, print material must provide unique forms of "added value"—information and insights not available elsewhere, at least not so conveniently. There must be a compelling reason for employees to pick up and read the print material. When competition in telecommunications became a reality at the former New York Telephone, management introduced a tabloid called *The Competitor*. The paper simplified the issues involved in competition and talked about them in a way that made the staff feel like they were "all in this together." The ragged appearance of the tabloid also communicated the message that the company was serious about being more cost-conscious. *The Competitor* became an important means of adding value, helping to change the mood of the company from one of fear to one of confidence.

Videos, Teleconferencing, Slides

We all know that we live in a visual society. And we all know the old saying "a picture is worth a thousand words." But the visual route is not always the most effective one. Suppose a chief executive wants to make a video explaining the company's new strategic direction to employees. It could be done and the time invested would be minimal. But the CEO would probably get greater commitment from the troops by addressing them in person at all company locations. As our workplace becomes more and more high-tech, the need for the personal touch is greater than ever. Your client in marketing can send you an e-mail thanking you for all the work you did on a presentation, or she can walk over to your desk, shake your hand, and thank you in person. You know which one would have the greater impact.

There is a place, however, for visual aids: on the intranet; on the screen via Microsoft's PowerPoint; in a video spoof of how *not* to talk with a reluctant customer; or in a videoconference that brings together twelve locations around the world. Video aids, though, can become oppressive if they're overdone. A director who sends out a video to the troops every week might become a joke throughout the company. Having a teleconference for every departmental issue can make participants resentful about how much they need to juggle their schedules and how much time they lose. Here you have to put yourself in the employees' shoes and figure out what kind of reception your visuals will have. In visual material today, less is often more.

Later in the chapter I go into the nuts and bolts of employee communications. But first I want to introduce you to the big picture.

Interview with Carol Kinsey Goman: An Overview of Employee Communications

Carol Kinsey Goman, Ph.D., is a consultant to organizations that need guidance on how to make their employee communications effective. Her work has been cited in *Industry Week, Investor's Business Daily,* and the *NBC Nightly News with Tom Brokaw*. The author of *This Isn't the Company I Joined*, Goman has served as adjunct faculty at John F. Kennedy University and the University of California, Berkeley. She is currently a faculty member at the Institutes for Organization Management for the chamber of commerce of the United States. In the following interview, Goman shares her experience and insights.

RLD: What changes have you seen in employee communications?

CKG: There has been tremendous change in employee communications. For one thing, the function now operates at a higher level in companies. Many in the organization consider employee communications a part of corporate strategy. At one company the new CEO included the vice president of employee communications in all the meetings. Another change is that we perceive employee communications as part of customer relations. Since employees are in the front lines serving customers, whatever we communicate to employees will have some impact on customers. At Levi Strauss & Company there isn't a whole lot of what we think of as "external communications." They're convinced that if they communicate effectively with employees, they're creating well-informed spokespersons for the company who will treat customers right. In other words, customer relations is part of employee communications.

Another change is what you might call the lessening of "spin control." Not long ago most employee communications were the mouthpiece of management. It used to be said that those working in employee communications serve two masters: management, who's paying the bill, and employees. The spin on the story could be just about anything management wanted, no matter how far-fetched it sounded. You'd rarely see negative stories about the company in employee communications. Frequently there was a big difference between the information in the company newsletter and in *Business Week*.

Now there's a new candor and a new commitment to be credible. At Weyerhaeuser, they reprinted and distributed a negative story about the company. Increasingly, you're seeing internal and external communications having the same content and tone. Finally, employees are being treated like adults.

RLD: It seems that technology is revolutionizing employee communications. Am I overstating things?

CKG: What technology has done in employee communications is give everyone in the company access to information that used to be restricted. This has leveled the playing field in a company. Everyone has been empowered. In addition to making information available, technology also allows employees to learn state-of-the-art concepts via intranets or video. All of human resources become more accessible and efficient; employees who want to find out more about their pension plans can bring it all up on their screens. And, thanks to technology, they can play around with "what if" scenarios about various investments. Companies that make this available to employees deliver a clear message: We care.

A lot has improved in the vertical stream of information. But we have a ways to go in terms of horizontal channels of information.

Technology—laptops programmed with Microsoft's PowerPoint—has also made it easier to deliver a pitch to employees. Additional equipment isn't needed and changes can be made in the visuals up to the last minute. The current technology provides a professional look without making employees go to a special room in another building to see the presentation.

RLD: Although management may not be putting so much of a positive spin on employee communications, they still are footing the bill. What does management want to achieve through employee communications?

CKG: That depends on the management. Certainly there is still some of the old guard who want total control of employee communications. Yes, they make communications their mouthpiece. But more often you find that management wants to use employee communications to reconfigure the social compact between employer and employee. Most of us remember the days when employers were paternal—sort of "father knows best." They provided for all our needs from the minute we entered the company until we died. In return, we were expected to be loyal, compliant, and willing to make sacrifices on behalf of the company. If the company needed our skills in North Dakota, we moved there.

Now, of course, that paternalism is gone. Global competition has made it impossible for corporations to offer employees security, either financial or emotional. But there has to be something put in its place. So, companies are experimenting with developing a new kind of social compact. It might take the form of promising employees that they will continue to develop new skills or of reassuring them that performance, not politics, will be rewarded. To bring about this new mind-set, employers are using all kinds of employee communications—from tabloids to expensive videos. The message is: We are partners in this. If the company does well, so will you.

In the communications there is nuts-and-bolts information about the strategic plan. That helps employees understand what they have to do on their jobs to affect the bottom line.

RLD: What tools are used in employee communications today?

CKG: There's a big change there. You're seeing less of the expensive glossies and more reliance on low-cost electronic communications. Through e-mail, a worldwide announcement can reach all employees in seconds.

We're also sincere about wanting to know what employees are thinking and feeling. That's why you're seeing so many focus groups and surveys. But focus groups and surveys won't improve management's relationship with employees unless there is follow-up. After a focus group or survey, tell employees what you've found and explain what actions you'll take.

RLD: Can an employee communications person conduct a focus group?

CKG: That depends on what kind of focus group you want. If the purpose of the focus group is simply to provide a transcript of what participants say, sure, someone from employee relations can conduct it. However, you might want a more sophisticated type of feedback, such as interpretation of body language. In that case you would have a marketing communications firm conduct the group.

RLD: Why are CEOs becoming more visible in employee communications? They seem to be conducting an unprecedented number of personal talks or town meetings with employees.

CKG: Way back in 1982, futurist John Naisbitt predicted in *Megatrends* that the more high-tech a society becomes, the more people will need the personal touch. Naisbitt called this "high-tech/high touch." In this world of e-mail it's good to have someone talk with you in person. That personal touch makes an impact.

In addition to CEOs, first-line supervisors are also meeting more often in person with employees. Surveys show that employees trust their supervisors. Therefore, information from a supervisor should ideally come in person rather than being delivered via a paper memo or e-mail. That bond between the supervisor and employees is another example of the new partnership in the workplace.

RLD: Small businesses now want to establish an employee communications function. How do they do that?

CKG: That function can be set up in marketing, public relations, or human resources. Frequently you see external and internal communications blended together in small businesses. When the function is established, those working in it have to decide what kind of vehicle they want. Will employee communications be the sounding board of management, or will it seek to truly inform employees?

RLD: Let's speculate a bit. What do you see is the future for employee communications?

CKG: Employee communications will be used more and more as a tool to help self-directed teams function. It'll also be more of a bottom-line issue. Employers will ask the employee communications staff, What can we do to help employees do their jobs better? In addition, employee communications will be a way to educate employees about the ramifications of a global economy. And you'll be seeing a loyalty compact replacing the old paternalistic contract.

More information will be presented experientially. For example, to communicate a number of points Rubbermaid held a fair featuring the competition's products. Each product revealed the cost involved and the selling price. Employees got immediate insights about how the company was positioned vs. the competition.

RLD: So if a corporation wants to get the message to employees to be more innovative, maybe they would set up a fair of new Microsoft products. Or have them watch the Disney movie *Toy Story* and analyze what made it innovative.

CKG: Right. You'll be hearing fewer speeches about the need to be innovative. Instead, employees will literally be getting into the act. Another change in the future is that those who want to communicate with employees will have to be emotionally literate—that is, they'll have to know to appeal to people's emotions, not just their brains. Part of CEO Lou Gerstner's success in turning IBM around was in knowing how to appeal to people's hearts, not just their heads.

"Staying on Message"

I remember working on employee magazines that were a smorgasbord of themes. These magazines were reacting to the news out there. Today that's too inefficient. Employee communications now has to be proactive or strategic. Every line in every paragraph has a purpose. This is what politicians call staying on message (see Chapter 4, Oral Communications). This was evident in Chrysler's turnaround. Employee communications—publications, meetings, videos—was used to reinforce the theme that Chrysler was the best in its class.

Jack Welch, CEO at General Electric, has been a master of picking a few messages to be communicated to employees and repeating and reinforcing them. Repeating the message might sound counterintuitive to communicators who are trained to be creative, to give a fresh point of view, to "break through the clutter" and get employees' attention. But repetition is one of civilization's oldest tools for getting a point across. Remember all the repetition in the Bible? In his oral epics, the ancient Greek poet Homer used plenty of repetition. Martin Luther King Jr. repeated, "I have a dream" in his famous speech at the Lincoln Memorial during the 1963 March on Washington. In its heyday IBM repeated the word "excellence." Advertisers keep repeating their commercials until the lines become part of popular culture.

The trick is to repeat lines in such a way that employees are pleased to spot a familiar message but also interested enough to pay attention. At Chrysler, Iacocca achieved that by making employee communications interactive. For the company newsletter, supervisors could nominate an employee who was "best in class." That best in class became a powerful message. Every month there was a new group of employees who were best in class. The theme was always the same. Only the details were different.

What messages should you select? This is where a business plan for employee communications comes in. And that plan should be integrated with the company's overall strategic plan. In that communications plan you want to emphasize:

- the mission of employee communications
- what role employee communications has in helping the company achieve its goals
- the goals of employee communications
- the objectives of employee communications
- what "push/pull" strategies will be used
- budget
- evaluation mechanisms, such as focus groups and surveys

Many employee communications functions are also adopting advisory committees. Those committees usually include employees, members of departments throughout the company, and (sometimes) representatives from outside the company. When advisory panels are in operation you can often prevent policies that will have a negative effect on the company. An AT&T newsletter once featured cartoon figures from around the world. The figure representing Africa appeared to be a monkey. The news media picked up the story and ran with it. It hurt the company's image. An advisory panel could have flagged this gaffe ahead of time.

Advisory panels are also useful in helping employee communications get support for its agenda. If employee communications wants to do an issue on the company's new marketing strategies, and someone on the advisory committee is a power in marketing, that person might help that special newsletter happen.

Accessibility

Whether it's *Hamlet* or the financial restructuring of the company, you have to make the story easy to follow. Americans never have been a nation of diggers who like to uncover nuggets of gold. We want things quickly and easily.

One of the biggest services employee communicators provide is accessibility. At the former Grumman Company, employee communications translated all complex concepts—from reorganizations to new high-tech products—into language that employees could understand. There was an unusual feeling of loyalty at Grumman.

How can you make your communications accessible? Here are some strategies:

Go to the experts

The expert in your company can explain the material to you as if you were a fifth grader. Whether he is the designer of a new platform for cars or the CFO brought in to save the company from bankruptcy, the burden is on you to get the information. If he isn't responsive to one of your questions, reframe it, and keep reframing it until he *can* respond in a way that will give you the information you need in the form you need it.

Think in terms of analogies

The new pension plan is like _____. The new service for banking customers is like _____. It's helpful when the analogies are drawn from popular culture and the history of the company. I remember the number of corporations that used the line "Where's the beef?" in their communications back in 1984, when it was part of a popular commercial. Analogies give people something familiar to hang on to.

Cater to people's desire for a story

The desire for a story is one of humankind's most primitive instincts. Advertisers tap into this need by making both print and electronic ads tell a story. If a new product is being introduced, scout around the company to find out the history of that project, its ups and downs, the breakthrough insights, what led to its development, the key players on the project team, and the company's hopes for the product's future. You might also research the history of similar products. The framework of the story will attract the audience.

Use graphics

Sometimes you want to do this in unconventional ways. For example, if a new tax on business is going to cost your company $1.1 million, depict that amount in terms of the number of cheesecakes in New York or the number of houses in Portland it could purchase.

Graphics give perspective to the words. If you're encouraging employees to write to their government representatives about an issue, think about depicting the debate as a scene from a soap opera or an old sitcom.

Know the demographics of your audience

Is the majority of the company's workforce under forty years of age? If so, you want your language and references to mirror the world young people live in. The newsletter you put on the intranet shouldn't sound like *The New York Times*.

Have something for everyone

For "scanners," it's a twenty-five-word abstract of the article right at the start. For those who want depth, it's sidebars with peripheral information. For those who want to pursue the topic further, recommend books, videos, and locations on the intranet and Internet.

Be interactive

Invite the audience to e-mail you with their comments. If people know they can have a say, they're more apt to expend the energy to understand a difficult article.

Financial Information

Employees want to know how the company is doing. One of the greatest services you can provide them is to package financial data in a way they can interpret it. There are many ways you can do this. Here are some suggestions:

- Invite financial experts who can simplify concepts as they brief employees. Videotape the presentation and make it available for all employees at all locations.

- Put on the intranet a simple, easy, and comprehensive discussion of basic financial concepts, such as ROI and retained earnings.

- Arrange special seminars at a local college for interpreting financial statements. All employees could attend.

- Have the CFO write a primer on financial concepts for employees. Help that person keep it simple.

- Have an employee learn the concepts and present them to other employees. This would be a form of self-help.

- Every three months, put the quarterly report, as well as the annual report, on the intranet. You might also want to post the quarterly and annual reports of major competitors. And you can set up a temporary hotline for employees' questions.

A Real Voice

In this digital age, a real voice is a prized commodity. The employee communications function should have real people to answer phones. These people should be liaisons between the company and employees. Employee communications is much more than the sum of its communications vehicles. It's a mind-set of caring. Employee communications serves management the best when it empathizes with employees.

Print vs. Electronic

Print isn't dead. And electronic communications isn't always the most satisfying way to receive a message. Brochures describing benefits, magazines with four-color pictures, a copy of the CEO's latest speech, and thank-you notes from the company president still play significant roles in many companies. People are fond of the rituals associated with handling paper. They can mark up a paragraph, display an article from the newsletter with their picture in it, pass the publication on to their family, and relax in an armchair at home with the company magazine. Paper hasn't gone away and won't. It's just that we have to constantly rethink how to use it.

Electronic communications is fast. It's all in one place: on your computer. If it's written well, it's meant to be an easy read. (It's been noted that you use much fewer words with electronic communications than with print.) Electronic communications also sends the message: We are with it.

However, employees can become bored on only an electronic diet. It's nice to alternate electronics with, say, an invitation from the CEO to a town meeting about the new corporate direction. In my experience, I've found that paper lets you break through the clutter. I could e-mail a colleague who helped me set up a client meeting, but it makes a greater impact when I send a letter on nice stationery to her home. That's a treat in her mailbox when she comes back from work.

Getting Employees Involved

Yes, employees can send e-mail to just about anyone in the company. But it isn't enough for them to feel part of the employee communications process. One consumer products company gives a U.S. savings bond to any employee who suggests a story for the worldwide newsletter. A telecommunications company helps employees write stories for the newsletter and gives them a byline. A TV network offers a catered breakfast for twelve to anyone who comes up with ideas for the company magazine.

You can turn employees into your most alert news agents just by finding meaningful ways to recognize their contribution. It may be an annual dinner with the CEO, or a Superman bulletin board where names of newshounds are posted, or a day off.

Approvals

Early in my career I realized that approvals of my copy were protection for me. If the law, finance, human resources, marketing, and sales departments checked my material for accuracy and political sensitivities, I knew there was less chance that I—or my client—would get into the soup. But it took a while before I recognized that the checking process should be interactive and that I couldn't just roll over—that if the law department said I couldn't use the word "new," it was my job to give them a list of alternatives.

For years I was so intimidated by the expertise of other departments that I didn't argue. One time a human resources department wanted to tout its performance appraisal system. At the time, I thought it was important for employees to know the pitfalls of the system: It wasn't as objective as human resources would have liked to think, and we needed to explain in detail how employees could try to redress a wrong. But I bit my tongue. In retrospect, what I should have done was explain that it was helpful for both managers and staff to present a balanced view of performance appraisal in order to help remove some of the negative feelings about the annual process. The article appeared, and it sounded like company pap. It did no one any good. Lesson: The burden is on the employee communications representative to make sure that a story is credible.

The CEO

The chief executive officer of a company has also become the chief employee communications spokesperson. Today there are many more internal than external presentations, and a significant number of the external ones are delivered by the CEO. Employees want to hear the news—both good and bad—straight from the horse's mouth. That means that employee communications has to have input in the remarks, from suggesting topics to discuss to actually drafting the speech or video script.

Recently, the CEO's speeches to employees have gotten mixed reviews. One CEO of a consumer products company in New York had to face the troops and announce that the company's parent was restructuring the entire firm. He didn't welcome the task. So he turned inward. He refused speechwriting assistance and came up with a bizarre talk on how bad he felt about the changes. He mentioned that when he heard the news, he "had tears in his eyes." He didn't empathize with the fact that everyone in the audience might get canned; the focus was purely on himself. The audience was furious that he hadn't reached out to them.

Another CEO started off strong: If the economic tides are going to be so turbulent, he said, it might be time for the company to take a new route. That energized the audience. But the speech fell flat when the CEO didn't give concrete illustrations of that new route. A year later, in a similar speech, he had, as in *Hamlet,* a play within a play. While he talked, his staff role-played the old and new ways of doing things. At a chemical company in Delaware the new CEO announced upcoming layoffs. He immediately followed this news with a description of the company's rosy future. His audience was devastated.

On the other hand, a very reserved executive started out his talk to employees with some professionally written humor that could have been straight from the *Tonight* show. That loosened up the audience. Then, in detail, he described the new social contract that he was establishing with his staff. You could have heard a pin drop. He triumphed because he was giving something to the audience. He was adding value.

If you guide the CEO or write the speech, you're going to be busy. Here are some tips:

Get the pulse of the audience

You can do that by listening to the grapevine, holding focus groups, or conducting a survey. You might set up a place on the intranet where employees can indicate what they would like to hear about in the speech.

Analyze what kinds of speeches work
for that particular executive

Read over his prior speeches and ask the staff which ones went well. Watch videos of those speeches, if they exist. What worked for one food company executive was a logical, sincere text that helped him conceal his boring personality.

Interview the CEO about the content and tone of the speech

Tape the interview so that you can capture the executive's speech mannerisms. Ask the executive if you should interview anyone else. Call your colleagues at other companies and find out how they handled similar assignments. Find out what worked and what bombed.

Give the executive a draft of the speech
earlier than you said you would

This gives the executive time to rethink his or her entire approach. Generally, there are many more radical revisions in internal speeches than external ones.

Confidentiality

A disgruntled employee at Microsoft can leak an internal memo from management to *The Wall Street Journal*. An unhappy manager at IBM can send a copy of an internal glossy magazine to *Moneyline* in order to show that the company is still wasting money. A laid-off employee at General Motors can deliver to the *Today* show all internal management communications about why staff reductions are necessary. You must be as cautious in internal communications as you are in external communications—perhaps even more so. The social contract is over, and many employees no longer feel loyalty to the organization they work for. Some are adept leakers. They know how to contact the right people in the media to publicize a negative story about the company; they usually know *not* to use a company phone; and they're experienced enough to recognize ahead of time which media will protect them.

In starting an employee communications function, I tell management to consider that what they say could appear in *Fortune*. This doesn't mean that the communications have to remain in safe "corporate-speak." Actually, plain speaking gets better treatment from the media. But it's important to review the material in detail and assess what could be taken—and quoted—out of context.

When it comes to rehearsing the speech you can either coach the executive or hire a consultant who can get away with telling the CEO, "You're boring."

Things to Remember

- Employee communications will never be the same after downsizing. The old social contract is gone and organizations are using employee communications to put another type of contract in its place.

- Employee communications is now a strategic function that affects the corporate bottom line.

- Employee communications representatives have to take control of the approval process. It's negligent to roll over and play dead.

- Helping the CEO communicate with employees is your number-one job.

- There's no such thing as confidentiality.

Notes

1. Gary Welz, "Newsmaker&A," *Internet World,* July 1997, 24.
2. Terrence E. Deal and Allan A. Kennedy, *Corporate Cultures* (New York: Addison-Wesley Publishing Company, 1982), 85.

Chapter 4

Oral Communications

Say to yourself that you are more qualified than any member
of the audience to give this particular talk and, by George,
you are going to do your best to put it across.

—Dale Carnegie,
*The Quick and Easy Way to
Effective Speaking*

When most people open their mouths, they fail. They fail to
get their message across, motivate others, or make themselves credible.
They fail to build confidence in their company or raise funds for their
nonprofit organizations. A poor performance in oral communications
derails more business careers than all the scandals, mistakes, and company
politics put together.

Why does this happen? Because many people don't realize that public
speaking—be it a speech or a conversation on an airplane—is a discipline,
just like athletics or the law. In public speaking, you have to
know what you're doing and why you're doing it, create strategies for
reaching your goal, and practice, practice, practice.

The Tale of John S.

In the seventies, I was working at a large public relations agency. One
of our clients was a major petroleum company. Part of our job was to

prepare the company's executives for their board presentations, road shows with security analysts, meetings with other departments, speeches at prominent forums, and videos for employees and the community.

Most of the executives didn't like to get up on their feet and talk, but they did it. Over time and with training, most got better. One president of a subsidiary, who had had a low profile until his alternative-fuel division was in the news, even enjoyed going out there and talking. One of his speeches was published in *Vital Speeches of the Day*; he was extremely proud of that accomplishment.

But not everyone was a good sport, like a senior vice president I'll call John S. John, who was a genius at getting out of his public speaking commitments. The strategy he used most often was having his subordinates address the board of directors or the chamber of commerce in his place because, he claimed, they needed the exposure. To give the illusion that he, in fact, was giving the presentation, he helped his subordinates prepare their remarks and even attended the meeting with them. Throughout the industry he was praised for supporting his people. Young MBAs wanted to get into his department. And those employees who went on to bigger and better things said that they owed their success to John.

I don't think too many of John's subordinates, or even his colleagues, realized that he was terrified about opening his mouth in front of more than one person. And John wasn't alone. Most executives fear public speaking about as much as they fear their own deaths. But not too many are as clever as John S. in shifting his public speaking responsibilities onto others.

John S. Today

John's scam would not work today. In fact, no sane executive would even consider trying it. You might say that the new mantra is "I'm ambitious, therefore I speak."

Being Seen

In today's age of talk and high visibility, John wouldn't get away with *not* talking. As Ted Feurey, speech coach to Fortune 500 executives, points out, we live in an era when people are seen. We see the president of the United States regularly on our television screens. Remember when it was a real novelty for First Lady Jackie Kennedy to show us around the White House on national TV? No more. O. J. Simpson's trial was shown on TV for months and months. Larry King and Barbara Walters interview just about anyone who's of interest at the moment. Troubled families discuss their problems on talk shows. *Moneyline* brings in CEOs as guests to tell us about their strategies and mistakes. More and more meetings are teleconferenced; we expect to and do meet electronically with the CFO or the vice president of marketing.

Yes, this is the age of fax and e-mail, but we still demand to see someone in person in order to do business. A naive colleague of mine moved his speechwriting business to a small town in Maine because he believed clients around the world would be happy to do business with him electronically. Wrong. He nearly starved to death. Since he charges about three thousand dollars for twenty minutes, customers want to see him. He moved his business back to a more central location in New York.

High Standards

Feurey also points out that in addition to wanting to see those we deal with, we expect them to present themselves with the same sophistication and polish as Katie Couric or Jay Leno. The standard for evaluating "how Joe did" in his presentation is now the same standard used on television: The presenter is supposed to be self-aware, focused, careful not to bore the audience, and able to provide something—knowledge, insight, inspiration—that people can take away with them. Even in ordinary conversation, such as talking to a superior in the corridor, you're supposed to be very polished. The bumbling characters played by Jimmy Stewart in old movies may be good-hearted, but they would have to be much more "with it" orally today.

Entertainment

Today's audiences also expect a presenter to entertain. The presenter doesn't have to be a Seinfeld; entertainment doesn't necessarily mean being a stand-up comic or even especially humorous. What entertainment *does* mean is holding the audience's attention. The burden is on the presenter to do so at all times. Whenever an audience gets bored, it's perceived as the presenter's fault.

Harvey Mackay, CEO of Mackay Envelope and author of *Swim with the Sharks without Being Eaten Alive*, gives business talks around the world. He uses a variety of techniques—humor, provocative anecdotes, contrarian thinking—to keep his audience mesmerized. What Mackay is doing is "adding value" to a business discussion that might otherwise be dull.

Show business is the name of the game, whether you're an international seminar leader or the keynote speaker of your company's board of directors. When the five top heads of a consumer products company gave their quarterly numbers report to the board, each made sure he or she had something entertaining to include. Several showed new commercials; two brought in new products that could be consumed in the boardroom.

You might say there is an element of theatrics in *everything* we do orally, including telling your boss about the figures that have come in about the new product. The trick is to find out what kind of theatrics you're comfortable with. An executive I coached found that he was comfortable working with props. One such prop was a small version of the old Underwood typewriters. He used it to demonstrate that all progress in technology is relative. And when he did, audiences kept that image in their heads. He repeated, "Remember when the Underwood was on the technological cutting edge!" like a mantra. Another executive worked well with offbeat slides, a foreshadowing of the Dilbert cartoons. A third executive got—and held—the audience's attention by asking, "Does your current reality measure up to what your fantasies depicted your life would be like by now?"

The number one crime in public speaking today is boring the audience, or the person sitting next to you on the plane. If you're going to open your mouth you have to obey the First Commandment: Thou shalt not bore the audience. My hunch is that Phil Donahue's television show was canceled because he began to bore the audience. The guy just got stale. Think over the conversations you've had at work with your colleagues. Do they indicate that *you're* going stale?

Are You a John S.?

Today John S., the oil company executive who continually ducked his speaker engagements, would be stuck in middle management. Without a good track record in public speaking, he wouldn't make it into the executive wing. No matter how talented, driven, or well connected, he would be forever limited by his lack of skills in oral communications. His superiors, colleagues, the board of directors, and members of other departments would want to see what he could do up on his feet. And if he couldn't show them something, they would write him off.

Surprisingly, I still meet plenty of John S.'s. They're in their twenties or thirties and graduated from colleges that had abandoned public speaking requirements. So in their most formative years, no one forced them to get up on their feet. They got the right degrees at the right schools and in some cases were able to get excellent entry-level jobs. But while their managers might have recommended they take a course in accounting for nonaccounting majors or learn a new software package, they didn't send them to a twelve-week Dale Carnegie public speaking seminar or recommend that they join the local chapter of Toastmasters. (Incidentally, at Mackay Envelope, Harvey Mackay makes sure that all executives are at least 9's on a scale of 1 to 10 in oral communications.)

Jane B., for example, would never be able to get a job at Mackay Envelope. When preparing for a meeting Jane spends all her time researching the topic. She chases around for all kinds of numbers inside the company and goes to superbookstores to load up on reading material. But she doesn't first ask herself what *message* she should be communicating, what the audience is interested in, and how to argue her case efficiently and interestingly. As a result, those who attend her meetings claim that she comes across as "being all over the place," "a flake," and "unable to see the forest for the trees." Jane B. isn't going anywhere in the organization because she's clueless about what a presentation is all about. If Jane B. worked even a few hours with a speech coach, she would realize the importance of having a focused message.

A good speech or presentation or a lively conversation with the CEO can put you in a whole different tier in your organization. I remember when my clients could make their mark if they turned in a thorough and brilliant report. But nowadays, who has time to analyze long reports? So clients have to present their findings in a manner that's brief yet efficient and interesting, spelling out all the important implications of the study. One client did just that at a board meeting. He used a slide as a prop, showing that the competition was beatable. He told his audience exactly what they needed or wanted to know. And he caught the eye of the chairman. It was a home run.

GE's CEO Jack Welch rose in the company partly on the strength of the way he presented himself. His no-nonsense manner in a corporation whose style was formal and statesmanlike helped him stand out from the pack. And he was so strong a public speaker that even his stammer didn't get in the way of his rapid ascent.

During the 1988 Democratic National Convention, Ann Richards, a not-very-well-known Texas politician, became a household name overnight. She did it by attacking George Bush in a funny, offbeat keynote address. At the 1996 Republican Convention, the highly respected General Colin Powell further enhanced his reputation with his "America" speech. Every day, in every organization, employees gain or lose points based on what comes out of their mouths. People remember bad presentations for months, even years. One new vice president of human resources at a company in the South wore casual attire when he made his first speech. People in the company never stopped talking about it.

Coaching—Now Part of the Public Relations Job Description

Do you work in public relations? If so, it's now part of your job to help your clients present themselves effectively. Those clients might be making a videotape on safety to send to all the plants. They might need some short notes scribbled on an index card to take along to a one-on-one meeting with a security analyst or a representative from a pension fund. Maybe they're delivering a big speech at the Detroit Economic Club, or they have to explain to the Akron chamber of commerce what it means to be a good corporate citizen today. Maybe they have to deliver bad news about layoffs to the employees. (If they're meeting with the media, see Chapter 1.)

Whatever it is, you'll probably be asked to help them. But even if you're not called on, you'd be wise to find a way to provide support for their oral communications. Oral communications is where the action is. Your support might consist of hiring a speech coach/consultant or simply videotaping the executives and giving them copies of the tape so they can see for themselves how they did. If you decide to get a consultant, ask your colleagues for a few names of reputable people. Call your professional association, such as the International Association of Business Communicators at (415) 544-4700. Take note of someone who made a good presentation and ask that presenter or the speechwriter for the name of the person who trained the speaker. Then ask those trainers about their track record. Request client references. Find out how long they work with someone before there are results (usually, results are immediate). And compare rates; the pricing is all over the place.

Oral Communications: It's All in the Delivery

Just about anyone who has worked with speeches, presentations, and videos knows that great scripts don't necessarily translate into great deliveries. And the delivery is the thing. No one cares what's on the paper; *everyone* cares what's coming out of your mouth. This is analogous to taking an exam. No one cares how hard you studied or how many useful reference books you used to prepare for the exam. All that matters is what you *produce* on the exam. Oral communications is a performance, and you'd better do well on whatever stage you're on.

I have known many executives whose oral material looks awful on paper. You wonder how it could keep an audience awake. But when the executive gets up to deliver it, the script comes alive. The script of a semi-retired executive at a petroleum company contained a smorgasbord of history, science, and management thrown together. When they read it, people giggled. But when that executive got on his feet, his audience was mesmerized.

Interview with Ted Feurey: An Overview of Oral Communications

Ted Feurey, speech coach to Fortune 500 executives, shares what he knows about oral performances.

RLD: Ted, why is there so much interest today in public speaking?

TF: It's all about how people *perceive*. People are not reading as much as they used to. Instead, they're perceiving through sight and sound. If you have a statement to make, it's probably more effective to make it in the form of a speech rather than an article.

Look at it this way: We saw Americans actually walk on the moon. We didn't wait to read about it in the next day's paper. We wanted that immediate experience.

RLD: What exactly *is* oral communications?

TF: Oral communications is a performance. Through that performance, the speaker informs, enthralls, and motivates. Good speakers, like Mario Cuomo and Barbara Jordan, understand this. They will throw themselves into the speech rather than trying to be cool and laid back. Remember Churchill's "Blood, toil, tears, and sweat" speech? Of course you do. But we usually don't remember speeches that are cool and laid back.

Preachers like Jesse Jackson are some of the best speakers in America because they know they're supposed to supply a performance. That performance isn't exactly the same as acting in a play or movie, but there are many similarities between what Laurence Olivier did in Shakespeare's *Henry V* and what executives do at the podium—or there should be.

RLD: If public relations people, administrative assistants, or friends want to help someone speak more effectively, what should they do?

TF: They should do two things. One, they should go through public speaking training themselves. They have to know what it feels like to get up there. That kind of training is available through consultants, community colleges, and organizations like Toastmasters International based in Mission Viejo, California [its 800 number is listed in most phone books]. Two, they should get a video camera. So much of public speaking training simply consists of looking at a videotape of how you performed.

   I would warn all speaking coaches to be careful how they approach this job. If they're training a superior, that superior can become very angry at criticism. That's why some assistants bring in consultants from the outside to do the hands-on training.

RLD: What will speakers learn as they train to deliver a speech or make a presentation?

TF: Basically, there are three things necessary to prepare for any kind of speaking engagement. The first is to have a goal. You have to ask yourself why you are doing this. What message are you going to send?

RLD: You can't just sit down to write your remarks and not have an agenda, right?

TF: Right. The second thing you have to do is decide how you are going to accomplish that goal.

RLD: We had a client who was announcing a layoff. We tried to figure out the best way to accomplish that. Should we recommend a short speech, in person, in each department affected, or an interactive videoconference throughout the company in which employees could phone in their comments? *How* you do it can make a world of difference.

TF: Right. And that "how" includes how long you will speak. One big pitfall in public speaking is speaking too long. Your speech is too long if the audience gets restless. Try out the speech before an audience of friends and see if the audience starts to become bored.

The third essential is practice. Practice puts the speaker in control. It's a proactive thing. All speakers improve—some dramatically—with practice. The most important equipment during practice is a video camera. It's during practice that people get to see the conflict between what they're saying and how they're saying it. They might be talking about making the company more open—and then stand there with their arms crossed which, of course, gives the shutout signal. When you train a person to speak, you diplomatically point out these discrepancies. And you ask that person if this message is what they intended.

RLD: I find it very useful to start my remarks with a story. What do you think about telling a story?

TF: Stories are great—if there's a connection between the story and the message. Incidentally, the reason the story strategy works so well is that we all have many stories within us. We have only to reach inside ourselves to get material for our conversation or our speech.

RLD: If you could specify just one thing about how to persuade an audience, what would that be?

TF: The best way to be persuasive is to put yourself in the audience's shoes. See the issues as *they* would see them. Former New York governor Mario Cuomo was very good at that. He could empathize completely with an out-of-work person in the audience.

RLD: Is there such a thing as charisma?

TF: Charisma is real. I define it as the ability to convey thoughts and emotions without words. You know it when you see it. It electrifies the room. Top speakers usually have it—at least when they're delivering a talk. Away from the stage they might be quite ordinary.

RLD: If someone is going to talk—to the boss, an audience of one thousand, or on a videotape—what kind of mind-set should they have?

TF: When someone speaks, that person should talk with the idea that they are going to inform, enthrall, and motivate. As for expectations, you shouldn't hope to be loved. If you get your message across in the way you want, you've accomplished your goal.

RLD: What kind of language should you use when you talk?

TF: One of the best guides for rhetoric is Winston Churchill. He used simple, short Anglo-Saxon words such as "sweat" instead of "perspiration." He coined the simple phrase "Iron Curtain." He also used simple, declarative sentences. He filled those words with passion.

RLD: We live in a visual age. Software, such as Microsoft's PowerPoint, makes it relatively easy and affordable to crank out plenty of slides. Do you see speakers using more visuals these days?

TF: For all the reasons you mentioned, there might be the temptation to have a lot of visuals for your speech or presentation. Well, *don't do it*. The audience usually recognizes that you're using these visuals as something to hide behind. Many speakers are overly dependent on graphics. Also, where do you want the audience's eyes? Do you want them to be on you or on the visuals? You can't have it both ways.

Frequently, visuals detract from the speaker. If you approach a speaking opportunity as if it's a performance, you won't need visuals. Your body language, gestures, facial expressions, and words will say it all. You can create your own atmosphere without props. Watch how Kenneth Branagh does this in the film *Henry V*. If you feel the need to pass out some visual material, do it after the talk.

RLD: What's the mortal sin of speaking?

TF: Separation. The speaker is unable to connect with the audience. Any connection can be lost if the speaker goes on too long. The rule of thumb for a speech is about twenty minutes. Bob Dole spoke for about an hour at the Republican convention in 1996, but I tell my clients: The day that *you* are nominated for the U.S. presidency, then maybe you've earned the right to talk longer than twenty minutes.

RLD: Is there any difference between a female speaker and a male?

TF: Barbara Jordan fully understood that she was giving a performance when she spoke. She enjoyed giving a speech and she knew where she was taking the audience. That should be the case more often when women go to the podium. But it isn't, and that is primarily because women hold back and don't seem to want to expose themselves in front of the audience. I advise women to study Lady Macbeth in the Orson Welles version of the play.

RLD: What about when one of those disasters happens—you lose your place in the speech or your mind goes blank?

TF: Simply give yourself permission to get the speech back on track again. Tell the audience you have just lost your place and you'll be back with them in a moment. If you can't find your place, then ask for their permission to start again.

RLD: How should speakers dress?

TF: They should dress as they wish to be seen. And they should avoid wearing anything, such as long dangling earrings, that could distract the audience.

RLD: Why is Colin Powell such an extraordinary speaker?

TF: It's his set of expectations. As a general, he expected that people would listen to him. People listen to generals. You should have the same expectation. If you cast yourself in the role of a victim and assume no one will listen to you, you will put in motion a self-fulfilling prophecy. What you want to do is assume a mantle of leadership.

What Oral Communications Entails

Oral communications breaks down into two essentials: deciding what you want to say and figuring out how you want to say it.

The two usually overlap. You really may not understand what you want to say until you try saying it. It's a bit like writing. Often you don't know what you're thinking until you try writing it. Or, while you're rehearsing, it might dawn on you that the strange entity who's making this speech isn't you. So you revise, making the talk a better fit for yourself.

For the Ear vs. for the Eye

You might have had a great teacher in your college Freshman Composition class who taught you how to argue your case—on paper. Well, the kind of speaking you have to do in corporate communications isn't like Freshman Comp. That was for the eye. This is for the ear. So, forget Freshman Comp.

Why Talk Is Different

Demosthenes, Cicero, Shakespeare, Winston Churchill, John F. Kennedy, Lee Iacocca—all of them understood that oral communications is very different from written communications. Therefore, they spoke differently than they wrote. Iacocca's speeches were full of "gots" and other in-the-trenches language. But his most famous print work, the "level playing field" op-ed piece on trade with Japan—was very statesmanlike.

Some executives still don't know that speech and print are different. A quick and effective way to demonstrate the difference is by reading an article from the newspaper aloud, then telling that story in your own way. Videotape both renditions. They'll be quite different: The reading of the article will be stilted; the story told in your own way will flow like normal conversation. It might even have passion and excitement.

The skilled oral communicator will use techniques that appeal to the ear. That's why, for example, you get so much repetition in a poem like Homer's *The Iliad*. It was meant for oral delivery. The ancient Greek audience was listening, and repetition kept their minds on the subject.

Here are some things you should know about oral communications:

Keep the subject matter relatively simple

Oral communications is meant for the ear—and the ear can take in just so much at one time. A book could cover the history of conflict from the time of Adam and Eve to World War II, but that would be too much to handle in an oral presentation. For a speech, you might focus on the factors that led up to World War II. The simpler your subject matter, the easier it'll be to communicate.

Keep focused on the message

This can't be emphasized enough. In politics they call this "staying on message." A book, report, or background paper gives you room to talk around your subject. Not so with oral communications. You have to be very clear what your message is and make sure that everything in the talk, whether it's a joke you tell or an example you cite, supports that message. People have a limited attention span when they listen. You don't want to burden them with too many messages.

Provide all the necessary data in an easy-to-process way

Remember that the audience, whether they're staff members at a meeting or a capacity crowd at Madison Square Garden, does not have a copy of your remarks. That means they can't go back in the text to clear up an ambiguity or check a statistic. If you're discussing the size of the widget industry in Indonesia, state that figure in round numbers—$1 billion—rather than specific numbers ($978 million) that can be quickly forgotten. If exact numbers must be presented, think about using visual aids.

Review your remarks and look for other sources of ambiguity. Is it clear that the "it" mentioned in paragraph four refers to the Salvation Army?

Present an image and a point of view

A conversation in the hall, a video, or a presentation represents just the tip of the iceberg, not the definitive last word on an issue. Executives open their mouths in public to show who they are and briefly express a point of view. They don't accept speaking engagements in order to demonstrate how much research they've done or to show off. Public speaking is all about presenting an image or a persona and offering a point of view. It's not about winning a contest for intellectual excellence. President Kennedy didn't have the highest IQ or the best grades at Harvard, but he sure knew how to communicate a message.

Keep it short

If clients give too long a speech, they immediately acquire the image of a windbag or someone who is out of touch. In my experience, I've found that executives who give unduly long speeches are in a downward career spiral.

Therefore, keep your or your client's remarks relatively short and make sure they are on message. Ted Feurey and other experts consider that twenty minutes should be the maximum time for a formal speech. There is no longer a hard-and-fast rule about that, but the human mind and ear are equipped to take in only so much information or new perspectives in one sitting. Try out the remarks on a real audience. Do the members of the audience seem bored? Do you lose their attention after five or ten minutes? If so, you'd better redo that speech.

Be clear in your message

Oral communications is often quoted out of context. That's why you must go over every sequence of words and see if they can be misconstrued. If they can be, reword that sequence.

An executive once said, "Although I can't condone welfare, I can say that welfare has a necessary function in capitalism." He was quoted in the press as praising welfare. The best way to keep the message unambiguous and avoid being misquoted is to talk in simple, declarative sentences. Avoid subordinate clauses that begin with the word "although."

Be open to making changes

Since oral communications is a performance, the speech, video, or point outline for the meeting is never "in the bag." No competent speechwriter hands in a speech a week before the event and assumes it's a done deal. The speech isn't 100 percent done until it's delivered. Many things can change. I remember when former president Ronald Reagan was shot in 1981. The speechwriters in our organization had to change the opening paragraphs of many speeches quickly. Suppose you discover that actor Tom Cruise is attending your executive's speech. That will change the nature of the event, and you will want to modify the remarks.

The Medium

What medium should you use to communicate your message? A speech, a presentation, a video, a point outline? Or should you structure the situation as an ordinary conversation—a casual chat in the cafeteria about the department's morale? To find out which medium is most appropriate, you might have to do a little audience research. If the audience is expecting a polished speech, you don't want to arrive at the Cleveland chamber of commerce with a brief point outline. It's up to you to find that out.

Suppose the Fairfield County Council of Product Developers wants your client to provide a description of how its best-selling product, Widget System 3000, was developed and marketed. That could mean they want the executive to present any of the following:

- A formal speech focusing only on the big picture in product development and marketing. No case study about how the project got off the ground. No slides.

- A detailed presentation, with slides, explaining all major aspects of the product development and marketing functions.

- A point outline, with or without slides, loosely structured to highlight the main points of the product development and marketing.

- An interactive presentation in which the speaker leads the audience to participate in a discussion of how Widget 3000 was developed and marketed.

If you select the wrong medium the audience will be disappointed, maybe even shocked. Inevitably, your reputation could be damaged. An executive from a consumer products company thought he was supposed to talk in depth about how consumer products were influencing world trade. He brought along tons of material packed with tons of numbers—and he looked ridiculous. It was an after-dinner speech and all the audience wanted to know was: Did Italians like American cheese and how was American beer selling in Germany? They expected something light. What they got was comparable to a *Harvard Business Review* article on change in the global marketplace.

So, how can you—or your client—be on target with the right medium in the right place?

- If time permits, attend some presentations that are given at the organization that is inviting you. This will give you a good feel for what works there. Check out the room. Is it conducive to audiovisual aids? What kinds of people attend? Is the audience serious about getting new information, or does it just want the illusion that it's being informed? Is this a crowd that wants entertainment more than information?

- You can also do some indirect intelligence-gathering. Ask your marketing colleagues what they think of the organization. Ask the organization for the names of past speakers and for a copy of their presentations. Call previous speakers. How did their presentation go and what would they have done differently? Did the audience give them a rough time during the question-and-answer period or was the group too polite to ask tough questions? (In that case, you might want to put some tough "plants" in the audience.) Was the audience bored by too much information? What kind of follow-up came from the audience?

  Imagine you have to present a reorganization plan to your company's board of directors. Contact everyone you know who might have information about the composition of the board. One member of the board might hate numbers. Another might like anecdotes about how other companies, especially Microsoft and Netscape, are doing things. A third member might want realistic, best-case and worst-case scenarios of how much money the reorganization will save.

  Also, you or your client should request copies of other presentations made to the board within the past year. What was their format and style? How much documentation was given? Was the tone personal or formal? How long did each presentation run? Were visual aids used?

  You or your client might also consider contacting the previous presenters. What advice would they give you? Who has the most power on the board? What types of evidence hold more weight with the key members of the board?

  Or let's say your client is making a video that will go out to all the company's plants. It will discuss the benefits and pitfalls of teamwork. If the budget allows, go to some of the plants and randomly interview employees about what they would, or would not, like to see in such a video. If that's not possible, you can do a survey via e-mail or the telephone. Should some workers be included in the video? Find out what rooms the video will be shown in. If it's in the plant garage, you might not want it to have a slick look. Talk to plant managers about what they would expect in a useful video. Would the employees and manager want to see supplementary materials accompanying the video? Should you include workbooks, for example?

In another scenario, you or your client has to give a five-minute presentation about human resources to the marketing department. Find out how marketing perceives human resources. If it's as a useless function, it might be disarming for your client to mention that as he or she begins the presentation. You also need to know what problems marketing has been having. Can human resources be part of the solution? How are presentations generally made in the marketing department? Ask to see some previous presentations. Contact the presenters. Ask them what they thought was on the minds of the audience. Should a presentation to marketing be made very quickly, or should it be presented in a slow, methodical fashion?

Imagine that your client has been invited to be a member of a panel at the American Medical Association. Your number one job is to find out what is expected of panelists. Are they supposed to come in with five minutes of prepared remarks, or just wing it? How long are they supposed to take to answer a question? How can nonmedical members of a panel make themselves more credible? Would it be useful if your client spoke with other panel members before the event to avoid saying something redundant?

What if you or your client meets, one-on-one, with a boss to ask for a promotion? You have to interview the client beforehand about what arguments have the most impact with this boss. Should you stress the results you've gotten or the amount of hours you put in? What pressures has the boss recently been under? What kinds of people has the boss promoted in the past? Have any of those promotions gone sour, and why? If so, how can your client demonstrate to the boss that he or she will not make those same mistakes?

Try out the draft of your or your client's remarks with actual members of the department. It's very easy for professionals to make fools of themselves when they're giving a presentation off their turf.

In short, you have to understand the nature of the beast. Addressing the conference board is very different than addressing the rotary.

What to Say

Some speakers like to talk from a formal point outline. That is, they have about twenty-five bullet points containing key phrases and data. Some have attended a Dale Carnegie public speaking seminar and learned to plan talks in their head without writing down a word. Others want every word written out and points that are to be emphasized underlined in red. Some want only a slide show that they can talk around. But what all have in common is that the message is the number one concern. The medium is less important than the message.

The Speech

You find out that the organization inviting you or your boss to speak wants a full-text speech. How do you go about writing it? Well, it is possible to put one together yourself. You can also hire a speechwriter. Many communications executive search firms, such as the Cantor Concern, have a list of freelance speechwriters. You can also put an advertisement in the paper for a writer or public relations professional. But no matter how you go about producing that speech, you had better do a good job. This assignment should be a priority to you.

The Stakes Are High

When it comes to a speech, the stakes are high. What you do will be seen by many people. Giving a speech is the ultimate networking opportunity. If you do well, this could be the big break you were waiting for.

Your Kind of Speech

Speeches, like everything else, have changed over time. Back in the sixties and seventies most executive speeches sounded alike. They were statesmanlike. Bad news and controversy were handled very carefully. Then in the late seventies Lee Iacocca came on the scene at Chrysler and introduced highly conversational speeches. He used unstatesmanlike words, and he didn't shy away from controversy. If the Japanese auto industry was eating the American auto industry's lunch, he flat out told the audience that.

Lee Iacocca changed the nature of the American business speech. Since then, there has been no one way to give a speech. Now you have to work hard to find what kind of speech fits you best. Start by watching speeches. Look in the business section of your newspaper, or read a publication like *Crain's New York Business,* which lists professional events. At many of those events someone gives a speech. Contact your trade association and see which speech events they have lined up. Often the C-SPAN network carries speeches. When the president makes a speech, observe how he goes about it. You'll find there are almost an infinite number of ways to communicate a message via a speech.

You can also read speeches. The library carries *Vital Speeches of the Day.* There are books containing collections of speeches. You can check the Internet to retrieve recent speeches. Analyze how those speeches might change a point of view. Which speeches work better than others and why?

After you find a few models you want to try out, write up a few pages of text in that style and then deliver them in front of a video camera or a live audience of friends. Do you like what you see? Do they? Keep working at it until the style you choose becomes a good fit for you.

Audience Analysis

As soon as you get a speech invitation, investigate who the audience is. If you don't have time to do this, have one of your assistants do the job. It's a task that has to get done.

You must find out: Will the speech be given after a big meal or just before lunch? Will drinks be served that evening? Did something happen in the organization that the speaker should be aware of? Maybe the president just died. Is there someone special in the audience who should be recognized? Does the group have any hostilities toward your company? Will there be any other speakers on the podium?

Research

Next, research the topic. First, ask the organization that extended the invitation if there is any background information you can read. Do they want you to meet with certain people inside or outside the organization?

You can explore the topic online on the Internet and not just retrieve information. While I was writing *The Critical 14 Years of Your Professional Life*, I chatted online with young people about what they were looking for in a career-advice book. You can call bookstores and see what they have in stock on the topic. Do you know people who work in think tanks or universities? They may be able to give you some input.

There are a number of goals in doing research. For one thing, if there's information that undermines your argument, you want to know about it. And you want the audience to know that you know about it. Second, you want to get beyond the clichés about the subject. Lee Iacocca was brilliant in retrieving and using information that would shock his audience. He had a number of character flaws, but boring the audience wasn't one of them.

Next, boil all that information down to one or two simple messages. And use those messages to organize your talk.

Formats

The question to ask yourself is, How can I best communicate this message? There are about a dozen basic ways to organize a speech.

The "problem-solution" model

You present the problem, and then you present the solution.

The reverse of the "problem-solution" model

You present the solution and then describe the problem.

The historical approach

Perhaps your message is that the business community must do more to help improve public education in the United States. You would present a chronology of problems in public education since the founding of America. Then you would, within that historical context, discuss a solution.

Variation

Another format is some variation of the present, past, and future option.

The personal-story approach

Perhaps you are a "victim" of public schooling and you can recount how that hindered you in your career.

The string of anecdotes

The speaker discusses how various famous men and women judged their educational background.

Mix and match

You can mix and match several of these. There's no longer one set way to do a speech. One executive used the "problem-solution" format plus numerous anecdotes about young school children in the inner city.

Tone and Timing

Who do you want to be during the speech? I think that we're finally giving up the notion that we all have only one true self. Back in the fifties, sociologist Erving Goffman pointed out that we all construct a different persona or image for each situation we enter. For example, we're different with our superiors than we are with our families. Many of us are also different people in different contexts on the Internet. According to sociologist Sherry Turkle, chatting on the Internet is helping us develop a number of distinct personae.[1]

In my years of working with clients, I've never found one with a true self. Successful clients are able to cultivate a variety of identities that are a good fit at particular times, such as when addressing the board of directors or meeting with their children's teachers. Finding that fit involves a lot of work. In becoming a seasoned speaker you may have to try out a number of identities, too. As the times change and you become more successful, your persona will change. The person you are now is very different from the person you were five years ago. But if you haven't changed how you give a speech, you're possibly falling out of touch. The odds are that people are whispering you're on the way out.

Every time you start a speech to clients, you have to figure out who they want to be for this speech and who they want you to be. You might need a consultant to work with you on this one.

The Opening

There are actually two openings of a speech. The first is what I call the "pseudo-opening." It's a minute or so of pleasant things to say. During this time the audience is settling down and the last few stragglers are finding their seats. Everyone's attention is starting to focus on the speaker. It is mandatory that the speaker doesn't say anything of consequence during this first opening.

Then comes the second opening. Here is where the speaker *really* begins. Many seasoned speechwriters write this second opening *after* the speech is otherwise done, because the speech usually keeps changing and therefore the opening will too—and because it's so important. If you work on it first, you may never even *get* to the body of the speech.

There are all kinds of ways to open. One is to simply state the problem. Another is to tell an anecdote. Perhaps for your speech on public education you saw a school principal on the *Larry King Live* show and were struck by her passion about her work. Some writers like to use a quotation. What about humor? If you're very skilled at oral communications, humor can work, but not everyone can pull it off. Remember that humor always involves risk. If it doesn't work out, the speaker will be off to a bad start. Failed attempts at humor stand in front of the podium like an elephant turd in the middle of the living room.

The important part about any opening is that it be sincere. An audience can tell if the speaker really cares about education or not. Dale Carnegie calls this "earning the right to speak about the subject." Carnegie noticed that many insincere speeches were simply the result of the speaker's lack of experience with the subject matter. Thus, they hadn't earned the right to speak about the subject.[2] If your clients similarly haven't earned the right to speak on the subject assigned to them, then they should reshape the subject into a topic they *can* speak about with conviction.

The Body

In the body of the speech your job is to persuade the audience to adopt your point of view. The techniques you use depend on what you're comfortable with. A member of the old guard in a manufacturing company spoke about quality with a string of personal anecdotes. Because of his credibility, this technique worked for him. But a less seasoned executive probably couldn't pull it off.

A professionally prepared speech usually includes a variety of persuasive techniques. Go to a bookstore or library and get books on persuasion. An excellent one is Roger Dawson's *Secrets of Power Persuasion*. Think back to incidents when others persuaded you to their points of view. What techniques did they use? Watch *Burden of Proof* on CNN. How do the hosts persuade the audience to a certain point of view? When someone gives a speech, what is it that makes him persuasive?

Some common techniques of persuasion are as follows:

Building common ground with the audience

If an executive is talking to a group of welfare mothers, he or she needs to bond with them somehow. If the executive has been no stranger to hard times, especially as a child, that would help, and should be conveyed.

Appealing to the higher self in each person

An astute fundraiser for an animal rescue group asks people to find room in their lives for an unwanted stray. But she doesn't leave it there. If they can't adopt an animal, she asks them at least give a small donation. She gets plenty. Sometimes appealing to the higher self means asking your audience to write their senators on behalf of their grandchildren.

Defusing hostility

One of the biggest barriers to connecting with an audience and convincing them of your point of view is unresolved hostility. It almost always pays to bring the hostility into the open. If someone from management is addressing the union, the speaker should acknowledge that things have not always been rosy between them but that now there's reason for cooperation. A very skillful orator could even inject a little humor—self-deprecatory wit, for example.

Using expert evidence

There was a time when citing experts was highly persuasive. But the public has become skeptical of experts and now know that an expert opinion is only an opinion. It's still useful to support some of your assertions with documentation from the experts. If your client is discussing reading scores for that speech on public education, it would be helpful to have data from an expert on the subject at the Harvard School of Education. But the audience also wants to hear what *you* think, not just what the experts think. It's frequently provocative to cite expert evidence, and then take issue with it.

Citing statistics

Statistics can be helpful. They support your argument. If you're talking about how many children don't attend school regularly, it's necessary to have some kind of statistic. But you have to be careful about statistics. Cite the source. That gets you off the hook if someone in the audience has different statistics. Check if the source is reputable; you can do that by calling the trade association that represents the industry. Also, make sure you have the latest statistics. If the only numbers you can get are for 1992, you probably shouldn't use them. Your audience will question your credibility. And round off most numbers. If there are 1.9 billion widgets produced a month, round that off to almost 2 billion. It's easier for the audience to remember that figure.

Turning around bad news

You can tell an audience any type of negative information as long as you can point to what good might come out of it. If you're announcing a layoff that will mean more work for the remaining workers, show them how the layoffs will protect their jobs, since the plant could close, eliminating all jobs.

Demonstrating your own expertise

Remember, you were invited to speak because someone believed you had something to say *based on your own experience.* You are doing a disservice to your expertise if you don't use anecdotes, express your opinions, and speculate about the future. As Dale Carnegie would say, you have earned the right to talk about your subject.

Introducing opposing viewpoints and arguments

One of the most disarming techniques is giving merit to the opposing point of view. This increases your credibility. After all, look at how objective you've been!

Positioning what you have to offer as a scarce commodity

Whether it's jobs or advice, increase the value of what you're offering. Suppose you are the dean of Harvard Law School trying to recruit students. You want the best and the brightest. Since a seat at Harvard Law School will seem more valuable if there aren't so many of them, you stress that there are only some 560 seats at the law school. That means only one in ten who apply will get in. Then you can explain strategies for getting into the school.

Adding humor

A dash of humor, especially if it's at your expense, can provide some comic relief to a very serious talk. The audience will be grateful that you gave them a chance to lighten up. It also shows that you don't take yourself too seriously. Not everyone—speaker or audience—can handle humor, however.

Involving the audience

It always helps to get the audience out of its passive role and participate in your talk. Maybe they can guess the number of personal computers that are sold each day. You can also involve the audience by calling for testimonials from the floor. For example, an unemployed fifty-year-old can recount how a job search is going.

Creating a sense of competitiveness

This helps establish a benchmark for the audience's performance. Did people in Minnesota donate $50 million to education? You can challenge your New Jersey audience to top that.

Telling moving anecdotes

President Ronald Reagan was a master of this. His researchers found just the right story, and his speechwriters inserted just the right level of detail.

Creating a sense of urgency

You have to get the audience to see the problem as a priority—one that must be solved in the very near future. The pictures of the wounded on the nightly news during the Vietnam War certainly brought a sense of urgency to the war.

If you accompany your clients on their talks you might also notice other persuasive techniques. For example, they may use body language to act vulnerable when they ask for cooperation. Remember those techniques and recommend that they use them again in the next speech.

Language and Sentence Structure

A speech is supposed to be conversational. That is, it's supposed to sound like someone is talking to someone else. But there are all kinds of conversations. You might talk in a formal way, like a statesman. Or you might have an informal style, like a TV talk show host. What's important is that the speech you use mirrors *your* style.

You don't need to use full sentences in a speech. For example, it's acceptable to say, "Shareholders' rights? What about employees' rights? The rights of people like you and me. Employees' rights—it's about time. Employees' rights—a battle already lost?" In normal everyday conversations, we don't use full sentences. We flit from idea to idea without introducing formal, full sentences.

In order to be conversational, your speech patterns should be very close to actual conversation. That means you'll use contractions, such as "don't" and "doesn't." The only exception to this is if the executive doesn't normally use contractions. I know a number of CEOs who feel downright uncomfortable with contractions and who insist they sound most natural when they say "do not" rather than "don't." Some of them are right. But more of them would make a better speech if they were a little less formal.

Analogies, Metaphors, and Examples

Your audience is trying to take in a lot of new thoughts. How can you help them? It's always useful to paint word pictures through analogies and metaphors. Instead of saying that a hamburger tastes good, say that it tastes even better than the way you feel when you win the lottery. Describe a reorganization as gutting an entire department and then come up with blueprints for the twenty-first century. Find out how to discuss your subject matter in ways that will let the audience think of it in new contexts. If your client wants to hype a bake sale, he can say it provides trips to paradise for fifty cents.

Examples are equally powerful. It's much more effective to illustrate a point than simply to say it. You can say that older Americans have never been richer, or you can cite both the number of people over fifty in New York State who are millionaires and how many cars and houses they own among them. If your client is arguing that another fast-food restaurant won't mar downtown Greenwich, Connecticut, have him or her describe the charm of Greenwich Avenue and show how it won't be affected.

Visual and Auditory Aids

It can be very effective to have appropriate visual or auditory aids. Some companies get legal permission to use scenes from a movie or music from a popular song. The audience identifies with these images and sounds and the speakers have an excellent introduction to their talks or seminars. Other companies create slides or overheads that help tell the speakers' story. The audience is grateful to have those visual aids and is more responsive to the speakers.

However, there are times when visual and auditory aids fall flat. Here are some guidelines for effectively using visual and auditory material:

Make sure they are integrally related to your talk

The two should fit like a hand and glove. If not, the audience will be distracted. One company's sales presentation introduced a new fitness device. The target market was aging baby boomers. To set the tone, the company got permission to use a few lines from a Bob Dylan song. Rather than create nostalgia for the sixties, however, the music angered the sales prospects, who felt that the company underestimated their knowledge of current music. This mistake could have been avoided if the music had a more direct tie-in to the product.

Make sure the visual aids do not inadvertently communicate the wrong message

The marketing department of a consumer products company used ornate-looking slides for a routine presentation to the board of directors. Since the company was in a cost-cutting mode, several members of the board made a reference to the expensive slide show. Ironically, those slides didn't cost more than less-ornate slides. What messages are you communicating with the visuals? The message in this case, unfortunately, was: We have money to burn.

Ask yourself if the visual aids really are necessary

Some speakers feel comfortable when they have visual aids to "talk around." That's fine if the aids really are needed. If they're not, the audience will realize that the aids are being used as a crutch for the speaker. And that will lessen the speaker's credibility.

Use slides only if there are enough of them to make it worthwhile to turn on a projector and dim the lights

One speaker felt that it was very important to show a picture of the coffee his company was selling in Asia. His speechwriter warned him that turning down the lights for one slide could annoy the audience. So the executive held up an actual bag of coffee instead.

Make sure the visual and auditory aids enhance the talk, not distract from it

It used to be that each slide had the speaker's exact words on it. That's no longer the case; now the slide can have slightly different wording. But it shouldn't be so wordy that the audience is too busy reading it to listen to the speaker. If your slides contain a lot of information, tell the audience that a hard copy of the speech will be available after the talk. This will ensure that they won't be preoccupied trying to remember everything on every slide. (Don't give them a copy *before* the speech, because they will be flipping through it as the executive talks.)

Use music carefully

Music can be so powerful that it turns the audience inward, not outward toward the speaker.

"Call to Action"

Here's where the rubber meets the road, where the client asks the audience to do something. In the speechwriting business this is referred to as a call to action. Maybe your client wants the audience to send an e-mail to their government representatives expressing approval of new highway funding; or to join community groups to help solve the solid waste problem; or to bring home a box of the company's new low-fat cookie.

Whatever the request, it should be spelled out in explicit, detailed terms. The client might say, "When you sit down at your laptop tonight and check your e-mail, I want you to do something for your grandchildren. Send an e-mail to your senator and congressperson. Tell them what you think about Social Security. And you might copy your grandchildren. They will someday realize what an important thing you did."

You also want the call to action to be easy to follow. Your client might give the e-mail addresses of the government representations, or print up the names of community organizations dealing with solid waste, or pass out sample boxes of cookies. You could also have all this information on your Website.

Presentations

A speech informs and entertains. But a presentation primarily provides information. Certainly it should be interesting, but no one expects a presentation to be the same "work of art" as a speech. I usually think of presentations as "no-frills talks."

Maybe you have to make a presentation to the board of directors to get more funding for a new product or present a possible joint venture to Ford. Your client might be addressing security analysts about the firm's current difficulties (see Chapter 2, Investor Relations), or explaining to a community board why the company is convinced its new facility won't upset the flow of traffic, or making a plea to employees to give all they can to United Way this year. Because there are so many things that have to be said and so many causes, executives are giving more presentations and fewer speeches. Often they give a new hybrid of speech and presentation. The presentation will contain some speech techniques—such as the use of quotations and inspirational reflections—but its basic goal will remain providing information.

What Are the Concerns?

In creating a presentation the most important question to ask is: What is the audience concerned about? Maybe the board of directors is concerned that a great deal of money is going into developing a new project and it doesn't see any payoff in sight. Perhaps employees are concerned that too much of the money donated to United Way goes into providing lavish lifestyles for its executives. The city of Stamford, Connecticut, may be concerned that the arrival of a new corporation in the downtown area will change the flavor of the community.

Addressing these concerns is what your presentation must be about. But how are you going to find out what's on people's minds? There are many ways to gather this intelligence.

- You may have to use your clients' connections. They may, for instance, know someone who knows someone on the board of directors.

- Security analysts often know more about what's going on in a company or an industry than executives do. Call them.

- Networking will inevitably turn up contacts who know where you can find out information.

- You can run an online literature check on the company or on the subject. You can use online services ranging from Dow Jones to CompuServe.

- You can search the Internet, but remember that there is no guarantee that the information is valid.

Tight but Interesting

One message you want to get across as you give your presentation is: I don't want to waste your time. Every sentence, every statistic, every example should be necessary to make your point. If there are two examples for a point and one will do, leave out the second one, no matter how interesting it is. The best way to find out what is not really necessary in a presentation is to put on the talk for a few friends and let them tell you what's superfluous.

You also want to be interesting. A finance executive at Chrysler could feel how bored the board of directors was during his bimonthly presentation. He went to the director of public affairs and asked for help. The director made these suggestions:

Use contractions

Using the contractions "don't" and "there's" is less formal than "do not" and "there is." Contractions make it seem like the presentation is moving along at a swift pace.

Use short examples

If the example requires three or four minutes to tell, then leave it out. If the appropriate examples require telling a long story, shorten that story. Boil it down to the essentials.

Use rhetorical questions to break up the text

The finance executive learned to ask, Why am I here today? or What does sawdust in a plant in Bolivia have to do with a 5 percent boost in profits?

Use visuals only if they really help tell the story

Visuals take time. The board has seen thousands of them.

Edit yourself

Go through the finished presentation several times, eliminating what isn't necessary.

Point Outlines

Many executives like the security of having a complete text for the speech, but they don't want to read the speech, since they might come off as too stilted. Therefore, they frequently have their staff create a point outline for them. There are basically two types of point outlines.

One type is the conceptual point outline. It breaks down the speech to five or six topics, then provides essential information, quotes, statistics, and key phrases for each topic. This gives the executive a big picture of the talk. Here and there the executive can digress to comment on other things. These outlines are only a few pages long.

The other type carefully follows the text of the speech. Each paragraph becomes more or less a bullet point in the outline. Therefore, every anecdote and every offhand comment would be included in the outline. These outlines can run up to ten or twelve pages.

Recycling Speeches and Presentations

Speeches and presentations aren't over after they are delivered. More and more, executives are distributing them to appropriate parties with little notes attached. It's become a way of getting out useful information—and getting your name noticed. If there's a budget for it, the speech can even be reprinted in the form of a brochure that fits inside a No. 10 envelope. If the content isn't confidential, the material can be put on the Internet. Some public relations executives develop the material into op-eds and articles under the executive's byline. In addition, the material can be sent to the media or made part of a media kit.

Speeches should be sent to *Vital Speeches of the Day*, P.O. Box 1247, Mt. Pleasant, South Carolina 29465. You do not have to be a CEO to be published in *Vital Speeches*. If your speeches are outstanding, send them in, even though you might be just a manager or run a very small company. If your speech appears in *Vital Speeches*, you can send reprints to a large mailing list, ranging from senators to your customers.

Videos

Your client is thinking about sending out a video on cost-cutting to all company locations. Your first job is to help the client determine if a video really is the best medium. Since cost-cutting will cause workers to worry about their jobs, it might be best if executives deliver this message in person in town meetings. Employees might also complain about all the funds being spent on the video. A more appropriate medium might be a memo or e-mail.

You and your client should also take into consideration the number of videos that were distributed recently in the organization. If there were quite a few, employees may not pay such close attention to yet another one. This is exactly what the public affairs department at a consumer products company in New York found when it centralized video production. They kept count of how many videos were being done and production dropped dramatically.

Standards

I remember the days when companies could get away with presenting their employees or the community with a talking head and some outdated B-roll film. Not anymore. Standards for corporate video are now identical to that of commercial television. Cable TV is probably your best model.

A video's worst pitfall is being boring. Fortunately, that problem can be remedied. A telecommunications company on the East Coast decided to discuss changes with employees via a live broadcast and a video. To make the video interesting, they featured not only executives but also workers and a live studio audience. There were also hookups throughout the company; anyone watching could call in. According to surveys taken afterward, the employees had enjoyed the show and had retained plenty of information.

The same telecommunications firm created a great video dealing with diversity in the workforce. The stage was set up like a talk show with employees representing all types of viewpoints. Some were minorities and women. Some were disabled. Some were traditional white males. The video was used as a catalyst for further internal discussion among employees. Surveys taken afterward indicated that this video had been closely viewed, and its points remembered.

The Right Kind of Tool

Videos can be a great tool if used appropriately. Unfortunately, they have a long history of abuse. Every senior in college who has applied for a job, every community activist, many car buyers, and many prospects for donations to charitable causes probably have vivid memories of seeing a lousy video. Maybe the video was poorly done or ran too long. Whatever the reason, these people still cringe every time they spot someone popping a video into a VCR.

If you're going to use a video, you need to know that your audience may not be delighted about watching yet another video. Explain to them the unique features of *your* video and why it's worth their time. Then, when you show the video, make sure you show only as much as you need to. The audience will be grateful. Like most speeches and presentations, most videos are too long.

Even when you explain all the pitfalls of using videos to clients, they may still insist that the new hires have to hear a few words from the CEO. In this case, suggest to them that the CEO's words can be imprinted on a T-shirt and would do just as well.

Getting the Right Resources

Videos are effective in companies whose powers-that-be have pumped resources into making those videos top-shelf. For example, some companies have hired humorist John Cleese, former member of Monty Python and a comedic film star, to liven up an otherwise boring training film. One auto company actually went through the trouble of filming a Native American religious ceremony when they wanted to make a statement about quality. And the audience for that video was internal; they were employees, not customers

Another key resource is a good video editor. Much of what is extraneous in your original video probably can be eliminated by a pro in the editing process. When getting a video into final form, more film should end up on the cutting room floor than in the video.

If you can't afford the right resources, maybe it's better *not* to do the video. An executive's reputation can be tarnished by being associated with a B-grade video.

Ordinary Conversation

You give speeches. You give plenty of presentations. And now and then you participate in a video. All of that shapes your reputation. But it's actually in everyday conversation that you develop the lion's share of your image. Your superiors, colleagues, subordinates, joint-venture partners, vendors, and customers judge you on the basis of what comes out of your mouth. I call ordinary conversation the "8-to-6 marathon." During those hours, including at lunch, you're in competition with everyone else who is trying to make a good impression. Just as if you were running a marathon, you must formulate strategy for how your conversations will go.

Spontaneous vs. Buttoned-Down

The myth that either you're real and your discourse is spontaneous or you're controlled and your conversation is buttoned-down or too carefully thought through has sunk many a career. Either the speaker was too loose and let too much information out at the wrong times, or he or she was so guarded that people became wary.

Conversation isn't an either/or proposition. You will be different people in different contexts. That's just common sense. As every schoolboy knows, his conversation is different when he's with the principal than when he's with his buddies in the schoolyard.

Prepare

My most successful clients prepare what they're going to say. If they're invited to a dinner party they don't walk in cold. They scan the news and the events of their own day for appropriate conversation pieces. That way, when they get to the dinner party they have a variety of possible topics of conversation. But they're flexible. If a flood at the Jersey Shore occurs while they're dining, they're skilled enough to ask the right questions of the person next to them: Do you own property near the shore? Do you have relatives or friends there? How serious do you think this flood will be?

They also prepare for unusual times. If there will be a major layoff on Monday, they conduct themselves with sufficient *gravitas* and respond appropriately both to those who were laid off and to the survivors. On such a day, you will be remembered—vividly—for saying the wrong thing.

If they're going to the company picnic they also get themselves into a playful mind-set and can connect appropriately about the food, the entertainment, the company, and future picnics.

In short, it's risky to walk into a situation cold. If you find yourself in an emergency, take time to survey the situation before blurting anything out. While you're gathering information you can say "I'm trying to get a handle on what happened" or "I don't know yet what the facts are." You *will* be judged on how well you handle yourself in an emergency.

The Food Chain

In the eighteenth century, the English poet Alexander Pope called the order of things the "Great Chain of Being." In the Great Chain of Being you have your assigned place, whether you're a country squire or an angel in heaven. Today we call this the "food chain." Our standing in the food chain determines how we conduct ourselves in conversations. This is a bitter pill for the free spirits of the sixties to swallow. They want to believe that all people are equal. Well, maybe we're all equal before our Creator, but in the world of work and social life, there's status to consider.

A man I'll call Jim L. was very successful at GE during the seventies and early eighties. He had the smoothness that the powers-that-be liked. He was from a wealthy family, but was relaxed and confident enough to be comfortable with everyone, including the CEO. Yet he was sophisticated enough to realize that he had to defer to those powers-that-be. Best of all, he knew how to defer without coming across as the Dickens character Uriah Heep.

Jim L. did well at GE. He knew his place and how to conduct himself. He didn't have any of that inner conflict that leads to abrasive relationships. But when promotions didn't come as quickly as he liked, he left GE and went to a chaotic entrepreneurial company. He simply didn't know how to conduct himself there. And his coworkers thought that with his prep-school pronunciation, he was putting on airs. Soon Jim L. realized he had made a mistake, a real whopper. His career never really recovered.

Corporate Culture and Organizational Norms

When you're looking for a job, listen to the conversations around you. What does the receptionist say when he or she greets you? What are the first five words out of your potential future boss's mouth? Do people talk in a style that you feel comfortable with? The same goes for the organizations you're considering joining, from the Public Relations Society of America (PRSA) to the Metropolitan Museum of Art. In the eighties we began to call this fit the organizational or corporate culture.

A writer went to IBM for a job interview in the late eighties. The conversation was very guarded; she didn't feel comfortable. That should have been a red flag to her. But she ignored her perceptions. She accepted a job offer when it was made and lived quite unhappily there until she could get another job.

Verbal Protective Coloring

We all make mistakes and get into situations in which we are misfits. Your goal is to exit that situation in good shape. You can do that if you verbally take on protective coloring: You may not like the pompous way they talk at a management-consulting firm, but you'll gain nothing by rebelling and using talk that is too down to earth. Blend in verbally until you can find something more suitable for yourself. One man I know spoke very much like a character on *Masterpiece Theater*. A certain marketing manager spoke like it was a crime to use more than five letters in a word. Hiding out verbally bought them the time they needed to figure out the next step—without being labeled a department misfit.

For the Fun of It

In his interview, Ted Feurey mentioned the importance of practicing. Most of my clients are always practicing. When they're on a plane they'll turn to their seatmate and try to communicate their message in a new way. At meetings they'll shift the agenda ever so slightly and observe what kind of effect they're having. When they have to give a speech, they introduce new anecdotes. One of the big kicks they get out of oral communications is that they're constantly growing. For them it's fun to see themselves becoming better and better.

Things to Remember

- How you present yourself orally determines much of your success.

- Today we live in an oral society, not a paper one.

- Before you do anything, determine the best medium for the occasion. Maybe it's better to talk to employees in person rather than make a video.

- In preparing a speech, the most important factor for success is understanding what your audience wants.

- Master the techniques of persuasion.

- A presentation is different than a speech.

- In ordinary conversation, prepare ahead of time what you might say. *All* conversation is strategic.

Notes

1. Paul C. Judge, "Is the Net Redefining Our Identity?" *Business Week,* May 12, 1997, 100.
2. Dale Carnegie, *The Quick and Easy Way to Effective Speaking* (New York: Dale Carnegie and Associates, 1962), 45–53.

Chapter 5

Crisis Communications

The primary rule of crisis communications is that stress makes
you stupid.

> —Chuck Rossie,
> specialist in crisis communications and founder,
> CMR Group, an executive public speaking coaching
> firm in Woodland Hills, California

C risis communications has come a long way. More and
more organizations now realize that they can't handle a crisis hap-
hazardly. Their approach must be *strategic*. They must develop a
core message and stay on message during the crisis. In addition, they
must demonstrate empathy. As soon as possible into the crisis, they
must present a plan about how they're going to resolve it and prevent another one from occurring in the future. This means that every
organization must be prepared for crisis long before one actually
happens.

In this chapter I discuss crises and how to use communications to
handle them effectively. Handled well, a crisis can be turned into an
advantage for an organization.

What Is a Crisis?

But what is a crisis? When former Walt Disney executive Michael Ovitz
abruptly left the company, was that a crisis? Was the bombing of the

World Trade Center a crisis? When the Dow fell 295-something points on February 18, 2000, was that a crisis? For a few years enrollment was down at Weight Watchers. Was that a crisis for the company?

Everyone has had a problem or accident from time to time, but a crisis is much more than that. According to crisis consultant Chuck Rossie, "A crisis is an event or series of events that may damage the health, success, or even the existence of an organization, depending on how it is handled and understood by employees, customers, shareholders, and the rest of the public." Important sectors of "the rest of the public" include the media, the government, and opinion leaders. In business, a crisis left unattended will jeopardize an organization's ability to conduct business normally.

Each Crisis Is Unique

No two crises are alike. Each has its own causal factors, ramifications, duration, rhythm, and unknowns. The whistleblower crisis regarding alleged price-fixing at Archer Daniels Midland was different from the whistleblower crisis regarding alleged theft of research at the University of Michigan.

But what all crises have in common is that if a company prepares itself for a crisis, it has a better chance of getting some degree of control over the crisis. I've helped companies handle every crisis—from building collapses to financial scandals. Companies that had a crisis plan in place always fared better with everyone—from the media and government officials to employees and customers—than those that didn't.

Communications—The Big Picture

When I say crisis communications, I'm not just referring to language and graphics. I also mean *action*. Actions talk. Actually, they *shout* during a crisis and become highly symbolic. The way First Lady Jackie Kennedy conducted herself after the assassination of the president in 1963 gave great solace to a nation. Her decorum symbolized all that was right about America.

It's What You Do, Stupid

Be proactive, not just reactive. During a blizzard in January 1996, one-third of the offices of MC2 Corporation, a computer network systems support organization, collapsed. Many of the company's seven hundred or so clients were without service. CEO Paul Lewis removed computers, files, and other key materials from the wreckage, set up shop in a small warehouse, and managed to restore service for many of his clients— even though the company's insurance didn't cover most of the disaster. Lewis's clients appreciated the extraordinary efforts he made to meet their needs and recognized his commitment to them. Through this experience, Lewis was also able to develop a new business providing disaster recovery packages.[1]

During any crisis, whether it's a scandal at The Prudential or financial losses at Apple Computer, actions will speak for you. What you do is far more important than anything you say. During the 1982 Tylenol poisonings crisis, Johnson & Johnson did something: It voluntarily removed Tylenol from store shelves. As a result, the company is remembered as being one of the most ethical pharmaceutical organizations in the world. Following the exit of its CEO in 1997, Apple did something: It announced a strategic alliance with Microsoft. The stock went up several points.

During the Great Depression, FDR did something. In fact, he did quite a bit. He pushed through legislation to help the country recover from the financial catastrophe and prevent one of that magnitude from recurring. His actions, though still controversial, worked. And in most circles FDR is still perceived as a great leader. During the crisis in President Bill Clinton's first term, when his ratings in the polls plummeted and the GOP seized control of Congress, Clinton did something: He changed his philosophical stance on issues. The public noticed, and re-elected him.

But action isn't always the best strategy during a crisis. After his fall from grace, Clinton aide Dick Morris should *not* have acted. He would have been better off issuing a statement and then keeping his head down. Instead, he appeared on talk shows and wrote a book. All this didn't help him reduce the damage to his reputation.

Action is important. But it shouldn't be premature or self-serving.

Words and Graphics

Words and graphics are also important. When a crisis happens, people look for words and images that will reassure them. When a brutal murder occurred in Central Park in Manhattan in 1995, Mayor Rudy Giuliani publicly declared that the park was safe. He kept the crisis at bay.

When students at Columbine High School in Colorado died from gunshots directed at them by fellow students, President Clinton appeared on TV and let parents—and the nation—know that he shared their pain.

What's at Stake in a Crisis?

Reputation

A crisis can affect a company's reputation positively or negatively. As James N. Sullivan, petroleum expert and vice chairman at Chevron, noted in a speech, about ten billion dollars is at stake if Chevron has an oil spill. That's the composite worth of its reputation.[2]

Crises can show if an organization has the right stuff, or they can make the company's executives look like the gang that couldn't shoot straight. How things turn out depend on how the crisis is handled.

Introducing Needed Changes

Smart organizations and people take full advantage of a crisis. After the alleged kickback scandal at the former Gulf Oil, management used the crisis to demonstrate how it was putting people—and systems—in place so that nothing like that would ever happen again. Among other things, a Catholic nun became a member of the board. Her perceptions of Gulf's policies were heavily covered in the media. As a result, Gulf developed a good reputation for integrity and social consciousness. Watchdog groups were assured that Gulf was now in good hands.

Public Support

As Hal Lancaster pointed out in *The Wall Street Journal,* "For alert managers, corporate crisis can be an opportunity for career advancement."[3] During any crisis, some players will greatly increase their power. Sometimes it's the company's counsel. Sometimes it's a plant manager. After he was shot in March 1981, former president Ronald Reagan was even more loved. During the Gulf War, former president George Bush's popularity soared. Remember how many heroes emerged from World War II?

Negative Impacts

But not all crises turn out so well. A crisis can plunge a company into serious trouble. Because of a crisis:

A reputation or image can suffer a heavy blow
Union Carbide, Exxon, and the United Way are still recovering.

A brand name can take a big hit
What does the brand name The Prudential mean to people now? Years of building the brand name through good service and advertising were nearly destroyed by the scandal regarding churning accounts.

Customers can go away
After the Exxon Valdez oil spill in Alaska, thousands of customers mailed back their credit cards to Exxon. When IBM went through its crisis of leadership under CEO John Akers, some customers went elsewhere. The challenge, of course, is to get those customers back. Chrysler did that basically by saying, We have sinned and we will sin no more. Under Lou Gerstner, IBM adopted a similar strategy.

Employees can lose their faith in the organization
During the 1997 crisis at Apple, many employees sent out their résumés looking for work elsewhere. That's why employees are an important audience to address during a crisis. Before a workforce reduction was announced during a departmental meeting at the former General Foods, both the vice president and the immediate supervisor spoke to employees. Employees

appreciated getting the information straight—before it appeared in the media.

There can be lawsuits

Everyone—from a shareholder to an employee—can decide to sue. Because of the critical importance of this legal aspect, there has to be a balance between what needs to be said and what the lawyers declare *can't* be said. This balance can be maintained. NYNEX was willing to talk candidly about layoffs and customer service and still protect itself legally. Much of this balance depends on good planning *before* the crisis.

The stock price can go down

The financial community doesn't like bad news, surprises, or uncertainty. A media company we handled received negative coverage in influential business media such as *Business Week*, and its stock went down. But the stock can be stabilized by one of the most important strategies in crisis management: Have a plan concerning how you're going to correct the situation. You'll be hearing a lot more about this later in the chapter. That media company now has such a plan. As a result, it's on its way back.

The community can become hostile

It's accepted now that corporations are social entities. What they do has an impact on the community. During a crisis, that community could withdraw its support. For example, since Kodak's series of layoffs, that great company town, Rochester, New York, has become a lot less like Jimmy Stewart's Bedford Falls. Something has died.

SwissBank's decision to relocate its headquarters from Manhattan to Stamford, Connecticut, might have been a "good" crisis—but it was still a crisis. The suburb of Stamford could have been disrupted by increased rental and housing prices. There could have been more traffic and more demand on restaurants at lunchtime. SwissBank's management got off on the right foot with the Stamford community by dealing with all these issues before laying a brick for its new headquarters.

A high-profile crisis can invite government intervention

One of the highest-profile crises ever was the publication of Ralph Nader's book about the U.S. auto industry, *Unsafe at Any Speed*. After its publication, safety became a burning issue in federal regulations affecting the industry. Crisis experts continue to debate whether the severity of that crisis could have been prevented if General Motors hadn't employed a private investigator to track Nader. The Nader case became a classic instance of a crisis that was poorly handled.

Interview with Chuck Rossie:
An Overview of Crisis Communications

Chuck Rossie trains executives how to present themselves during crises. He has coached more than four thousand executives and is an instructor at the California Office of Emergency Services Program for law enforcement, public safety, and government. From 1977 to 1985 he was the senior vice president of the Foundation for American Communications. He has worked in television for more than fifteen years and received an Emmy Award for the KNBC-TV local newscast in Los Angeles. In addition he has worked at the *Los Angeles Times*, the *Fresno Bee*, the *Modesto Bee*, the *Sacramento Bee*, and KOVR-TV in Sacramento. He provides coaching services through the CMR Group in Woodland Hills, California.

RLD: We're hearing a lot about crisis communications. What does it entail and what can it accomplish?

CR: My definition of crisis communications is the communication that takes place prior to, during, and following a crisis.

First, let me say that there are a variety of crises. For example, there are financial, environmental, weather, crime-related, and technology crises. There are also various definitions of crisis. However, what they all have in common is that they all involve *risk*. When a company downsizes, jobs are at risk. When a company closes, moves into a new community, or experiences growing pains, there is risk. In an oil spill, the lives of wildlife and marine life, the lifestyle of the community, the company's reputation and its ability to do business, and the stock price are all at risk. Usually, the higher the perceived risk to the public, the greater the sense of public outrage and the lower the trust. Three Mile Island was an example of perceived high risk and low trust.

There is a growing body of academic scholarship on crisis communications and risk that can help corporate communicators to expand their thinking on the topic. The textbook *Crisis Communications: A Casebook Approach* by Kathleen Fearn-Banks is an example. In the publication *Reporting on Risk: A Journalist's Handbook on Environmental Risk Assessment* [produced by the Foundation for American Communications and the National Sea Grant College Program (ISBN 1-885756-08-09)], Peter Sandman of Rutgers University, a former journalist, points out that one of the major jobs in crisis communications is to assist the media in understanding the nature of the risk.

When it comes to risk—any risk—in a crisis in which there is public outrage, you must focus on the human factors of the risk and try to reassure people.

Your first concern is empathy, empathy, empathy. Rule number one is to communicate immediately—no matter where you are—your concern for lives, property, and the rescue efforts. The technology is in place to broadcast a press conference or an interview from any corner of the globe. This is what TWA's CEO could have done after the crash of Flight 800. Instead, he waited until he returned to the United States from Europe to make a statement and answer questions from the media.

You can inform people about how they can lower their exposure to the risk. If you explain to them how to prepare chicken or beef in order to prevent food poisoning, they usually will feel more secure about the risk. For example, there has been a long-term educational campaign to educate the public not to eat uncooked chicken or beef. And there are specific rules on how to prepare these foods.

You can also explain what's being done to lower the risk. For example, after a terrible crime the mayor of a city might put more police on the street.

You can also identify alternatives to the source of the risk and the risks associated with the alternatives. For example, during a downsizing crisis you might compare the risk of losing a job to the risk of having one's hours cut.

Moreover, you can find ways in which people can participate in eliminating the risk. During a quality crisis in a company, management frequently will establish quality teams to help investigate the problem. The same type of process can be used for a health or product process.

I need to emphasize here that all of these strategies address what's going on in people's *emotions*. You *must* deal with the emotions. This is a rule. Companies that don't deal with emotions receive bad publicity during a crisis. Notice how the news media usually displays emotion during a crisis. After the crash of TWA Flight 800, CNN news anchor Bernard Shaw let the strain and his sadness show. The media certainly understands it can't be totally objective, or totally unemotional, during a crisis. The anchors *always* pick up on the appropriate emotion. We the audience expect that of them. And this input of emotion makes the story more interesting.

In addition to emotions, there's the more objective or factual side of the crisis, the nuts-and-bolts information. In your crisis training preparation you should have on hand appropriate statements for various crises that would be available *immediately* in the event of an actual crisis.

You can address people's need to know by helping the media understand the nature of the risk, and providing all the necessary background material about that. For example, explain to the media how the risk is measured and monitored, what the possible ramifications of the risk are, how the public is being protected, if the standards being used are controversial, and the legal issues involved.

Through these two approaches to risk you cover both bases: the human and information factors. One without the other will get you in trouble. I'm sure you've encountered engineering or scientific types who coldly present data after a crisis; that's not the way to do it. During training you must help your scientific staff to learn to speak in simple English. Overall, the government agencies involved in investigating the explosion of TWA Flight 800—the National Transportation Safety Board and the FBI—understood both the human and the informational parts of their jobs during the crisis. Two of a very close friend's relatives were killed on that flight. When he returned to Long Island for a one-year anniversary of the crash, everyone gave the government agencies a standing ovation. They are the best role models I know for how to communicate during a crisis. For years students of crisis will be studying the TV clips of how these professionals handled themselves.

RLD: Are there more crises now than there were in the fifties and sixties?

CR: Probably not, but there's a much greater chance that we will hear about more of them. In the seventies there were the Vietnam War, Watergate, and the end of respect for privacy. Those social phenomena changed the way we perceive events and how the media covers news in the United States. They ended the age of innocence. Now many people are suspicious and feel that it is normal to be skeptical. Everyone seems to be looking under the surface of things, trying to spot problems. And whenever anything goes wrong, everyone is quick to point a finger at what or who appears to be at fault. The news media reflects those attitudes and routinely assumes that there's a big story lurking behind any business-as-usual image.

RLD: How does business prepare for a crisis?

CR: In two ways. The first way is to build a climate of trust, give-

and-take communication, a reputation for fair dealing, and caring about people over time. Johnson & Johnson went into the Tylenol crisis with an excellent reputation. It earned that reputation by taking the time to establish its core values and by educating employees about those values.

When Johnson & Johnson—a blue-chip, responsible pharmaceutical company—discussed its crisis, people were predisposed to listen to what the company had to say and believe it. The second way companies can prepare for crises is through crisis communication training. Stress makes us stupid. In a crisis there's plenty of stress. But executives handle the stress better if they've been, as they say, through the drill. For example, in training they might practice how to handle hostile media questions or reframe a question that has been asked of them. They can also practice how to deliver bad news and what to say to shareholders. The best type of training simulates real crisis conditions and includes *all* the important decision makers. During training, the appropriate executives are all in a conference room—we call that tabletop exercise training—and they establish the communication policies that will be used during an actual crisis.

RLD: Can you describe in more detail what this drill is? What happens during training for a crisis?

CR: A tremendous amount goes on in crisis training. The key decision makers literally walk through a set of crisis scenarios. One of the things they do is make a series of decisions: Who will be the major spokesperson and the backup spokesperson if the major speaker isn't available? Often that spokesperson is the CEO. When the CEO steps forward, the organization is giving the message that it's taking the crisis very seriously.

In the case of the Exxon oil spill, it was logistics that made the company appear to be insufficiently concerned about what had happened. Exxon had established Alaska as the central point of information. If someone called Los Angeles for information about the oil spill, that person was directed to

Alaska. Obviously, that sort of system wasn't conducive to getting information out sensitively and quickly.

There are occasions when other spokespeople may be more appropriate than the CEO. When a nonprofit organization's accounting system was being questioned, the CFO was the spokesperson. That worked out well. For that particular situation, the CFO had the most credibility on the issue, more than the organization's executive director.

Some individuals, including CEOs, may simply not be as comfortable as others at being spokespeople. In some cases, you will have to designate a different spokesperson. It could be the head of an individual business involved in the crisis. It could be a board member. It could be the top scientist in the organization. But, again, you must be careful. As a corporation in crisis, you want to be perceived as working hard to resolve the issues. If the CEO isn't directly involved in the crisis, the public might conclude that nobody at the company cares. So it's advisable to use the CEO, even in a limited way, to symbolize the importance to the corporation of solving the problem.

With training, almost every spokesperson can become better at presenting the right information with the right tone of voice and body language. Training also helps the spokesperson take an empathetic approach to the situation. I call this approach the empathy grid, or getting on the right side—that is, the human side—of the question. Applying this grid is especially important in high-risk, low-trust situations. In matters of potential public outrage, you *must* use empathy or else people won't hear what you're saying.

RLD: What's the best way to show empathy?

CR: The secret to presenting your information in an empathetic way involves a five-part process.

In part one you demonstrate how you personally, and your organization, have a stake in the question. You don't want to be perceived as distant. For instance, a company involved in distributing tainted hamburger meat would have to demonstrate its concern about getting to the root of the problem and not resting until all the questions are answered.

In the second part you answer the questions asked of you and don't try to duck the issues on the public's mind. This shows that you're sensitive to what's bothering people. This works best if the organization has anticipated the kinds of questions that could be posed in various kinds of crises.

In the third part you present whatever information supports your answers. This includes testimonials, statistics, research findings, and endorsements. It may be useful, for example, to cite research that found that after X number of years following a plant-wide layoff, the laid-off workers found comparable jobs. If John Jones conducted that research at such-and-such a university, *say* that. Citing your sources shows that you respect people enough to explain to them why you believe what you believe.

In the fourth part you identify your significant message and keep repeating it. Your message might be that the safety of the public and your employees is important to you, or, if you are a utility, that restoring service is the number one goal of the company. This message has to get hammered away in all kinds of communications during the crisis, from TV interviews to e-mail to employees. As they say in politics, stay on message. Staying on message demonstrates to your constituencies that you cared enough to think the issues through.

The fifth part of the process involves looking toward the future. The future may be tomorrow morning or the year 2025. Your reference may be an offer to hold news briefings every couple of hours as long as the emergency or crisis continues.

RLD: How else can an organization prepare for a crisis?

CR: It's important for an organization to establish its values or philosophy of communications *before* a crisis happens. The organization must decide *how* it will present information. For example, smart organizations have communications values that determine that spokespeople will not make things worse by speculating, telling untruths, saying that things are OK when they aren't, or raising false hopes.

It sometimes happens in training that the company CEO asks corporate communications to come up with the questions that might be asked in a financial or environmental crisis. At this point, some communications executives or CEOs might decide that a certain question is "too hot to handle" and that the organization doesn't want to deal with the issue. When the crisis happens, that very question comes up and the organization is unprepared to deal with it.

During training, executives also learn that it's imperative to solve the problem *before* they tell the public that it has been solved. In other words, learn not to be the bearer of good news until there *is* good news.

RLD: What you've said gives us a good framework for dealing with the media. Can you now be more specific? Slivers of glass are found in the jars of General Pickle Company. Three people are in the hospital. The media—print and electronic—have descended on the company. How can General Pickle effectively handle the media?

CR: In crisis communications, the two most powerful media tools are preferred access and preferred information. As long as the media believes the best information and the best access come from the company, they will cooperate with the company. However, if the media thinks it can get better information from other sources, or simply on its own, the company's influence on it declines, or even evaporates. If the company is silent, the story that comes out could be about the company, but the company is not the primary source. The company can usually continue to be the primary source of information if it keeps itself focused on news coverage.

But back to the pickles. The first thing the company does is communicate its concern for public safety and product integrity and its willingness to cooperate with all constituencies to solve the problem. Next, the company asks consumers to help protect themselves. If you look in your pantry you'll notice that most food containers have small numbers on them. Once the pickle company can identify the source of the contamination it announces certain batch numbers and asks consumers to check if they have those batch numbers in their homes.

For the remainder of the crisis the company stays on message, communicating its commitment to safety in food production and distribution. It also answers questions, provides support for those answers, and explains its plan to prevent this problem from happening in the future. It lets consumers know where they can get more information. It delivers updates when new information is available.

But the question is: Will the world hear what the pickle company is saying, or will it hear what it wants to hear? Odds are good that the world will hear and believe what the pickle company has to say if the company is open, empathetic, and tells its story in its own terms. That applies to both the context of what's being said and the language used.

Seasoned corporate communicators know that they can define the story in any way they see fit. They can also use the kind of language they want in order to tell their own story in their own words. Lee Iacocca and his turnaround team were masters at this. They defined the Chrysler story in terms of international trade and they used the language of the people rather than traditional "corporatese." That was highly effective. The pickle company can define the story in terms of the safety of the public. If the company is located in a small town, it can use the folksy language of small-town life rather than the more formal linguistic style of a large urban area.

In the event of leaks from within the pickle company, the best defense is preferred information and access to more of the story from official sources. If the company is offering good information and making it easily available, the media is apt to pay less attention to the rumors. Here it's important to practice vigilant rumor control without using the word "rumor" in public or with the media. The very term "rumor" gives an untruth a life of its own. It is better to say "unconfirmed information" or "false information."

The pickle company must look upon the media as an information distribution system. Journalists are doing a job, passing along information to the public.

RLD: What's the most common problem you've found in getting a company's story out accurately?

CR: There are two major problems. The first is that you're suddenly in a crisis mode. You may have worked a long time building relationships with the media, but you've probably had little experience dealing with world media in a crisis. There will be many new faces out there you've never encountered. You have to adjust to the crisis conditions. If you've had some crisis training, you'll be better equipped to deal with the content and pace the crisis.

The second problem is that every corporation has a personal style, and that style is set by the CEO. If the CEO is open in communicating, then the organization is probably open. That openness is very useful during a crisis. A history of two-way communications between the company, employees, the community, and customers can make a world of difference.

However, those organizations whose personal style is a guarded one are closed systems. It's difficult for them to get information out or to take new information in. These corporations have difficulty during crises. Usually they have low credibility with all constituencies, from government agencies to employees. The media will get frustrated and will get its information by going around the company.

RLD: In addition to the media and the public, what other groups might a company in crisis have to address?

CR: Depending on the circumstances, the company may have to tell its story to government agencies, shareholders, customers, employees, the local community, and suppliers. Just who needs to be reached, and in what circumstances, should be part of the crisis planning.

Procedures

A company needs detailed procedures for its crisis communications plan. Fortunately, many companies have emergency response plans in place that help speed up action during a crisis, including the roles that the CEO and corporate communications will play and a one- or two-page description of everyone else's roles.

In formulating a plan, a company must pay attention to a variety of areas.

Defining a Crisis

A crisis for a mom-and-pop deli in Manhattan might not be a crisis for General Motors. Each company has to define for itself, ahead of time, what would constitute a crisis. For example, if the brokers at a Wall Street brokerage house are being investigated by the U.S. Securities and Exchange Commission, would that be a crisis?

Declaring a situation a crisis will have ramifications throughout the company. Some officers will have to drop what they're doing and devote their full attention to the emergency. Normal productivity might be decreased.

The Key Players

The company must decide who will be part of the crisis team. Normally, this includes senior staff, legal counsel, and the highest-ranking members of the public relations department (or, if an outside PR firm is used, members of that agency). Depending on the nature of the crisis, the team might also include representatives from the human resources, labor relations, customer service, environmental affairs, and manufacturing departments (in a major recall, for example, manufacturing would definitely be involved).

Key Tasks

During a crisis there are a number of jobs that must be done. In the pre-crisis planning process, those tasks should be specified and assigned to designated people. Their names, addresses, and all their contact numbers—ranging from office telephone numbers to e-mail—should be on record.

Before the planning starts, it's useful to talk with all employees about the kind of disasters that could happen. Someone in manufacturing would know how an act of terrorism might occur in a plant. Someone else might recognize how customers could be overbilled.[4]

Here are some of the typical tasks in a crisis:

Creating the overall message for all communications
Usually this core message has to be consistent with the culture of the company. If a company puts customer service above profits, that will be reflected in its message. Should there be a product defect, for instance, the company might announce—along with the recall—that customers will be given an extended warranty for the inconvenience.

Determining the appropriate spokespeople
The right spokesperson is not always the CEO. In some cases it might be the president of the workers' union or the vice president of quality. Get those people trained and ready.

Collecting information as it becomes available
It is also often necessary to supply background details. This will probably require a team of people who should understand company policy relating to disclosure. They should be fully briefed by legal counsel.

Marshaling resources to assess the risk
This might require retaining an outside consultant, particu-

larly if the company wants to be perceived as 100 percent credible. A management consultant, for example, could be brought in to comment on the company's financial controls.

Creating a plan of action to resolve the problem

The plan might be as simple as preventing further deaths or establishing multicompany committees on safety or the environment.

Identifying and contacting supportive third parties

A company in an environmental crisis might reach out to supportive "area groups" to speak about the company's long history of environmental concern.

Communicating with key audiences

Whether you're communicating with media and government officials or employees and customers, detailed information must be assembled on how to contact all relevant people, both in the office and at home, including their e-mail addresses. Certain people, such as the mayor of a city or the head of a large pension fund, should be contacted in person. The names of these people should be determined beforehand.

Monitoring the situation

It might be more effective to hold regular press conferences than to handle individual calls from the media. During part of the TWA Flight 800 investigation, regular press conferences provided a handy way to give the public up-to-date developments. After a Seattle TV station reported that a local couple had discovered a syringe in a can of Diet Pepsi, Pepsi Bottling Group's CEO Craig Weatherup found that it was best for him to take every individual media call as it came in. One day, the company handled three hundred such calls.[5]

Continually assessing resources

The public relations department might decide to bring in an outside agency to help with the media. The legal division might need an outside law firm to help clear everything from white papers to statements to the media. The safety committee might need to contract with a think tank for leading-edge thinking on safety.

Evaluating how the team did

A committee should be appointed beforehand to analyze how well—or ineptly—the crisis was handled. This information can be valuable in planning for future crises.

Delivering the Bad News

Whether it's a layoff of eight hundred people, two deaths in a fire at a manufacturing plant, or moving the company's headquarters from Ohio to California, the information should be delivered completely—and all at once. The sooner the information is out, the sooner the company can put that part of the crisis behind it and move on. When Delta Airlines reshuffled its management in 1997, it released the story in pieces. As a result, a negative story that would have been news for *one* day became a story for several days. A partial release also makes the company appear like it's manipulating information or is disorganized.

It's not always possible, of course, to deliver all the bad news at once. You might be receiving it in bits and pieces. In that case, it's important to tell your publics that the information is partial and will be updated. Then *immediately* update the bad news as information comes in. If one hundred more bodies were found in the plant fire, announce that, but with each announcement, reiterate the core message. For example, in the case of a disaster at one of its plants, the core message could be that the company's first priority is prevention.

Bad news by itself usually will not destroy a company. As we saw with Watergate, what destroyed the players was the attempt to cover up negative information. In *Nation's Business*, Roberta Maynard cites a survey by the public relations firm Porter/Novelli in which some 95 percent of respondents claim they're more offended when a company lies about a crisis than about the crisis itself.[6]

When It's Over

A crisis doesn't have to leave a black eye on the organization. After the 1993 terrorist bombing at New York City's World Trade Center, the managers of the Port Authority of New York and New Jersey were able to retain many of the building's tenants. Seven months after the bombing, the occupancy rate was 92 percent vs. lower Manhattan's normal occupancy rate of 80 percent. Part of that success was due to the great location of the World Trade Center. But part was also due to aggressive postcrisis communications efforts. Immediately after the bombing, Port Authority management explained to tenants the building's inherent safety.[7] Today, the World Trade Center remains one of Manhattan's great building complexes.

After a contamination scare in 1990, Perrier re-established its market leadership and returned to the sales volumes it had previously enjoyed. The company attributed its success to its alert response. Although it had a crisis plan in place before the emergency, the company was flexible. At first, it adopted a calm facade in all public appearances. When that didn't work with either the public or the media, the company got real and talked with the members of the media, individually, from 4:00 P.M. one day to 10:00 the next morning. The media became sympathetic.[8] Instead of being the end for Perrier, the situation became a classic example of how a company handles a crisis. In fact, as Bruce Jacobs pointed out in *Industry Week*, "A crisis handled effectively can become a public relations coup."[9]

After a crisis, companies want to put the experience behind them. But first they can get excellent PR mileage from telling their publics what they learned and how it led them to change. The 1996–1997 menu and discounting crises at McDonald's could have been turned into advantages if the company had simply told its customers, "Now that we gave you what you don't want, here's something you might want very much." That would have predisposed consumers to be receptive to what the company then had to offer.

When the board of directors at General Motors ousted the CEO, the company positioned its leadership crisis as a fresh start. And under new CEO Jack Smith, GM did do better. IBM and American Express adopted similar strategies. It's up to the organization to turn the aftermath of a crisis to its advantage.

On the Lookout for a Crisis

If management is alert, there are signs—admittedly sometimes faint ones—that problems are brewing. All the excesses of the 1980s should have been red flags to managers that some of their financial services staff might be playing too fast and loose with accounts. The managers could have introduced closer supervision and perhaps prevented some scandals.

In *Nation's Business*, Steven Fink noted, "You and your managers should understand that anytime you are not in a crisis, you are in a precrisis mode."[10] If a company can pick up on that and address the situation, it can head off a full-blown crisis. Let's say a customer service clerk notices a growing increase in customer complaints and informs the manager. The manager analyzes the letters and sees that one product is generating about 60 percent of all the complaints. He brings this to the attention of quality control, which evaluates all the production systems and identifies a problem. The problem is fixed. A full-blown crisis is avoided.

Today we hear a lot about learning organizations. Well, corporate America may become more profitable—and less stressed-out—if it learns to prevent crises. In my public relations work, I talk to many rank-and-file employees at many large and small companies. Each one of them knows the crisis that is about to happen. They know the arrogant design team that has forgotten the customer. They know who's near the cash and is improperly supervised. They know the shortcuts that are taken with product and employee safety. If this information can bubble up in the organization, many crises can be prevented.

Things to Remember

- There's no one definition of crisis. What constitutes a crisis for a small business might not be a crisis for General Motors.

- The most difficult crises are those involving high risk and low trust.

- Every organization must establish a plan for dealing with a broad range of possible crises. That plan includes which individual will handle which tasks, the philosophy on open disclosure, and public speaking training for the designated spokespeople.

- In a crisis, the spokesperson's job is two-fold: Communicate the organization's human side and provide useful, detailed, and timely information on a continuous basis.

- A crisis can lead to a public relations coup for the organization.

- Some crises can be prevented. Put systems in place that can identify the red flags.

Notes

1. Julie Androshick, "Kaboom Crisis Management," *Forbes*, November 18, 1996, 19.
2. James N. Sullivan, "Crisis Management: Prevention and Preparation," *Vital Speeches of the Day*, November 1, 1996, 65–68.
3. Hal Lancaster, "A Company Crisis Could Be Your Chance to Make Your Mark," *The Wall Street Journal*, August 26, 1997, B1.
4. Roberta Maynard, "Handling a Crisis Effectively," *Nation's Business*, December 1993, 54.
5. Androshick, 19.
6. Maynard, 54.
7. Minda Zetlin, "The Twin Towers Rise Again," *Sales & Marketing Management*, October 1993, 116.
8. Daniel Butler, "Perrier's Crisis Management Strategy," *Management Today*, August 1990, 72–74.
9. Bruce A. Jacobs, "Beating Back a Crisis," *Industry Week*, March 23, 1987, 93.
10. Steven Fink, "Planning for a Crisis," *Nation's Business*, April 1986, 49.

Chapter 6

Community Relations, Government, and the Global Marketplace

My father took me aside . . . and told me, "All politics is local. Don't forget it."

—Tip O'Neill,
All Politics Is Local

Maybe you want a stop sign on your corner. Maybe you're a big company like Disney that wants to build houses on the Florida wetlands. You might be a global pharmaceutical company that wants to switch a nasal spray from prescription to over-the-counter status. Or perhaps you're a small business in White Plains, New York, that wants to establish a joint venture with a company in Japan to distribute designer shoes.

In any case, you're going to have to be very savvy about your relationships with the stakeholders, whether they are the local community, the state, the U.S. government, or foreign companies and foreign governments. Whenever you deal with them you'll always have to act local; that is, be intimately familiar with their needs and with how you can best fill these needs. You'll also have to understand the customs and laws of the area you live in. If not, you could end up not only out in the cold, but also making an enemy. The halls of business are filled with war stories of executives who didn't do their homework before dealing in Egypt or Japan and who really alienated some people. Local knowledge is as much a prerequisite for doing business in the community of Latrobe, Pennsylvania, as it is in the global marketplace.

The Shoreham nuclear power plant on Long Island, New York, was never finished because the lighting company and local public officials couldn't agree on a suitable evacuation plan. But the standoff was just a symptom of a larger problem: the poor relationship between the company and the community. On the other hand, Disney knew what to do when building Celebration, a twenty-thousand-resident community in Florida that entailed destroying five hundred acres of wetlands: The company worked on its relationship with the community.[1] In this chapter I explain how to develop relationships so that you can obtain what you want.

Being Strategic

At one time it was enough to be a good corporate citizen. You did good deeds with, say, your joint-venture partner in Japan, from building housing for employees to technology transfers. In today's global marketplace, however, your entire approach to structuring and nurturing a relationship has to be strategic. It has to be an outgrowth of your own strategic plan that also makes your constituents feel that they are getting their fair share.

As you read this, many companies are creating strategic plans to define their relationships with all their constituencies. Gone are the days when a company doled out fifty thousand dollars to the local symphony orchestra just to be a good guy. Today, such a donation is usually given to help the company carry out a strategic goal. Instead of bestowing favors to create goodwill, a company has to judge which of those favors have a strategic purpose.

Before I go into more detail, I want to give you an overview that sets a framework for these issues.

Interview with James W. Hart Jr.:
An Overview of Community Relations,
Government, and the Global Marketplace

James W. Hart Jr. was vice president of public affairs for Duke Energy Corporation, where he received extensive recognition for his public affairs projects, including three Silver Anvils from the Public Relations Society of America and two Golden Quills from the International Association of Business Communicators. Prior to that, he was senior vice president and general manager of Hill & Knowlton in Denver. He is a member of the American Bar Association and three state bar associations. In 1996 *PR News Magazine* voted him outstanding public relations practitioner of the year.

During the volatile oil embargoes of the seventies, Hart handled community, state, and federal relations for the former Gulf Oil Corporation. One of his major projects was gaining acceptance for the production of such alternative fuels as synthetic fuels, coal, and solar and nuclear energy. At a time when many thought that production of synthetic fuels would ruin the environment, he helped prepare the way for a proposed synthetic facility in West Virginia. On a host of other energy issues, he used diverse strategies, including third-party advocacy and op-eds—at that time uncommon practices of governmental relations departments.

RLD: We hear the term "good corporate citizen" quite often. What does it mean? I remember the days when IBM used the term as a major strategy for increasing its global business. For example, IBM hired and trained many local nationals.

JWH: In my experience, "good corporate citizen" means that the organization discharges a certain amount of responsibility that goes hand in hand with the privilege of operating a franchise in a public marketplace. In other words, if a company is granted the opportunity to make a profit in the United States, India, or China, it will share some of that profit with the various stakeholders. If a company is constructing a new plant in

North Carolina, those stakeholders might include the people who live near it; those who've been inconvenienced by the construction of the plant; local government, which has to provide roads and schools for the population increase; the residents of the county, whose way of life is being disrupted; and local social service agencies, which will have to provide additional services.

Who looks at whether or not you're a good corporate citizen? Lots of constituencies: government entities; stockholders; parties with whom you've formed alliances; local communities; opinion leaders; third parties that might have supported you in the past; and your own employees, vendors, and customers.

Today, some of these constituencies—such as stockholders—may be adverse to your generosity. In a *New York Times* op-ed piece, a CEO declared that for him, being a good corporate citizen concerned only producing profits. He believed that if he produced profits, all the constituencies would benefit and the heck with philanthropy. Incidentally, Duke Energy still believes in philanthropy, but now makes its contributions in conjunction with its overall corporate strategies.

RLD: Yes, Jim, I read that op-ed piece. Being a good corporate citizen is not always a plus in many constituencies' eyes. But many companies still use good citizenship as a strategy to achieve their goals. One of my clients is an energy company that has had to learn to compete in this era of deregulation. One tactic they've used is brand-name development: They engage in philanthropic activities to help create a good image. They believe, all else being equal, that customers will choose the good corporate citizen over another company that has its eye only on the bottom line.

JWH: This has become a complex topic, both in the United States and abroad. First let's look at the United States.

The old social contract between the corporation and community has broken down. For example, since the time of Henry Ford and the development of company towns, companies took good care of their employees in return for employee loyalty and community support. Often that meant everything—from lifetime employment to contributions to the local art museum. Well, that modus operandi is fast becoming an anachronism. With global competition, you're focusing more on earnings per share and keeping the *financial* community happy. CEOs like IBM's John Akers and American Express's Jim Robinson lost their jobs because of disappointing earnings. In evaluating a CEO's performance, how much weight will be given to how equitably they shared the profits? That depends on what company you're at.

On the other hand, troubles with the community or the local government can impede a company's ability to do business. CEOs who create bad relationships will probably be judged harshly. Whatever the company, it has to devote enough attention to community or government relations to prevent hostilities or an "us vs. them" attitude from forming.

RLD: If I can paraphrase what you've just said, it seems that many companies now want good corporate citizenship to fit well within their overall strategy.

JWH: Exactly. In many American companies, the thrust of good corporate citizenship is strategic. The thinking is: We'll do A, B, and C in the community in order to accomplish X, Y, and Z in our strategic plan.

In other countries it's a mixed bag. IBM built its business around the world in the sixties, seventies, and eighties on the platform of good corporate citizenship. But other companies haven't done that, because the host country just didn't have a highly developed notion of social responsibility. That can backfire, of course. We all know the damage Union Carbide suffered—economically, and in terms of its good name—when there were problems with one of its chemical plants in India. Smart companies take a preventative stance. They anticipate where there could be problems with the community or government and do what's necessary to ensure that those problems don't develop.

RLD: In this country, some business people feel that there is an excessive amount of government regulation. What do you think?

JWH: Certain segments of the business community do feel that government regulation is excessive in some areas. If you were to talk to representatives of a company that manufactures chemicals or paper products and has to comply with air-emission, water-pollution, and other environmental standards, they will probably tell you that they are paying too much to clean up a small amount of pollution. They don't mind cleaning up 98 percent of the pollution; the additional 2 percent that regulations might dictate is too costly. This 100 percent approach to cleanup, they feel, is excessive, overzealous, and misguided.

On the other hand, if you look at the communications, transportation—from railroads to the airlines—and the energy industries, you see many of the positive effects of decontrol or deregulation. These industries *can* become more competitive and the price *can* go down for the consumer. This current era of decontrol began in 1981, when former president Ronald Reagan, in his first executive order, took price controls off gasoline. And you mentioned, Bob, that one of your clients is in the energy industry. Here we're seeing the early signs of decontrol. Competition is making the companies smarter and giving consumers choices. When that started happening in natural gas, it was an exciting time for my company and for our customers.

RLD: There are those experts in government affairs who say that if you want to change a government policy, go directly to the people, not the intermediaries. What do you think of this strategy?

JWH: Whether this strategy will be effective or not depends a lot on the particular issue. Remember when the Clinton administration in its first term tried to revolutionize health care by appealing directly to the people via television? The administration received a totally negative response. This issue was so sensitive and so complex that it couldn't be reduced to a headline for television consumption. Complex issues are best put in the hands of lawmakers.

Another constraint on presenting your ideas directly to the people is image. Companies with a bad image or track record in social responsibility will not be successful if they make a direct appeal to the people. If you're not a good corporate citizen, you're going to have a hard time selling your point of view in the court of public opinion.

But there *are* clear-cut issues that can be brought directly to the people. The pharmaceutical companies are doing that sometimes.

RLD: Why do you think NAFTA won? And don't tell me it was because Ross Perot was against it—only kidding.

JWH: Why did NAFTA win? I have an opinion on that—only an opinion. NAFTA won primarily because you had a unique combination of Republican legislators at the federal level who saw it as an opportunity for American business to expand, reduce regulation, and improve world competitiveness and a Democrat president who was willing to fight for the bill. That's how NAFTA got approved.

RLD: In your experience, suppose you were lobbying for some federal legislation. Would you use print media or just stick to electronic media, ranging from TV to the Internet?

JWH: Print is still an important tactic in any government relations strategy. The use of print media—from editorials to reports— to reprint, copy, and circulate your message is much more efficient than radio or TV broadcasts. The fact that fewer newspapers exist today means that the power of each newspaper has proportionally increased.

If you look at what is happening in the profitability of print media today, you see that newspapers are more profitable than they've been in a generation, even though the circulation may have gone down.

RLD: We hear quite a bit about the Washington news corps. How do you deal with it?

JWH: I don't think that American business has much opportunity to deal with the Washington press corps. Our channels of communication in Washington are through newsletters and the trade press. But if you're talking about the *Washington Post* or the *Washington Times* it's very difficult for business to penetrate that type of media. That's primarily because the Washington media's focus isn't on business, it's on what happens inside the Beltway. And it's been brought about by years of muckraking and exposés. I don't know if you've noticed, but very few businesses are headquartered in Washington.

RLD: How does power work in Washington, D.C.?

JWH: The most powerful people in Washington are those *outside* of government—that is, outside the circles of elected or appointed officials and even outside those who work for senators and Congress. They are men and women who have been in the area long enough to have grown up with those who now hold leadership positions. For example, suppose that I had gone to D.C. as a young lobbyist representing a company or an industry, and at the same time the current Speaker of the House arrived as a freshman. We might have worked together on projects. We might have socialized. Our wives may have become good friends, and the current speaker may be godfather to my children. Over the years, we maintained this relationship. Well, today I would have a very powerful friend in government. This person would take my phone calls and pass along information I could use. This person might make phone calls on my behalf. Through this access to power, I would have incredible power. And there might be four or five of these kinds of relationships that I developed during my many years in Washington.

The second most powerful people inside the Beltway are those who head up associations, organizations like the American Association of Retired Persons (AARP), the American Medical Association (AMA), and the National Association for Small Business People. The leaders of these organizations have power by their ability to influence the membership. Associations have become very adept at working at the grassroots level, which has increased their influence.

Among an association's members are people who are influential in their own right. They might be active in local or national politics or significant contributors to political and social causes. Their power enhances the association leader's power. It's no accident that there are so many trade associations physically located in Washington, D.C.

RLD: As a nation, we have become very sophisticated about lobbying. How exactly do you lobby the federal government?

JWH: There are many ways. How you approach lobbying depends a lot on the particular issue. Suppose the issue only concerns you or a handful of companies. In that case, you're going to have a hard time being heard. But you *can* be heard. If you're imaginative and relentless—like Mothers Against Drunk Driving (MADD) was years ago when few cared about its issue—you can get attention. Here you would learn a great deal by analyzing the tactics of people or groups that, against all odds, developed a local or national profile. You can do an online search or check out what the bookstores have on the topic.

But suppose your issue is broad and sweeping. Suppose you are committed to getting medical insurance coverage for part-time and contract workers who put in at least twenty hours a week. As we saw in the UPS strike, there is sympathy for this issue. Here you would start to assemble your advocacy groups. They might include unions, trade associations, retired workers, mothers, social workers, college students, sympathetic opinion leaders, and government officials. From these you would put together a coalition. You might call it Equity in Health Care or the Health of American Workers. This coalition will give you a base for fundraising. Once you have money, you can start to get the resources you need. For instance, you would hire an expert in demographics and an expert in direct mail. You would purchase media.

Simultaneously, you also would develop grassroots support. There may be many individuals out there who have a reason to identify with your cause—anyone who's been unemployed and used the COBRA option to maintain health coverage, for instance. You want them to embrace your issue.

RLD: Ok, you're finished planning and now it's time to act. How do you approach local, state, and federal government officials?

JWH: Usually not in the same way you approached them twenty-five years ago. Today they're very sophisticated about developing and maintaining a political network. To reach them, you have to penetrate that network. Also, there's technology. How do officials use technology? Do they have Websites? Should you send a fax? Should you call them on their cellular telephone number? And should you be using technology to encourage your members to contact the officials? Maybe you have a Website, or send e-mail, or give members updates via an 800 number.

Another big challenge is selecting the appropriate media. I remember when there were three major channels on TV and you could watch the famous Kennedy-Nixon debates on those channels. Now the media marketplace is much more fragmented. You have to know enough about your supporters and those you wish to reach to be able to select the right media. For instance, with cable you have a large number of channels. Do you need to target those who exercise in front of the TV at 5 A.M. *and* those who drink beer in front of the TV at 5 P.M.? Then there's radio. Do you need to reach the executives who only listen to radio while they're commuting to and from work? That means you should be buying drive time. Do the officials you need to influence read the *New York Post* instead of *The New York Times* every day? If so, you're wasting your time publishing a brilliant op-ed in *The New York Times*.

In evaluating which media to approach—and spend any money on—you have to get the facts. People think that CNN is very powerful. But the fact is that NBC still has more people watching its evening news show than does CNN. *Oprah* might be the most popular talk show, but the target audience you might want to reach may be loyal viewers of *Charlie Rose*.

The same need to get the facts applies to all tactics you use. I've heard that direct mail is ineffective. The fact is, if you do your mailing in the right ways, you're going to reach people—and do so cost effectively. So do your research and talk with people who have used these tactics. Experiment. Send out one hundred pieces of direct mail and see what happens.

RLD: Is it a lot different lobbying on the state vs. the federal level?

JWH: There are similarities between the two. In both cases, for example, you have to be able to tap into the network and know how the official communicates. Should you try to get in for a one-on-one interview or would it be more effective if two thousand of your supporters sent e-mail? What TV channels or print media influence the official? In addition, in both cases you need to have the kind of supporters who have unique access to the official and can get you on his or her agenda.

In general, there are a few differences between state and federal lobbying. On the state level, it's all a little more personal. An individual lobbyist will probably develop a relationship with state officials and meet with them one-on-one. As a result, that lobbyist could have quite a bit of influence.

How much influence will depend on the persuasiveness of the lobbyist and what that lobbyist has to trade. Another difference may be in the ease with which the lobbyist can garner support from one specific geographic area.

Power

Whether you're going to approach the mayor about the dog pound or the president about medical insurance, the relationship will involve power. One of the best definitions of power I've ever heard is that it's the ability to get things done. Suppose your son needs a summer job in your hometown. You can approach the situation cold and have him fill out applications for work throughout the town, or you can get in touch with the chair of the chamber of commerce and have her call a fast-food place about hiring your son. The odds are that your use of power will get the kid a job. It will accomplish the goal, whereas the routine procedures will probably not get results.

There are all sorts of power, and all forms of power are used to influence events in the community, state, federal government, and global marketplace. In 1988, Washington journalist Hedrick Smith did a brilliant job in discussing the different kinds of power in his book *The Power Game: How Washington Works,* which helps us see the "soft" side of power.[2]

We all know the "hard" side of power. That's the side of power you can't miss. It's the power of position. The person in the Oval Office has it by virtue of being president of the United States. It's the power of authority. There's also the power of money. The royal family in England may eventually lose the power of position, but it will retain the power of money. There's the power of the facts, as when MADD conducted a study of the number of children killed by drunk drivers.

We probably haven't given much thought to the softer, less obvious types of power. Yet they often have more influence than conventional ones. Just think of the power of beauty (and this applies to both genders). In any workplace, highly attractive people have more power than others. Could Mary Cunningham at Bendix have influenced CEO Bill

Agee if she hadn't been beautiful? The late Princess Diana captivated the world through not just her vulnerability, but also her beauty.

In his book, Smith points out the various types of power[3]:

- visibility
- a sense of timing
- trust and integrity
- physical energy
- self-confidence
- showmanship
- likability
- access to power
- the ability to obstruct and delay
- winning
- the illusion of power

John F. Kennedy, one of the most powerful people in history, had the power of position *and* the power of money. He also had the power of information; he was a genius at marshaling just the right data to support his arguments. But that wasn't the whole story. He also used the soft side of power. His personal energy was his trademark. His self-confidence was abundant. He could put on a good show, as we saw during the presidential debates and his trip to the Berlin Wall. He was likable. He was also a guy whose family trained him to win—and to savor that victory. And because of his family and his experiences at Harvard and in Congress, he had access to a lot of powerful people.

If you're going to influence others and persuade them to your point of view, ideally it would be great to hold an important position, be highly visible, and know how to get your cause on the media.

Community Relations

Actually, the word "community" should be in the plural. There are now many communities in which companies have interests. They include:

- where their headquarters are located

- where they actually manufacture
- where they distribute and sell
- where they are considering doing business
- where they do business that could create a crisis
- where they no longer do business because there *was* a crisis

A Changing Landscape

What a company did in community relations used to be almost formulaic. It donated money to various causes. If there was a major event, a representative of the company was always there. Some of its executives served on various nonprofit boards. Many of its employees did volunteer work.

Now companies are redefining what they want to do in community relations. As Sandra Waddock and Mary-Ellen Boyle point out, "As we move into the twenty-first century, one of the central issues facing companies will be how they define their relationship to their communities."[4] Most companies will now take a strategic approach and consider which stakeholders they most need to influence.

Key stakeholders may be residents of the community who initially had little power but, because they are so vocal and know how to use media, have obtained clout in the community. They may be the heads of businesses or government officials. A mayor who's up for reelection and whose polls show she is vulnerable might be a stakeholder you want on your side. That's because she could become a loose cannon in her attempt to regain a favorable rating. The key stakeholders could be the most respected people in the community who exercise power behind the scenes, or members of certain ethnic, racial, or age groups.

For example, Coors Brewing Company recognized that African Americans were not consuming their products in 1984 after Chairman William Coors allegedly made remarks that gave the company a racist image. To build market share among African Americans, Coors's community relations department used a three-pronged strategy: It sponsored community events, from sporting activities to art festivals, which gave a "face" to a regional brand that wasn't widely known outside the West; gave financial assistance to groups promoting social issues such as literacy; and developed targeted advertising and promotions for

African Americans. Over a ten-year period, sales to African Americans rose from about 0 to 6 percent of the company's total sales.[5]

Another factor that guides the strategies is the ongoing financial pressure on companies to increase profits. As Judy Stringer points out, "As companies redefine their interest in corporate relations, they seem to be moving away from simply being a good corporate citizen toward a role that combines being a good corporate citizen and a global competitor."[6] It's up to the community relations representative to advise the company where the dollars would make them look caring *and* how it would affect the bottom line.

A good portion of community strategies should be preventative. As with crisis communications, in community relations it's imperative to anticipate what could happen and then do whatever it takes to stop that from happening. This can also prevent coalitions from forming against you. As David McDermitt and Tony Shelton emphasize, "Waiting to become active until after strong opposition surfaces is a costly and often fatal mistake. Your community relations should be as integral a part of early project development as engineering and design."[7] In this, community relations has followed the lead of manufacturing companies. Before the project is even named, a cross-functional team meets to plan how to prevent problems.

Tactics

Companies that are effective in their community relations use the human touch. Their top executives are available, accessible, and visible in the community. The CEOs of PepsiCo and Perrier were visible in the community during their companies' crises. If you're moving a plant out of Akron, Ohio, to Indonesia, don't send a middle manager to make the announcement and answer questions. Send a top executive, preferably the CEO. As G. Pascal Zachary points out, "CEOs are stars now and have emerged as a kind of royalty. People expect to see them."[8]

As in global relations, another important tactic is to think on a national or global basis but act locally. In other words, put your focus on your own little sandbox. Prospective clients come to me desperately stating, "I need to be in *The Wall Street Journal* or *The New York Times*." They're dead wrong. In 90 percent of the cases, what they really need is *local* exposure. They need to cultivate the local newspaper, radio, and public access cable TV. They need to be visible at the chamber of commerce and to serve on local boards. They need to buy a house in that community. One of the best bits of community relations they can do is jog on a popular path in their town or neighborhood. Ross Johnson, former CEO of RJR Nabisco, refused to become part of the Atlanta community when the company relocated there. Bill Agee, former CEO of Morrison-Knudsen, let people know that he didn't like Idaho, where the company was based, by conducting company business from California. Both lost their jobs, in part because they never developed community relations.

Another effective tactic is recruiting local champions. They may be welfare mothers or the presidents of local banks. Take the time to explain your positions to them and enlist their backing. They are key ambassadors. When a consumer-products company produced a controversial product, it relied on a civil rights organization that it had continually supported to rally behind it in its time of need. Smart companies treat their employees so well that the employees themselves become their champions in the community. This was the case with the former Gulf Oil, which paid its employees slightly higher salaries than other employers in Pittsburgh and which provided outstanding training. During the 1974 oil embargo, amid rumors and accusations that the oil companies were holding back the oil, Gulf employees stood toe-to-toe with the company's critics.

It's also effective to have a sustained interest in philanthropic projects or much-needed research. Everyone is familiar with the *Hallmark Hall of Fame* TV series, which has presented top-quality dramas that have further enhanced the brand name Hallmark as a class act. This wouldn't have happened if Hallmark had intermittently sponsored different programs. Carefully choose the areas *you* will support and stick with those. It may be the art museum, or a shelter for battered women.

In addition, maintain ongoing community advisory panels (CAPs). These panels should contain a cross section of ordinary citizens and community leaders. As Stringer points out, such CAPs provide a forum for discussing past mistakes, present conditions, and future problems. They bring sensitive topics into the open—and they ensure that you know what's on people's minds.[9]

Many of the tactics you'll be reading about in this book are also useful in community relations. For example, in Chapter 4, Oral Communications, you learned how to package and deliver information in a way that persuades the audience to your point of view. In Chapter 5, Crisis Communications, you learned what to do during an emergency. In Chapter 10, Small Business Communications, you'll learn how even a little organization can get community attention through a special event.

Government

Ever since the Boston Tea Party, Americans have been trying to influence our government. Sometimes we got our message across, sometimes we didn't. But it wasn't until the sixties that government relations, both federal and state, became a serious discipline.

During the sixties, muckrakers showed us what was wrong with life in the United States. To correct these ills, ordinary citizens learned the fundamentals of lobbying. They got in the habit of contacting their federal and state representatives. On the other hand, companies affected by the protests told *their* side of the story to government officials. Another powerful force during the sixties was the utopian orientation of Lyndon Johnson's administration, which sincerely proposed that by funneling in enough money and sustaining your efforts, you could create the perfect—or at least "The Great"—society. Those who wanted to help shape that Great Society quickly learned how to influence Washington, D.C., and the state capitals.

During this time, American business wasn't one of the good guys. It was accused of environmental violations, safety violations in plants, and misrepresentation of products and services. Initially, it went on the defensive. Eventually, it learned how to go on the offensive with political action committees (PACs) and other weapons.

By the mid-seventies, business was beginning to get the hang of how to influence government. Corporations moved the game to their own playing field. They issued high-powered white papers about the cost of regulation to business, spoke about how regulations could eliminate jobs, and documented how many new jobs were created in an industry that wasn't highly regulated. No longer were they merely whining about how awful all the new regulations were.

From the years of the Carter administration through the Reagan and Bush administrations, business began to succeed in its quest for deregulation. This success gave it the confidence to then seek out laws to help American business in a global marketplace. Along the way, corporations learned to center the argument on issues, go directly to the people, tailor issue campaigns to the findings of opinion polls, and form coalitions with other interested parties.

Understanding Washington, D.C.

Inside the Beltway, most everybody knows how Washington, D.C., really works. They have an in-depth knowledge of the legislative process and are up-to-date on the status of every bill or the proceedings in every hearing room.

You can get some of this same knowledge. You can learn how bills get through the Senate and Congress, who is sponsoring those bills, where those bills are every day in the legislative process, which committees and subcommittees handle which issues, why two or more committees might handle similar issues, and where the power is— including which aides to senators and congressmen have the best access. To accomplish this, it's important to read the daily *Congressional Record* and the *Daily Digest*. The *Record* contains a comprehensive report of the action in both houses, including speeches. The *Digest* publishes a summary of each day's actions and provides a weekly schedule for both houses, including committee hearings.

You also need to find out what will influence someone you want to persuade. Suppose you want to approach a senator about increasing the tax on gasoline. Such a tax could, of course, eliminate jobs. If this senator is from a state with relatively high unemployment, you have to be prepared to address the unemployment issue. You should have the same sort of information about all relevant participants in the legislative process, from heads of committees to aides to government officials. The *Yellow Book* directories provide you with this sort of information about many of the players. You should also check the *Congressional Staff Directory*. You must also often understand what is going on in cabinet-level positions. You can read the media daily to get a handle on who's who and what's what in the thirteen cabinet-level departments, and for more specific information you can consult the *United States Government Manual* and the *Federal Yellow Book*.

All this knowledge is a prerequisite to doing business in Washington, D.C. But it's only a beginning. You will also have to understand, in detail, each issue that affects you.

You may not have the resources to dig for this type of information and monitor the legislative process that intensively. That's where a public relations agency comes in. There are a number of PR firms that specialize in governmental affairs. You can get information about them through the grapevine or by ordering *O'Dwyer's Directory of Public Relations Firms* from the J. R. O'Dwyer Company, 271 Madison Avenue, New York, New York 10016.

Public Opinion

The key driver in Washington, D.C., is public opinion. How people see things will largely determine how an issue gets decided. The pharmaceutical industry, which was under attack for alleged excessive profits, has aimed its recent advertising directly at the average citizen. If these ads—which show how the industry is trying to put a human, caring face on what it does—are successful, the industry can probably avoid excessive regulation.

The number one strategy in government relations is to tap into public opinion, because it is public opinion that will usually determine how your legislator votes. Therefore, a company's governmental affairs staff works on two levels. The first is to help shape public opinion; the second is to bring the facts about public opinion to the halls of Congress and the state capitals. If 87 percent of Americans strongly want a cure for AIDS, legislators will think long and hard before cutting funding for AIDS research.

There are almost an infinite number of ways to influence public opinion. You can write a book such as *The Death of Common Sense*, which attacked overzealous regulations. If you aggressively promote your book—going on talk shows, getting reviewed in publications that opinion leaders read—you have an excellent chance of influencing how people will see an issue. To show that the diet industry isn't exploitive you can hire a well-known spokesperson, as Weight Watchers did with Sarah Ferguson (Fergie) the Duchess of York. You can issue brochures, deliver speeches, enclose inserts in customers' bills. You can attend lots of events relating to the issue and become very visible. You can think up interesting angles about the issue and appear on TV and radio. You can sponsor a celebrity-studded rock concert to benefit your cause. And you may get some movement of the dial in public opinion.

The former Baby Bells got results in their campaign to "reach out" and inform customers that competition in the telecommunications industry didn't necessarily mean great service with great savings. As decontrol now sweeps the electricity industry, power marketers such as Enron are trying to convince the public that it's an attentive and caring company. By withdrawing its controversial diet medication from the marketplace and setting up an 800-hotline for consumer questions, American Home Products is trying to win the public opinion battle.

Influencing the Powers-that-Be

Many of the same tactics that influence public opinion also influence government officials. That's because officials read, watch, and listen to the same media as the public. I like to use this image for how this process works: Congressman Jones was watching a discussion on CNN about the late Princess Diana's fatal car crash and her allegedly drunk driver. As he watches, he constructs for himself what the public might be thinking about alcoholic beverages (or the paparazzi) as a result of the accident. He might call for a poll. He might make use of others' polls. Then he starts to form a position.

Suppose you're a beer manufacturer and you want to prevent further regulation of alcoholic beverages. You would be wise to form a coalition with others who are concerned about the same issue. Coalitions will increase your power and give you more resources to work with. You would work with the media. At the same time, you would visit with governmental officials or their aides to present your point of view personally. Perhaps those meetings would take place in the officials' home district, where they have more time and are more relaxed. So, how do you get in to talk with the appropriate people?

From doing your homework, you should recognize that all access is not equal. You don't necessarily want to go to the highest level; you want to go to the point people on the issue. That might be an aide instead of a committee chair. Remember, it's easiest to get in if you do so through one of the official's constituents.

You want the arguments you present to the official to be well researched. As you present your case, you must cover the highlights of your opposition's point of view. Do this fairly; you will lose credibility if you misrepresent the other side's case. If previous errors have appeared in your material, make sure that they are corrected.

If They Ask You to Testify

The powers-that-be may ask you to present your point of view before a committee or before Congress. The ball is in your court now not to make yourself or your client look foolish. The testimony could turn up on national TV or in the *Washington Post* or *The New York Times*. Remember, you're appealing to at least four distinct audiences: members of the committee, the committee staff, the media, and any interested observers.

Before you testify, understand thoroughly how the group works, what its biases are, and who your potential supporters and foes are. Sit in on a few meetings to get a feel for how sessions are conducted. Notice which committee member asks the most questions and what kind of questions they are. Does the committee lean more toward presentations based on fact, experience, or emotion in testimony?

Keep your remarks brief. You can always hand over background material to the committee after you speak.

The State Level

Since the early eighties, power has been moving from the federal to the state level. This trend shows no sign of reversing. As a result companies are now paying as much attention to the state arena as the federal and there has been a corresponding growth of issue advocates at the state level. Therefore, in much of what you do at the state level, you must take into consideration a variety of audiences. These include government officials, both appointed and elected staffs; special interest groups; the media; and anyone who is observing the legislative process, from professors to the public.

As Jim Hart pointed out, a lobbyist can have more influence at the state level. Access is easier, and there are fewer players to get to know.

Global Relations

As the late Speaker of the House Tip O'Neill often said, "All politics is local." That adage applies—in spades—to global relations. Former McKinsey consultant Kenichi Ohmae called it being an insider, the term "insider" referring to everything, from the language and the cuisine to how goods and services are marketed and distributed.

To succeed in a foreign culture, Ohmae has emphasized over and over again, you have to work your way inside all the host country's systems. One way IBM did this was by training local nationals to run the entire business. The enterprise in Japan, for example, might have started out with an American manager, but eventually the operation was turned over to someone from the local population. That made IBM a real insider. In addition to being a smart business maneuver, this tactic also showed that IBM was a good corporate citizen. After all, wasn't the company training the local population for sophisticated professional jobs?

In the mid-eighties, business thinkers such as Harvard Business School Professor Michael Porter began using the term "global" rather than "international," which denoted a sea change in how business was being conducted across borders. As Porter points out, "Today global competition can rarely be dealt with simply through exports or with free-standing foreign subsidiaries."[10] At one time, international trade meant exporting cars or Cartier jewelry to another country. Now global relations means an integrated system that includes design, production, marketing, distribution, and after-market activities, some of which could take place in a variety of settings around the world. This system has become so highly integrated that business theorists may wonder if companies have *any* type of national identity anymore, or if they are now all truly global companies in a borderless world.

What's the Message?

Public relations is usually difficult in a global environment. As the United States itself becomes more and more diverse, it, too, can be considered a global environment. In fact, throughout corporate America managers are now regularly trained in diversity issues. This will only continue. That's because in this world of rapid change and intrusive technology, many people are putting a higher value on what differentiates them from everybody else in the world.

Meanwhile, instead of melting pots around the world we now have what etiquette experts Barbara Pachter and Majorie Brody call "salad." The diversity is retained, intact.[11] Since the world is less likely to adapt the Western model of how to act in business, no one model exists for the proper business behavior, in either foreign or domestic markets. This ambiguity factor makes business relations—and all forms of public relations—more problematic than ever.

There are all kinds of configurations of the global environment for you to consider. As an American, you could work for a global giant like IBM at its domestic headquarters in Westchester County, New York. That would seem easy enough. But it isn't. When a company is global, you have to deal with many intersecting systems: brands of capitalism, commitments to work, time zones, languages, cultural habits, ways of viewing the world, types of etiquette—even different kinds of sexual communications.

A colleague of mine handled special events for IBM in Japan and Latin America. Her job took longer than other people's jobs because first she had to think through everything she said and did. Like a Nelson DeMille novel, in which different countries have different agendas, she had to balance her words and actions to reflect all the agendas. She had to listen to the news in these other countries, analyze their stock market, keep abreast of any emergencies, and then ask herself, What's the mind-set in Japan today? In Latin America? That was how she had to think on the macro level. On the micro level—the level of company politics—she had to figure out how Japan and Latin America would view the company's new laptop or its discount pricing. And with the time differences between the United States and Japan, she worked the second shift at home, where she placed international calls to Japan.

There are also those American public relations people who work for non-American companies. Their work involves constantly translating the company's real message. They first have to understand what their company wants to say and then package it in such a way that's acceptable to both the client (a foreign company) and the audience (American). A colleague of mine worked for the former American Motors after it was taken over by a French company. His stay there was brief. He felt that he would never be able to penetrate the French mindset and think like them. Had he learned more about the French language and culture he could have improved his position. He could have appreciated—maybe even admired—how the French approached business.

Then there are PR people who work for an American company in another country. When they write a press release, they have to be aware how the release will sound in the United States, where the top brass will read it. They have to monitor the rhythm of life in two different countries and learn how their types of capitalism differ. Along the way they have to figure out if this German subsidiary is the division of an American company or a German company with a U.S. parent. What's the message here? Did parent company General Sign develop the new process or did the German subsidiary?

Getting Up to Speed

If you live and work in a foreign environment, there are many things you can pick up by osmosis. But you're bound to be more productive if you enter the game with a body of knowledge. Pachter and Brody cite a study by the Business Council for International Understanding Institute, located at the American University in Washington, D.C. The council found that employees who work abroad without cross-cultural training have a failure rate of 33 to 66 percent. Those with training have about a 2 percent failure rate![12]

You have to learn how to decode another culture. Usually you need someone to guide you as to what is important and why. The Japanese have made a fine art of this and are trained early in their careers "to watch for the little nuances that differentiate cultures."[13] Of course, we all know about those differences—from body language to how direct you can be when doing business. However, there are less obvious but nevertheless highly important characteristics, such as ethical beliefs. As globalization consultant Patricia Digh points out, "Doing business across borders requires . . . new ways of thinking about what's right and what's wrong. Or what's right and what's right."[14]

In global relations, ethics really isn't a case of one person being right and the other being wrong. It usually happens that *both* parties are right—given their ethical underpinnings. In those cases, recommends Digh, the participants need "moral imagination" rather than "moral imperialism."[15] Suppose Worker A wants a bribe to do what you need him to do. You don't believe in bribes. If you're morally imaginative, you can come up with a way to encourage his cooperation without breaking the law or violating your own code of ethics. That could mean helping Worker A understand computers or something else he needs to master in order to get ahead.

There are good books that help you get past the ambiguity about global relations. One is Pachter and Brody's *Complete Business Etiquette Handbook*, which has a comprehensive global section. But you will usually need a guide to walk you through the recommendations for behavior. When you're dealing with something as complex as the intersection of two cultures, there'll be plenty of gray areas. Your guide has to understand both cultures.

The Media

In just about any country, you have to use great judgment in dealing with the media. If former New York police commissioner Bill Bratton had been wiser in handling the media, he might still be commissioner. But it didn't dawn on him often enough to mention in media interviews how much of the credit for fighting crime belonged to his boss, Mayor Rudy Giuliani.

In global relations, dealing with the media is even more sensitive. As a globalization public relations expert, the late Kathleen Connelly, pointed out, the media tends to be idiosyncratic in each society. There are even big differences within the nations of the European Union.[16] This means you have to approach worldwide media on a country-by-country basis. For example, since legislation and regulatory advertisements differ from one country to another, you'll have to seek advice from local legal experts.

Connelly cited some of the cultural differences in global media relations. In Egypt, interacting with the newspapers is so volatile that public relations people are better off bypassing them and getting publicity directly through special events. In France, using general newspapers for communicating business news rarely works out. Because the newspapers have such small circulation, it's more effective to discuss business news through special events, salons, and trade fairs. As television advertising grows more popular in China, the country's fourteen thousand newspapers are becoming less influential.[17]

Things to Remember

- Every relationship boils down to the specifics of a certain time, place, and agenda.

- In lobbying, don't count out the print media.

- Increasingly, community relations is run as a strategic discipline.

- Monitor public opinion. It's the platform for most legislation and regulation in the United States.

- Learn how Washington, D.C. works, and you'll find yourself working with others instead of alone.

- The reason global relations is so challenging is because it involves the intersection of two or more distinct cultures.

Notes

1. John Koenig, "Company Woman: Walt Disney Co. Senior Vice President of Government Relations Diana Morgan," *Florida Trend,* September 1994, 48–53.
2. Hedrick Smith, *The Power Game: How Washington Works* (New York: Random House, 1988), 41.
3. Smith, 42.
4. Sandra Waddock and Mary-Ellen Boyle, "The Dynamics of Change in Corporate Community Relations," *California Management Review,* summer 1995, 125.
5. Shari Caudron, "Creating Customers by Making Friends," *Black Enterprise,* November 1995, 70.

6. Judy Stringer, "A Hard Look at Community Relations," *Chemical Week,* August 23, 1995, 21–22.
7. David McDermitt and Tony Shelton, "The 10 Commandments of Community Relations," *World Wastes,* September 1993, 48–52.
8. G. Pascal Zachary, "CEOs Are Stars Now, But Why? And Would Alfred Sloan Approve?" *The Wall Street Journal,* September 3, 1997, A1.
9. Stringer, 21–22.
10. Michael Porter, *Competition in Global Industries* (Boston, Massachusetts: Harvard Business School Press, 1986), 11.
11. Barbara Pachter and Marjorie Brody, *Complete Business Etiquette Handbook* (New York: Prentice Hall, 1995), 271.
12. Pachter and Brody, 272.
13. Majorie Sorge, "Move Over James Bond," *Automotive Industries,* August 1997, 5.
14. Patricia Digh, "Shades of Gray in the Global Marketplace," *HR Magazine,* April 1997, 90.
15. Digh, 91–92.
16. Kathleen Connelly, "Global Public Relations," *Dartnell Public Relations Handbook,* fourth edition (Chicago: Dartnell, 1996), 103.
17. Connelly, 103–4.

Chapter 7

The Nonprofits

Identify a seasoned public relations pro who is deeply committed to your charitable mission and recruit him or her to join your board of directors.

—Roy Clason, former vice president
for communications, the American Red Cross

Relationship marketing, unbundling of services, thinking out of the box, asking, "What business am I really in?"—these were all concepts that took a lot of Dave Hilliard's attention in the late eighties. As CEO of the Wyman Center, a nonprofit camp for troubled children, Hilliard was trying to improve just about everything related to his camp: attendance, contributions, revenues.[1] So are the 1.4 million organizations in the nonprofit sector.

Nonprofits, which employ about 16.4 million paid and volunteer workers, have had to adopt the tools of management to survive.[2] Why? Nearly 60 percent of all nonprofits were founded in 1970 or later. This means there are more organizations competing for corporate, federal, state, and individual dollars. In addition, downsizing in the corporate world has cut some of the flow of funds from corporations and from the individuals who used to work there.

Hilliard's story has a happy ending: In the first half of the nineties, contributions increased 36 percent and earned revenues grew 152 percent. Other nonprofits, such as Mothers Against Drunk Driving (MADD), the American Red Cross, the Salvation Army, and Harvard

College, are also thriving. They've adjusted to the new realities of the nonprofit world and are eclectic in the tools they use.

In this chapter I candidly discuss public relations tools you can use. Some, such as branding, are also used in for-profit business. Others, such as public service announcements, are restricted to nonprofit organizations. All of them can get you publicity cost effectively. Other chapters of this book, such as Chapter 6, Community Relations, Government, and the Global Marketplace, also discuss topics relevant to your nonprofit work. But first, with the help of Roy Clason, here's an overview.

Interview with Roy Clason: An Overview of the Nonprofits

Following distinguished service in the Reagan and Bush administrations and as a Pentagon spokesperson during the Persian Gulf War, Roy Clason worked closely as a long-term policy and communications adviser to Elizabeth Dole at the American Red Cross.

During his tenure at the American Red Cross, I worked with Clason as a board member at the National American Red Cross in Washington. At the time, the organization experienced unprecedented fundraising success and favorable media exposure. Public opinion surveys showed that it had become the most respected national charity in America, and *Money* magazine named it its top-rated charity.

RLD: Today we hear so much about fundraising by the nonprofit. If you do an online search of the literature on nonprofits you'll find article after article about how nonprofits can improve their fundraising. Why is this happening?

RC: A number of forces are converging. Of course, we're hearing about corporate cutbacks in charitable donations. I think *Crain's New York Business* once cited the statistic that corporate contributions to nonprofits had declined 18 percent since 1987. Along with the cutbacks, contributors are discovering more and more new nonprofits that they can support. The number of agencies funded by an umbrella organization such as United Way keeps growing, stretching the already limited charitable dollars even further. Many of them are competing vigorously for the same corporate, federal, state, and individual dollars. The challenge, if you are a nonprofit, is to differentiate yourself from the other nonprofits, strategically positioning the importance of *your* mission or cause and demonstrating your proven track record of using donors' gifts wisely and efficiently.

RLD: So nonprofits, you might say, are in the same position as business. They have to break through the clutter of all the other nonprofits out there in order to be noticed by funding sources. People need to know why they should give to their alma mater—which is a nonprofit, of course—rather than to the Salvation Army, which is also a nonprofit.

RC: Exactly. That's why the role of strategic positioning, through effective public relations, has become so important to nonprofits. Through public relations, nonprofits can work to create a distinct, honest image, or, as we say in business, a brand identity.

RLD: In addition to the tools of public relations, aren't nonprofits also adopting the tools of management? And is there a dark side to that?

RC: Nonprofits have found that they have to, and should, operate internally as a tightly run, efficient business. But at the same time they cannot forget the core service they ultimately provide—helping people. The problem is, how are nonprofits going to learn about business? To tap into that expertise, many nonprofits have invited savvy business people to join their boards so that they can learn from them. They also have taken seminars in subjects like accounting and marketing. In addition, more business people are leaving the corporate world to take jobs at nonprofits.

However, no nonprofit, I'm convinced, wants to be perceived as a business per se. For those in the nonprofit arena, the mission is what makes them special and also what affords them the privilege of tax-exempt status. Nonprofits never want to lose that deep sense of mission. It might be to provide a roof over the heads of the homeless, teach a child to read, or provide lifesaving blood or valuable research to help cancer or AIDS victims. Nonprofits can never get to a point of satisfaction merely by paying all their bills and having a surplus. There's always more work that can be done to advance the important goals of the nonprofit.

RLD: What about scandals in the nonprofit sector?

RC: I think scandals—such as the ones at the United Way and NAACP—though extremely infrequent, give the public pause and create some skepticism. It was a shock to many people that donors' dollars weren't being spent wisely. This tested public trust, the most valuable asset to a nonprofit, and for a brief period hurt contributions. But I think that most consumers are very sophisticated, and have come to see these scandals as isolated instances, not as indicative of what's going on throughout the nonprofit sector. A nonprofit must consistently demonstrate its integrity, in the sense that its mission is absolutely critical and will continue to earn the public's trust and confidence.

RLD: If you were associated with an organization that had a scandal, what course of action would you recommend?

RC: If the organization is in error, then the best course of action is to admit it. Come clean immediately, both externally and internally. Be ahead of the curve. Share your findings and plans fully with the media, your board of directors, employees, and donors. However, before the discovery of a problem, you should have developed positive, honest relationships with *all* your key constituencies—the public, your board, the media, government agencies, etc.

You also have to determine where the system failure occurred, devise strategies to correct the problem immediately, and publicly outline plans to prevent such a failure in the future.

RLD: How can nonprofits work with the media most effectively?

RC: First, nonprofits have to remember that one of their most important audiences is local, and, in fact, most nonprofits are local or at least have local, community-based chapters. Some of your best sources of local coverage would be your hometown newspapers and radio and television stations, if they exist in your community.

Whether nonprofits approach local or national media, one of the most appealing stories is the human-interest story. Instead of saying the organization collected so many units of blood this year, put a personal face on it. Explain how the blood was used to save a life and, if possible, give testimonials from those whose lives were saved by the gift of blood. Nonprofits must be direct in how they present their stories. Another thing the media is frequently interested in is results—results in programs and in efficiency. Another item of interest is research. Nonprofits are frequently partnering with businesses and other nonprofits to sponsor critical research and can join forces to publicize the results.

One question that comes up often at nonprofits is: When do you hold a news conference? The answer is when you have *real* news. In general, press conferences are overused. Before a nonprofit calls one, it should be certain it's offering something important enough for the media to attend. Often it's more appropriate to call individual media outlets with the announcement, follow up with a news release, and make your appropriate spokesperson available for interviews. Then the media can decide if it wants to follow up on the story.

In dealing with the media it helps to be mindful of the tight deadlines that reporters, editors, and producers are under—and what other stories they may be working on.

Those other stories could be competing with your story for the news media's attention. If you waste the media's time, you'll risk losing credibility. Whenever possible, it's a good idea to give the media a lead time of several days and it's best to call in the late morning, not late afternoon when most reporters are working on a tight deadline to file their story. You can send them the appropriate information ahead of time and arrange for advance interviews—all on an embargoed basis until the release date.

In dealing with the media, it's also useful to make third-party experts available to the reporters and producers. Suppose the organization's mission is to support gun control. The organization might let the media know sources of information and individuals they could turn to for background information or interviews.

If the nonprofit links up with a local radio or TV station or a local newspaper, it may receive tremendous publicity. Ask for their support for your cause or an upcoming special event, such as the 10K run to benefit breast cancer research. The news media can be, and frequently has been, very helpful in fundraising.

RLD: So much of what nonprofits are doing today, whether it be MADD or the March of Dimes, is education. What's the best way nonprofits can educate?

RC: The key is to identify and then reach your targeted audience. If you want to deter children from using drugs, you probably will be most effective if you target your message to the parents. Identify the most likely stakeholders and then target your message to them and enlist their involvement and support. Identifying the right audience may take some advance, but relatively simple, research.

RLD: How can nonprofits get the public relations help they need at an affordable cost?

RC: Just ask. Nonprofits can identify seasoned public relations pros in the community—just as the American Red Cross tapped you, Bob, and sought your expert counsel—and invite them to join the board of directors. Also, there are a number of retired or semiretired public relations pros who will lend their time. In addition, nonprofits should get media representatives on their team. They can invite a member of the media to serve on the board or join forces for a special event and serve as an on-call adviser or a strategic planning assistant.

Another excellent source of help is the marketing and communications departments of local corporations. As you know, Bob, the line between public relations and marketing keeps blurring. If nonprofits want to excel in public relations they must understand the tools of marketing and market research—everything from developing a credit card program that benefits consumers to using direct mail.

RLD: Are there any pitfalls in doing a bang-up job in public relations/marketing?

RC: Nonprofits have to be mindful about the appearance of a campaign and using donors' dollars wisely. The materials used in a campaign, such as videos and glossy annual reports, may appear expensive. That could turn off donors. An effective campaign need not be glitzy or expensive. Incidentally, businesses face the same concern now.

RLD: What are some specific public relations/marketing strategies you would use in nonprofits today?

RC: There are a number of them. Since the public is concerned with donor dollars, it's wise to publish an annual report that fully discusses expenditures, income, and liability. This report should also be put on the nonprofit's Website.

Also, link up with partners, both in the nonprofit sector and business. If you want to sponsor a day of education about nutrition, you're going to get more local and national reach through partners. Celebrity spokespeople can be very effective, especially if they have a special interest in the problem. Celebrities are famous for being good media and fundraising draws.

Improve the usual techniques of direct mail and strategically target, target, target. For example, some nonprofits fail to contact former donors and just try to obtain new ones. That's a mistake. Former donors are more likely to give again if asked. And follow up immediately with a thank-you letter. Establish a credit card partnership with your local bank and MasterCard International. Sponsor some breakthrough research and then share the results with the media. Promote your program results, specifically highlighting actual individuals or families, to the public via the new media. Research cyberspace to get ideas about promoting your cause. You may want to put an inexpensively produced video version of your annual report on the Web.

Now that we have the big picture, we'll look at the nuts and bolts of media relations—everything from the technology to what directories to use.

Technology

Let's discuss the basics of getting publicity in a world where it's harder and harder to get people's attention.

Resources—and the Favor Bank

We've already mentioned recruiting a public relations/marketing champion to join your organization. Don't stop at one. The more public relations/marketing people you can attract to your cause, the greater access you have to their resources, ranging from knowledge to media contacts. Even if you're a small organization, you can establish a volunteer public relations/marketing advisory board.

What's in It for the Volunteers?

To attract new members, you must be able to offer them what they want or need. I usually call this the favor bank. People help people who can help them. You can't participate in the favor bank unless you have something to trade.

For example, an animal rescue organization in Manhattan offers volunteers high-quality training about how to deal with the animals. Through this training volunteers can:

- find out if they'd like to make a career in some aspect of animal handling
- develop actual skills that can be marketed, such as teaching obedience to dogs
- feel a sense of satisfaction that they have done something to improve the lives of animals who have no home

Other kinds of organizations can offer volunteers or board members opportunities to network. Usually it's a high-caliber person who volunteers or is invited to become a board member. Frequently in our busy lives, we might not run across these people had we not volunteered. If you are a nonprofit organization, don't be shy about pointing out the networking possibilities.

Service in a nonprofit organization can also provide volunteers and board members with media exposure. You've probably seen many newspaper photos of volunteers or board members presenting a check or announcing that the organization has reached its fundraising goal.

Before you start a recruiting drive, think: What's in it for the volunteers and board members? It could be very effective to put the reasons for joining in a recruiting brochure or video.

How to Recruit

The best way to recruit members for the board and for rank-and-file volunteer activities is to contact local businesses, including the mom-and-pops. You can also contact public relations agencies, even small shops. Ask them to donate some pro bono time. I know from experience that public relations/marketing people are usually pleased to be invited to participate. It's a chance for us to do community service and network with other professionals. You might even look for help on the Internet through search engines and key in "nonprofit," "nonprofit and paid media," etc.

Cyberspace is a gold mine for nonprofits. For example, in surfing the Internet I found out about the Benton Foundation, 1634 Eye Street, Washington, D.C. 20006; Tel: (202) 638-5770; http://www.benton.org. This organization gives you access to publications such as *Electronic Networking for Nonprofit Groups: A Guide to Getting Started* and *Media Advocacy: Reframing Public Debate,* which it produced in conjunction with the Center for Strategic Communication, 72 Spring Street, New York, New York 10012; Tel: (212) 965-0180; http://www.csc.org.

If you search databases, such as the magazine research section of CompuServe, you can retrieve articles that explain what other nonprofits are doing. In addition, you can network with your colleagues in other nonprofits.

If you have a specific need, such as to set up a speaker's bureau, you can contact both profit and nonprofit organizations and ask how they went about doing that. You might be able to reach them online. Learn from their mistakes; for example, many speaker's bureaus usually discover at the outset that the speaking scripts are too long and stilted.

Most of the small business seminars and lectures given in your community would probably be applicable to your needs. Like a small business, you're on a tight budget and you have to learn to maximize the use of the resources you have. For example, the course "Marketing on a Shoestring" is frequently advertised in local business papers such as *Crain's New York Business.* That sort of thing would be worth looking into.

Since corporate pockets are no longer as deep as they were, you might try to start a project with multiple sources of funds rather than just one. A corporation might be willing to give you ten thousand dollars instead of the hundred thousand dollars it donated in the past. You might also try partnering—joining with another nonprofit (or even a for-profit) to raise money. A radio station might help you raise money for a specific cause, such as toys for children on Christmas.

Branding

The same tools that built Procter & Gamble, Hewlett-Packard, and Johnson & Johnson can make your nonprofit unique to your clients, board of directors, donors, volunteers, and community. Those tools are the public relations/marketing strategies used to create, nurture, and, when necessary, reposition brands.

Basically, a brand name—Heinz or Colgate, Anderson Consulting or Stanford University—differentiates your product or service from all the competition out there. It gives you a clear identity and makes the purchaser feel positive about making the transaction. Bonds are established between the brand name and the buyer. We've all heard the story about the man who feels so good whenever he buys a Cadillac or something from Ralph Lauren. With the proper brand name, you can create that same feeling in the people you wish to influence.

Go Shopping

One good introduction to brands is David Aaker's *Building Strong Brands*.[3] But perhaps the best introduction is simply to go to your local supermarket and mall. Look at the well-known brands. Then ask yourself:

- Why does a particular brand name stand out on the shelf? Is it the national advertising supporting this brand? Is it the local supermarket's forty-cents-off promotion for this brand? Is it the packaging? Is it the fact that this brand is situated on the shelf at eye level, not on the bottom shelf? Maybe it's all of these.

- What personality does the brand have? If I have to write up a personality assessment of Tide, I would use the words "straight shooter," "gets the job done," "environmentally OK," "can get out those hard stains," and "my friend during emergencies like the flood we had last year."

- What associations does the brand bring up? When I think of Tide, I think that it's a name my wife trusts. I think that it's backed by the resources of a giant corporation. I think that if I had a problem with the product, the company would listen to me. I associate Tide with no surprises. In short, my experience with Tide has shown that it's reliable.

- How does the brand improve or add value to your life? Because Tide is reliable, it gives me peace of mind. That added value makes me reluctant to switch to another brand. When I send a Hallmark card instead of one of its competitors I feel assured that the card will make a good impression on the person who receives it. That assurance is the added value I want from a greeting card company.

Who Are You?

A brand-name identity for your nonprofit can give it a unique identity, the kind that the Salvation Army and the American Association of Retired Persons (AARP) have.

The first step in brand building is to find out how you're perceived right now. You can do this in a number of ways:

Conduct focus groups

Invite present clients, people in the neighborhood, those who no longer use your services, employees, volunteers, and donors to participate. Get a facilitator—perhaps from outside your organization, so as not to inhibit participants—to ask open-ended questions, such as how the group sees you now and how it would like to see you. The facilitator can put all this feedback up on a chart so that the participants know their feedback is important. Then analyze this material. If your budget permits, of course, a marketing firm can conduct your focus groups professionally. This will allow you to obtain a more sophisticated analysis.

Conduct surveys

Surveys can go out with your monthly mailer or be conducted on the phone. You can create the survey yourself or have a marketing firm do it. Surveys can also give you a good idea about what your publics want from you that you may not be providing.

Once you've canvassed others' perceptions of you, take into consideration the feedback you're getting from the outside. You've got to do some soul-searching to determine who you are and who you want to be. Think about what "share of mind" you want to occupy. What niche out there in the nonprofit sector do you want to represent? Do you want to be known as the most results-oriented provider of mental health services for adolescents or the best-equipped nursery school in the county? Do you want to be positioned as the leader in ethical studies?

A gas-and-electric company in the Midwest that was facing the same problem you are—competition—held focus groups, conducted surveys, and really looked at itself. What it found was that the customers and the community perceived it as the "trusty old electric company." The company realized that in order to compete it needed to be seen as an *innovator*—the kind of company that would develop products and services before customers even realize they want them. To help establish an innovative brand name the utility changed its name. Have you considered getting a new name? The utility also adopted bold public relations strategies, such as buying the right to put their name up in a sports stadium. It sponsored car races and cutting-edge philanthropic projects. Along with those externals, it changed its systems inside the company to make it capable of producing added-value products. As a result its identity has changed from being an electric company to a Microsoft of energy.

How can you achieve this transformation? The utility called in an identity consultant. You may have to do the same thing. Or, if you have a talent for positioning yourself, you might be able to do it on your own. One of the most successful nonprofits of all time, Alcoholics Anonymous (AA), did its own positioning. It occupies a unique niche in the substance-abuse field. There are a number of books from AA that describe how it established its identity. Also, check out AA's 12 traditions. You can reach AA at P.O. Box 459, New York, New York 10163; Tel: (212) 870-3400.

Two good books to help you think about brand identity are *Positioning* by Al Ries and Jack Trout and *The New Positioning* by Jack Trout.[4] Scan *Adweek* and *Advertising Age* to monitor how brands are doing. Is Coca-Cola getting the edge on Pepsi? If so, why do you think this is happening? Why did Kodak lose ground as a brand name, and has it gained back its momentum?

Once you decide on your niche—and what messages your name will communicate—you can roll out the new identity. We discuss some of the tools by which to do this in later sections of this chapter. But you must also bring all your internal systems into alignment to reinforce that brand identity. If part of your identity is about caring, then you'll probably want to answer your phone with a human voice rather than a machine. If you're known for being efficient, you'll want state-of-the-art equipment. If you specialize in services to the elderly, you'll want access to the best experts on the topic—and you'll print their names and credentials on all your materials. *If your systems don't match your claims, there's going to be a disconnect.* Disconnects happen when what the brand name says you are and what you are don't match. Behind every brand name that has endured there has been substance. Clauson Pickles have lasted because they taste the way a premium pickle *should* taste.

Changing a Brand Name

Brand names are living, breathing entities. Their value can fluctuate over time. At one time Snapple was hot. Then Quaker Oats bought it and suddenly it was not so hot. The advertising agency Young & Rubicam invented a system to measure the value of brands called the Brand Asset Valuator. You can read about it in the book *Building Strong Brands*.[5]

As brands lose value, marketers may cancel the brand or try to reposition it. Let's say you represent an organization named United Charities of Fairfield County, Connecticut. Historically you've served a lower-middle-class population. Now you see the need to help upper-middle-class professionals who are out of work. You have all the services in place but few professionals are coming to United Charities. You want to know why.

You can have telemarketers call certain ZIP codes and find out how people living in those affluent areas perceive your company. You can hold focus groups. You can simply contact professionals you know and ask them if they would use your services if they were out of work. Based on the information you get, you can decide if you want to extend the identity of the current brand name or create a new brand name, such as Partners with Fairfield County.

You now have to decide what niche you want to occupy. Most non-profits can't be all things to all people. You might test out various identities with focus groups and find out which one is the best fit for both the organization and the people it serves. You can run a pilot program to see what does and doesn't work.

Now let your target audiences know who you are. Many organizations go through this, sometimes several times. For years Weight Watchers was the number one name in sensible weight management. Then focus groups showed that the Weight Watchers brand name seemed dated to a new generation of those concerned about their weight. Weight Watchers did its homework: It studied the marketplace and discovered that the new generation wanted more private counseling, ready-to-eat foods that could be purchased at a meeting, more flexibility in menu choices, and shorter meetings. Weight Watchers decided to keep its name but made major changes in its operations. The organization has gone through other periods of asking itself how it is perceived.

What are the signs that your brand name may not be serving you well? As in business, there are red flags indicating that your brand name may be stale or has become an outright liability. Here are some of them:

- Donations are dropping off, and new sources of funding aren't emerging to fill the gaps.

- It's become difficult to recruit for your board of directors.

- The number of clients and volunteers is declining.

- You've had a series of negative articles or TV coverage about your organization.

If you're adjusting your brand name or trying to maintain it as a winner, there are a number of proven strategies to create the identity you want. The following sections discuss them.

Free Media Coverage

Nonprofits are at a distinct advantage in dealing with the media. Despite its current fame and power, the media is a service organization. Its first job is to deliver information to the public. In the *Public Relations Quarterly*, Doug McPherson stresses the importance of having nonprofit status in getting special attention from the media. He advises nonprofits, for example, to write "nonprofit" on the press releases they send.[6]

The Media Is Rooting for You

During my pro bono work for nonprofits, I often dealt with the media. I found it was almost as if the media—yes, the sophisticated, all-powerful media—was rooting for the nonprofit and would go out of its way to try to place a story about us. The president of a small women's college in Pennsylvania submitted an op-ed on women and entrepreneurship to a major business daily. That paper was willing to work with her until the piece had been shaped into something they felt they could use.

You can cash in on your nonprofit advantage if you provide the media a package of information in the form it needs. First, when you think you have a story, gather any relevant background information. If you are a mental health agency, get the statistics on how many cases of bipolar disorder are diagnosed each year. How much does bipolar disorder cost employers? What is the cost-per-patient to treat the illness? Then gather your *internal* statistics. How many cases of bipolar disorder does *your agency* treat each year? What is the average recovery time? What is the success rate, as you define success? Next you will need sources of information for the media to interview. Perhaps you rely on a consultant who is a professor at Tufts University. Is the professor willing to be interviewed? Find that out *before* you contact the media. Who at your agency should be interviewed? What about clients—are any willing to be interviewed either by name or anonymously?

You'll also need an angle or a hook to capture the media's attention. Maybe the actress Patty Duke, who wrote two books on her bipolar disorder, is visiting your agency. Maybe your agency has just treated its thousandth client. Maybe a former client of yours who's been treated for bipolar disorder has been admitted to Yale Law School. Package this information so that it's an easy read for the media. Attach any background information on the illness that might be useful. For example, Patty Duke's book *A Brilliant Madness* might help the media get a feel for the disease. You might include a short video on the subject. You can begin to pitch the story over the phone. If an editor or producer is interested, you can messenger or FedEx the material. If the story is time sensitive, ask them to please get right back to you. If it isn't, and if they don't get back to you, call them in about ten days.

After a Mistake

Repositioning a brand name warrants notice by the media. Explain to the media why United Charities is changing and who will benefit from those changes. Since the public should know about these changes, the media probably will be receptive.

If your agency has made mistakes, admit them up front. Explain that you have a five- or ten-point program to prevent those mistakes from happening again. Lee Iacocca and his turnaround team at Chrysler made the best such apology to the media. They admitted what Chrysler had done wrong. They corrected the mistakes. And they said that they were vigilant that those mistakes wouldn't happen again. This is a proven tactic in winning the media over to your side. From my experience, I'm convinced that nonprofits have to be even more direct than corporations in stating that they've been in error because they rely on the goodwill of donors.

Public Service Announcements

You can also obtain free media coverage with public service announcements (PSAs). Usually these are fifteen- or thirty-second spots the media gives you free of charge. The trick is to have your PSA accepted by the stations. You can increase the odds that this will happen by precisely following the station's directions. If they want a color side with blue and green, make one like that. If they say the PSA should be fourteen seconds, make sure it is exactly fourteen seconds. Also, avoid making direct sales pitches in your PSA. The PSA should simply present information. As its name indicates, the PSA performs a service. Before you send it, identify the person at the station who is in charge of this function. Talk to that person and explain *why* your PSA is helpful to the public. If they use the PSA, write a thank-you note to the station and invite them to visit your agency.

Op-ed

If you look at the op-eds (opinion-editorials) on the editorial pages of national and local newspapers and magazines, you'll find many written by someone from a nonprofit organization. It might be a think tank in Washington, a university in Massachusetts, a government agency, or an organization serving citizens with mental retardation. Many influential people read these op-eds, which are worth millions of dollars of free publicity to your organization. Studies even show that nonprofit op-eds are more likely to be published than op-eds by business leaders. Yet not enough nonprofits take advantage of this opportunity. You can get into print, in the publication of your choice, on the topic of your choice. Maybe you want to discuss the dark side of current capitalism in *The Wall Street Journal* or the rights of prisoners in *The New York Times*. Here are some tips on how to break into a national or local publication:

Read the editorial pages every day
Study what kinds of pieces get in. How long are they? Analyze what techniques the author has used to persuade the audience about a certain point of view. Does the author use statistics, appeal to common sense, cite personal experience, or allude to a recent tragedy? Which of these techniques persuaded you? Which fell flat and had no influence on you? Two books you might want to scan are *Influence: The Psychology of Persuasion* and *Secrets of Power Persuasion*.[7] What types

of persuasion does the publication seem to favor? Personal experience? Statistics? Follow this model in drafting your own op-ed.

Prepare to be timely

If Father's Day is in five weeks, now would be a good time to prepare an op-ed on the importance of fatherhood. Send it to the publication as soon as possible. If Congress is going to consider a bill soon, now is the time to comment on that bill. If it's the anniversary of your daughter's death from an auto accident, now would be the time to write an op-ed about auto safety and how that death could have been prevented.

Focus the topic so that it is of maximum interest

Rather than just writing an op-ed on students who are graduating from college, you might include all kinds of graduates—young and old, from grammar to graduate school.

Write from the heart

The op-eds that get published are usually sincere, or at least they sound that way.

Be conversational

Print communication has become much more like oral speech than like the kind of stilted prose you used to find in *The New York Times* a decade or so ago.

If your target publication doesn't accept your op-ed, try others

Editorial tastes differ widely. An op-ed submitted by a woman to *Newsweek* was rejected, but it was later accepted by *The New York Times*. A well-written op-ed usually finds a home.

Paid Media Coverage

Nonprofits are now opting to place paid advertising. At one time, that strategy was verboten. Donors cried foul and claimed that the organization was wasting their money. But advertising has become a standard tool of nonprofits. Most donors understand that the competition for funds makes it necessary to get exposure through such advertising. Some of the space is paid for by the publication or the TV channel, through grants for public relations, and largely out of the coffers of the nonprofit.

For many nonprofits advertising is an important investment. But it has to be done right. Here's how:

Test out an ad in a focus group

Your graphics and words may be missing your target audience entirely. Also, ask your focus group about the placement. Maybe the ad belongs in the *New York Post* rather than *The New York Times*. You might find out that your focus group doesn't even read the *Times*.

Pay attention to the day of the week that you run the ad

If you're interested in recruiting housewives and househusbands as volunteers, you might run your ad on the day the supermarket discount coupons appear in the paper. It's also usually effective to run an ad more than once. A university that was recruiting for its continuing education program ran a series of ads several weeks before the peak enrollment seasons and received a good response.

Track the responses to the ad

You might put numbers on different ads and ask the public to bring the ads in for a free gift. By tracking its ads, one university found that it got its best results in the weekly suburban papers, not the big downtown daily. Tracking also helped determine the recruiting cost per student. That's the kind of statistic you'll need to explain to any skeptical donors why you're using paid advertising. You might discover, for example, that the cost per new student is lower because of your advertising than it would have been using workers in the agency for that purpose.

Cyberspace

MADD has at least four homepages in cyberspace. One page gives general information about MADD. Another allows visitors to the site to obtain more specific information about its activities. A third provides information about local meetings. And a fourth allows families with loved ones killed by drunk drivers to post their pictures and provide a short biography.

This efficient use of technology certainly makes MADD seem like a right-on-top-of-things organization. Members, legislators, donors, volunteers, and newly grief-stricken families can all access MADD easily and cost effectively. Many other nonprofits also have Websites. According to *Business Wire*, more than 7,500 nonprofits now have Websites.[8] If you don't have one you could be at a competitive disadvantage in getting the public's attention.

How much does it cost to have a vendor create a Website for you? Prices range from less than a thousand dollars to hundreds of thousands of dollars. One nonprofit called upon a vendor in Queens, New York, who charged under two thousand dollars for graphics, animation, and posting of materials. Shop around and get different prices. Ask to see Internet work they have already done. And talk to their customers. Study the Websites of other nonprofits and for-profits to help you decide what approach you want.

Partnering

Organizations in the vanguard of fundraising techniques know how to partner. MADD partnered with VISA and MasterCard to put its logo on "affinity" credit cards; each time the cards are used, MADD gets a donation. Many wildlife organizations are using the same tactic. The Charlotte Merchandise Mart of North Carolina partnered with the Shelter Medical Clinic for the Homeless to put on a concert series. There's an increasing sense of social responsibility among American consumers, and businesses that partner with nonprofits for the sake of a good cause discover that they can come out ahead.

If you have a partnering idea, approach the marketing department of your potential future partner. You might want to draw up a business plan for the joint venture. That means you'll have to do research on the kind of influence you and your partner could have on various target groups. If the marketing department is interested enough in your idea, it might help you develop the most appropriate business plan. There are books that explain how to draw up such a business plan.

However, national partnerships with large companies comprise only the tip of the iceberg. More nonprofits are partnering with local organizations. The community newspaper might sponsor a walk for mental health. A radio station might sponsor the Eagle Scouts' "hire-a-kid" campaign. Jeb's Book Store, Grand Union Supermarket, and CVS Drug Store may sponsor a "sober prom" for the senior class of Meyer High. One woman began her nonprofit career with a grassroots organization that fed the hungry simply by going from store to store and asking for food. Most stores made a donation. In return, they received a tax deduction—and the goodwill of the community.

A group of local colleges can partner to offer a high-powered lecture series with names such as Alan Greenspan and Harvey Mackay. Such a joint venture would boost the image of all the participating colleges. Then the colleges can distribute copies of the talk to prospective students, graduates, legislators, and the media.

Speaker's Bureaus

Speaker's bureaus are nothing new. During the oil crisis in the late seventies, the former Gulf Oil's dynamic speaker's bureau, which was composed mostly of dedicated employees, told Gulf's side of the story. The approach was successful; audiences at least listened to Gulf's point of view. It also indirectly may have prevented some further legislation from being enacted against the petroleum industry.

Today, however, speaker's bureaus have to measure up to the standards set by television and the Internet. Speakers have to present information faster and in an entertaining format. There can't be too many words, or even too many visuals. The sooner the speaker finishes, the better. Then the audience can comment and ask questions. The sooner you involve the audience, the sooner you have a complete hold on their attention. How can you ensure an effective speaker's bureau?

The point outline

It's standard practice to provide volunteers for your speaker's bureau with a set text. This often gives the speakers a feeling of security. However, in my experience, speakers who rely on a set text usually do a mediocre job. For example, they can't react rapidly to such audience cues as boredom or restlessness. It's far better also to provide your clients with what I call a conceptual point outline. This outline sums up all the important parts of the speech and organizes it according to topic. A point outline on bipolar disorder, for example, might include the following topics:

- the emotional and financial costs of the illness to the individual and society
- what we presently know—and don't know—about its causes
- standard—and promising—treatments
- how to help people with bipolar disorder

Under each bullet point would be key words, relevant statistics, and useful anecdotes. The point outline gives speakers flexibility to adjust the text to the mood of the audience.

Visual aids

Visual aids in a speaker's bureau? They can be useful if they don't dominate the talk. For example, if your hospital is building a new wing, you would want to show the artist's rendering of that wing or a plastic replica of what it would look like. If you're trying to recruit volunteers for the ASPCA's Dog Walk in Central Park, you might show a short video of last year's Dog Walk. But if your Dog Walk video runs five minutes, you might shut it off after two or three. Your objective is to reach the audience, not to preoccupy the audience with visual images. You want the audience to relate to you, not to pictures.

Props

Props usually work well. If your nonprofit just licensed two mascots, bring them along. If you can manage it, bring some mascot images along to sell. The speaker's bureau can be a good opportunity for fundraising.

Audience participation

The most productive part of the talk is when you *stop* speaking and ask for audience participation. You can get the questions and answers rolling if you throw out some comments such as, "You might be wondering if the ASPCA has a 'no-kill' policy. Let me tell you a little about that. And you might have some questions about that or other policies at the ASPCA."

Print Material

This may be an era of electronic communication, but many people still want some paper in their hands, especially if they're expected to donate money to a cause. Your print material should be concise, however. Boil down your material for a brochure or a flyer to the essential elements. Your tone should express your grave concern about the problem. You also want to provide the facts; expert testimony will give your brochure more credibility. You might also want to include testimonials from clients; depending on their illness and wishes, their identity can be either revealed or concealed. Lastly, offer suggestions to readers about what they can do to help.

The graphics should correspond to your demographics: If your target audience is over forty, you should have more staid graphics; but if your target group is young, your graphics might be typical of the Internet or *Wired* magazine. If your cause lends itself to pictures—as the ASPCA's does—you might include some.

Special Events

Special events, such as a breast-examination day or adopt-a-dog Sunday, are a multipurpose tool. They help the image of the organization: If a big hospital participates in a health fair in the mall, it will appear to be responsive to the community. They also deliver a message in an experiential way: Instead of just saying, "You should have your blood pressure checked," the organization actually *checks* your blood pressure. The message is: Checking blood pressure is important. Additionally, special events help the organization to network; people will come up and offer to volunteer or donate money.

Special events can involve enormous coordination. But that burden can be shared with your partner. And having a partner can make the event seem bigger and more festive.

The public now *expects* outreach from nonprofit organizations. Your absence from sponsoring special events will be conspicuous. Some events work out better than others. Ask your colleagues in other organizations what events and places drew crowds—and why.

Advocacy

Increasingly, nonprofits have a legislative agenda. Since at least the seventies, organizations have realized that operating on the micro level—that is, tending to clients—usually is not enough. The organization must also operate on the macro level and work to change society. Some of the most effective advocacy organizations are AARP and MADD. In fact, they *attract* new members with their reputation for being able to influence the way things are. Nonprofits would be wise to highlight their advocacy work in their materials.

Because nonprofits have a clear and usually a popular mission, they can often make more of an impact than businesses in state capitals and in Washington, D.C. Yet you're free to adopt all the strategies of business and politics for your own agenda (see Chapter 6, Community Relations, Government, and the Global Marketplace).

Things to Remember

- The world of nonprofits has become a dog-eat-dog arena. You must use the most sophisticated tools of public relations.

- In your campaign to obtain funds, develop a brand name, recruit members or enact legislation, and don't forget your mission.

- There are already more than seven thousand nonprofits in cyberspace.

- The media is on your side. Use it.

Notes

1. Donna Fenn, "The New Dog-Eat-Dog Nonprofit," *Inc.*, July 1995, 45–50.
2. Judith Miller, "Harvard to Establish Center to Study Nonprofit Sector," *The New York Times*, April 12, 1997, B7.
3. David Aaker, *Building Strong Brands* (New York: The Free Press, 1996).
4. Al Ries and Jack Trout, *Positioning* (New York: Warner Books, 1981), and Jack Trout, *The New Positioning* (New York: McGraw-Hill, 1996).
5. Aaker, 304–13.
6. Doug McPherson, "Twelve Tips to Stretch Your Nonprofit Media Relations Dollar," *Public Relations Quarterly*, fall 1993, 41–42.
7. Robert B. Cialdini, *Influence: The Psychology of Persuasion* (New York: William Morrow, 1984), and Roger Dawson, *Secrets of Power Persuasion* (Englewood Cliffs, New Jersey: Prentice Hall, 1992).
8. "Nonprofits Hit the Web," *Business Wire*, July 2, 1996.

Chapter 8

Promoting Yourself through Print

One of the major benefits of publishing a book is that you put your message out in a permanent form. A book lends solidity to the message.

—Reid Boates,
literary agent

 $\mathbf{B}$ ack in the late eighties, when I was writing my first book, *Power and Influence: Mastering the Art of Persuasion*, well-meaning friends and colleagues told me that I was wasting my time. Some claimed that print was dead and no one would bother to read my book. Everyone, they said, was watching TV. Even a top executive at a major computer company claimed I was making a big mistake. I guess they hadn't noticed how management consultant Tom Peters had become a household word through his books.

Others thought that I shouldn't use my precious professional time sitting alone in a room writing a book; my hours, they claimed, could be better spent networking to get me the contacts I needed in business. Some warned me that no matter how good the book, there was no guarantee that it would sell. They advised me not to take such a big risk.

Well, I persisted. I wrote the book and it changed my career. I sent it to clients and prospective clients. Having produced a real book made me more credible in their eyes. In addition, overnight I became an "expert" on power and influence. The media, which had had no great interest in me before the book, now sought me out. If there was a power struggle in midtown Manhattan or faraway Hong Kong, the media wanted to hear what I had to say about it. My superiors and colleagues treated me with more respect. And when I left the public relations agency where I had worked for many years and started my own business, the book gave me name recognition, making it easier to get the new business off the ground.

In short, appearing in print can help your career or whatever cause you represent. Print includes books, articles, op-eds, letters to the editor, newsletters, and all sorts of material on the Internet. Print may be under attack these days, but it's still a formidable weapon in promoting yourself and your organization. CEOs, opinion leaders, government representatives, the media, and most white-collar professionals still read print—and will continue to do so.

In this chapter I explain how you can break into print, or, if you're already in print, how to graduate to more influential publications. It's a skill you can learn. But first here's an overview.

Interview with Reid Boates: An Overview of Publishing

Reid Boates is a literary agent who has handled many of my books and many best-sellers, as well as TV and general-interest films. He's provided corporate consultations to Booz-Allen & Hamilton, Credit Suisse Boston, Ford Motor Co., the University of Notre Dame, and the American Red Cross.

Boates is a shrewd judge of what will sell. That's what an agent is for: to help you get your ideas into marketable form so that a publisher will be interested. Then he or she presents the proposal to editors and negotiates advances, royalties, and rights and territories.

RLD: There seem to be more books out there today. Is that so?

RB: Yes, there are more books out there. But there is a major change in the kinds of books they are. At one time, much of the market was dominated by so-called vanity books. These would include a biography about your father, whom no one else ever heard of; the history of your company, which interests very few people; or an autobiography of yourself when you really have little claim to fame. Sometimes you yourself would pay to have these books printed. That's called self-publishing, or vanity publishing.

Today's readers are very sophisticated about what books offer. They want a book that can enlighten them or provide new insights. They're busy and they probably won't spend the time to read a self-serving vanity book.

RLD: Suppose someone out there is considering writing a book. What's the first step?

RB: The first step is to come up with an idea. That idea should have a sense of purpose. Maybe you are addressing a problem such as unemployment and providing a solution.

RLD: I mentioned earlier how writing a book benefited me. In general what are the benefits of going through all the angst of writing a book?

RB: When authors get published, most of the time they get attention. They get noticed. As you would say, Bob, they break through the clutter. In addition, when people write books they put out their message in a *permanent* form. A book gives solidity to the message. A good one lands and stays in libraries forever. Also, a book is frequently used as source material, which gives you additional exposure. Books are used as primary sources for documentaries and a variety of television formats. They're already well established as source material for CD-ROMs and multimedia.

RLD: But what are the pitfalls to publishing a book?

RB: There are a number of pitfalls. Your book could receive negative reviews. That's bad for sales of the book and can be embarrassing to the author. Also the whole project could backfire. For example, a major corporation allowed itself to be the source material for a book. When the book came out, it was not at all what the corporation had expected. If you agree to be part of a book project, you have to make sure you protect yourself. That means that you put *all* the terms and conditions in writing, with the underlying goal of a fail-safe out.

RLD: Do you think an author should collaborate? Or is it less cumbersome to work on your own?

RB: Not all of us are natural writers. We may have a good idea that should get out there, but we don't have the writing skills. Or maybe we just don't have the time to write a book. That's when it's useful to collaborate with a professional writer. A professional writer can organize your material in a way that tells a good story. Where can you find such a writer? Agents like myself know of them. What do they cost? Now more than ever, you get what you pay for.

RLD: Okay, let's say you have an idea. What do you do next?

RB: After you have the idea, the next step involves getting feedback on the idea. Talk with trusted colleagues and experts on the subject. Determine the level of interest in your idea and if it has a chance to succeed.

RLD: There's a lot of buzz about the formal book proposal. Is that important?

RB: If authors are known names, they probably don't have to submit a formal proposal. They can dash off a few pages describing the idea and the market. But most new authors have to submit a formal proposal. There are no right or wrong ways to write a proposal. Bookstores carry books that discuss the nuts and bolts of writing a proposal. *The Writer's*

Market, a Boston-based publication, also gives you tips. There's also a helpful book by Susan Page, *The Shortest Distance between You and a Published Book*.

RLD: I came across a series of useful books about publishing written by Jeff Herman. One of them, the *Insider's Guide to Book Editors, Publishers, and Literary Agents, 1996–1997*, provides an example of a formal book proposal. His approach is that the proposal is essentially a sales tool. Is Herman on target?

RB: Yes, he is. Basically a proposal is a marketing document. You are trying to convince first an agent, and then a publisher, that the book you are thinking about writing will sell. Today the most important parts of the proposal are a clear, succinct theme and title and a savvy marketing analysis.

RLD: What's the role of the agent in preparing a formal proposal?

RB: If agents are interested in working with you, they will help you get your proposal into a form that would interest a publisher enough to buy it. Good agents are able to put themselves in a publisher's frame of mind and make sure the proposal is rock solid. Agents know that most nonfiction proposals get rejected because they have either a half-formed premise or a poor marketing analysis. Agents can guide you in presenting both clearly. They might help you sharpen your focus as to who is the reader and why this book addresses the reader's needs. A good agent will insist that you, as the expert in your field, present an intelligent and thorough knowledge of similar recent books, both successes and failures.

RLD: Most books fail. Why?

RB: In the publishing business there is little or no test marketing before a book is released. Therefore there's no way to determine where a book is lacking or to fix it once it's committed to print.

RLD: What helps a book become successful?

RB: There are a number of factors that help a book succeed. Concept: Is it solid? Is it of interest to others? The title and subtitle have to attract attention. Organization: Is the book well put together to tell the story it's telling? The writer William Goldman calls this the book's "backbone." Voice: Does the person telling the story or explaining the material have a unique approach? We call this the "voice." Definition of the market: What is the focus? In your book, *The Critical 14 Years of Your Professional Life*, Bob, you defined your market as young adults who were just getting into their careers. That's where your focus was. Utility: What does the reader get from the book? Informing the publisher: Does the publisher understand what's unique about the book? The burden is on you or your agent to make sure that he or she does. Logistical support: Are all your systems in place to help promote the book?

The Book Business— The Agent/Publisher Route

Because writing is an art, it's easy to forget that publishing is a business. Publishers are looking to make a profit on the books they publish. They have to focus on the bottom line, otherwise their business would fail. If you want to deal in this business, you have to learn all you can about it. You can scan the media journal *Editor and Publisher*, and articles in newspapers and magazines that discuss the publishing industry. Educational institutions frequently offer seminars on how to get published. Reid Boates, for example, has spoken at the publishing programs at Columbia University and Radcliff, the Southwest Writers' Conference, and elsewhere. As he points out, the bookstores have a number of up-to-date selections on the topic.

If you're monitoring the publishing industry, you'll find out that it's going through tremendous change. According to the consultancy Open Book Publishing, (203) 316-8008, consolidation continues to be a major trend in publishing. In 1997 the twenty largest houses in the industry accounted for 85 percent, or seventeen billion dollars' worth of sales.[1] There is also consolidation in how books are distributed. Superbookstores, such as Barnes & Noble's typical 150,000-title store, are dominant distributors. And, more recently, online book retailers, like Amazon.com, with close to a million titles in stock, have become major players.

Consolidation in both these sectors of the food chain means that it could be harder for a new author to get a book published and distributed. The burden is on you as never before to explain in your proposal *why* people would buy this book. That's why Reid Boates emphasized the marketing aspect of your proposal. You can't write a proposal in a vacuum. You have to present it to the agent and the publisher in the framework of its marketability. That marketing analysis includes who your competition is and how you plan to promote the book. Publishers have been downsized too and rarely have the resources to aggressively market what they print.

Also, publishers are breaking with the traditions of the past. In June 1997, HarperCollins announced that it was canceling 103 titles prior to publication because it believed they wouldn't sell. Although those books had already been announced in the company's fall catalogue, the cancellations were part of a plan to reverse the publishing house's seven-million-dollar loss in that fiscal quarter.[2] Loud and clear, publishing houses are sending the message that the concept for a book must have commercial possibilities.

Planning Your Book

So how do you go about planning a book that will sell? As part of your investigation of the book industry, you should invest time analyzing what books are selling well. Ask yourself:

To which target markets does this book appeal?
Perhaps those target markets tend to be big book buyers.

Why did the concept catch on?

A good part of the answer is timeliness. Michael and Mary Dan Eadeses published their brisk-selling diet book *Protein Power* at a time when Americans were watching what they ate yet were still gaining weight. The villain, said *Protein Power*, was the high-carbohydrate diet that had become fashionable. The book found an audience.

How did the author organize the material?

Did the author, for example, talk about a scandal on Wall Street as though he or she were telling a story? Was there suspense and excitement in the narrative? What if the author had told about the scandal in a dry, factual manner?

What kind of added value did the author give the reader?

The Eadeses, for example, shared their long experience with nutrition and unique insights on how people lose weight.

Was the price for the book a fair one?

If *Protein Power* were priced at $10.99 instead of $21.95, would readers think that the lower price indicated that the book wasn't any good?

Your next exercise, as Boates advises, is to try out your ideas with others and see what their reaction is. When I was planning my book *The Critical 14 Years of Your Professional Life*, I personally asked young people what they would like to see in such a book. I went online to a career chat room and asked whether there was a gap between what young people *needed* to know and what kind of information was available. I learned plenty.

Next comes writing the proposal. Occasionally, some agents will accept a short query letter and one chapter of your planned book. You can find out which ones will do this by surfing the Internet or looking into an agent guide, such as *Guide to Literary Agents*. A young man planning to write an ethnic cookbook took that route and it saved him months of work on a proposal. Some new authors also go directly to the publisher. That can work, but it's a long shot. Perhaps you met an editor at a seminar who indicated interest in your idea. Find out if the editor wants to see a proposal. You may be able to make a direct connection with a publisher that way.

Most new authors, however, find it useful to go through the intellectual exercise of writing a formal proposal that they'll submit to an agent. This proposal gives them the opportunity to think about the book and its markets in depth.

There is no one way to write a proposal. In the *Insider's Guide to Book Editors, Publishers, and Literary Agents, 1996–1997*, Jeff Herman recommends that your proposal contain:

An overview

Give a complete picture of what the book will be. Remember, this is a sales document. You might want to mention that your book is like another best-selling title in such and such a way. Highlight the commercial possibilities of your book.

A biographical section

Present your credentials for writing the book. If you were in the Foreign Service for thirty years, you probably have the necessary credentials to write a book about life in the Foreign Service. If you have no paid experience in financial planning, you might have a hard time trying to attract an agent to a book you're writing on how to plan for retirement. There are exceptions, though. If you somehow managed to save five million dollars for your retirement on a salary of forty thousand dollars per year by shrewdly picking high-tech stocks, some agent might be interested in hearing about your story.

A marketing section

Here you outline the market for the book. If you are writing a diet book, do research and find out how many people are on a diet at any one time. How many of those people have experienced failure—that is, gained back the weight after a year? How many people have given up on diets? Why would your book offer new hope to these readers?

A competition section

Examine other books on the market dealing with your subject and show how your book differs. Explain how you're adding value.

A promotion section

Here you would explain how you intend to promote the book. Suppose the book is on retirement, and you have published numerous articles in *Modern Maturity*. Emphasize the contact you have with a retirement-oriented publication. If you have already lectured at one hundred retirement clubs, offer to promote the book at these and other retirement clubs. Do you have contacts at talk shows? Will you contribute a percentage of the sale of each book to establish a foundation for the elderly poor (that can get you publicity)? Do you plan to visit states with high percentages of retirees? Do you know any celebrities or well-known people who will endorse your book? Are you willing to create a homepage on the Internet and put excerpts of the book on it?

A chapter outline

There is no set length for a chapter outline, but, remember, the outline should attract an agent to your proposal. Describe in detail what will go into each chapter. Give each chapter a title. When you're describing the contents of the chapter, keep your marketing cap on. Ask yourself, Why would a reader be interested in this chapter and be willing to buy a book to read it?

Sample chapters

Agents usually require two sample chapters to get a good idea of how you intend to handle the writing of the book. These chapters are not cast in concrete and will probably change as you get input from the agent and the publisher. Since the agent is looking for both marketability of the material and writing skill, if you can't write, consider hiring a professional writer or ghost writer to compose the material for you.[3]

Rewrite Hell

Good agents or publishers will make many suggestions about how you can improve your material—at every stage of the book. In the final phases of writing my book *The Critical 14 Years of Your Professional Life*, the publisher recommended that I delete two chapters, substitute two new chapters, and rewrite several chapters. The publisher was right. The changes made the book easier to read and therefore more marketable.

The point about criticism is not to take it personally. If you disagree strongly with the agent or the publisher about revisions, you should choose another agent or publisher.

Creative Marketing

Many new authors think they will get on talk shows and be able to promote their book via television and radio. It's a good strategy to send a copy of the book, with a personalized letter, to members of the media. Explain why their audiences would be interested in your book. You can also send a series of press releases to selective media.

However, don't put all your eggs in that one basket. You have to be more creative about getting your book noticed. One way to get attention is to send the book to opinion leaders. If they find the book useful, they will recommend it to others and maybe even order copies for their organization. If your book deals with careers, you can send a copy to professionals who oversee career development, from the placement director at universities to the development experts at corporations.

This kind of distribution costs money, but I've found it to be a worthwhile investment. If you have connections at associations such as the chamber of commerce, try to get them to invite you to speak about your book. In addition, you can write op-eds or other short articles with a viewpoint for local and national papers. In the piece, or at the end where the author is identified, you will be able to mention your book. I submitted an op-ed to one newspaper that was picked up by a syndicate with three hundred newspaper subscribers. About one hundred of those papers published my op-ed.

The Book Business—Self-Publishing

Self-publishing used to be primarily restricted to vanity books. Those books are of little interest to the general public. But with the consolidation in the publishing industry and the proliferation of publishing technology, more authors are opting to publish their books themselves. Some publishing experts predict that in the next decade about half of all books published will be self-published or published by small presses. Not surprisingly, the Internet contains a significant amount of information about self-publishing. If you use one of the search engines, for example, you could turn up <http://www.megasuccess.com/pubmp.html>—Melvin Powers's discussion of his book *How to Self-Publish Your Book and Have the Fun and Excitement of Being a Best-Selling Author*. Powers self-published *How to Get Rich in Mail Order* and claimed to have made two million dollars from the venture. You can order *How to Self-Publish* with your credit card online or by calling (512) 719-3595.

Why Self-Publish?

Preparing a book proposal, submitting it to fourteen or fifteen agents, and then receiving rejections can be a heartbreaking experience. I've seen proposals with definite commercial possibilities that were never picked up by an agent or publisher. Self-publishing gives you more control over the fate of your book. By approaching a few printers, looking over their work, and then getting price quotes from them, you can at least guarantee that your book will be published. That represents an investment on your part, but you bypass all the costs of having an agent and all the costs at the publishing house. By the time a big publisher prints and distributes your book, you may make only 5 to 10 percent per book. By self-publishing you can have a bigger share of the profits—at least potentially.

But self-publishing doesn't mean you can't get into bookstores. Melvin Powers's book explains how to copyright your book, secure a Library of Congress Catalog Number, and obtain an International Standard Book Number (ISBN)—all of which are necessary if you want to have your book in Borders or Barnes & Noble.

How to Self-publish

Self-publishing isn't a whole lot different from the process of approaching an agent. Before you write a word of your book, you want to test out your idea. Are people interested in yet one more diet book? You can find that out by talking with friends, holding rudimentary focus groups, conducting a survey on the phone, and placing an ad in the paper asking people to contact you about how they feel about dieting. This market research, no matter how crudely done, is imperative.

If there's interest in your idea, you can go ahead and think about how you will write the book. Go to the bookstore or library. Find books that can serve as models for yours. Analyze how the author has organized the material, worked in the research, conducted the interviews, and written the ending. Such a model will keep your book on track.

In writing your book, don't aim for the perfect beginning, the perfect chapter, or the perfect ending in the first draft. In a first draft you are trying out different approaches; you may keep some and discard others. Be willing to keep revising. In my experience books evolve; they don't just spring to life. Have other people read the chapters. Does the material hold their interest? Is your message clear? Are they getting something special out of reading your book?

While you're still working on the book, start thinking seriously about strategies for distribution and marketing. You might have to take an elementary marketing course in a local college or marketing institute. Monitor the print and electronic media. See how other authors are marketing their books. It might be smart to set up a homepage on the Internet. Talk up your books with people who can help you through word of mouth.

Now shop around for a printer. You might need to get help from someone who knows something about the graphic arts. Print, just like architecture, is a specialty. Very few of us really understand it. I would never go to a printer without an expert in graphic arts.

When the book is done, pull out all stops. Probably no marketing idea is too crazy. One psychologist loaded his van full of his self-published books and headed west. He stopped along the way at just about every radio station; frequently, they were willing to interview him. Word of mouth soon created demand for the book, and the bookstores began ordering it.

Reevaluate your marketing plan on a weekly basis. Do more of what works, and stop doing what is getting only mediocre results. And don't worry about racking up big sales early in the process. Some books are sleepers and take time to catch on. Many self-published books have a long shelf life. And time is on your side.

Articles

Publications—from *The Harvard Business Review* to *The Public Relations Quarterly*—take articles from people like you and me. This increases our name recognition, enhances our credibility about the topic, gives us reprints of the article to distribute to just about anyone we want to influence, and encourages other editors to invite us to write for their publications. Because articles take time and might involve rewrite hell, many ambitious people don't take advantage of this opportunity. That's a big mistake. One article can be a significant career boost, such as the piece by Harvard Business School's Ted Levitt on globalization in *The Harvard Business Review*. One relatively unknown woman published an article in *The Public Relations Quarterly* on how to promote onself. She heard from the heavies in the field and received not only recognition but business. After that she regularly published in *The Speechwriter's Newsletter* and received more business. An article in a magazine or newspaper under your byline can be a great marketing tool.

So, how do you get in? The first step is to analyze the publication. *The Writer's Market* contains descriptions of magazines in your field, but it's wise to contact the magazine directly and get a copy of the publication to inspect. I've sometimes found that *The Writer's Market* is a little out of date; since it was published, the publication might have changed owners and therefore its direction.

What are you looking for as you inspect the magazine? Here are some of the things that will help you decide whether what you write would be a good fit for the publication:

The tone

Is it very earnest? Is your point of view more balanced? Are you willing to adopt the publication's tone to get published?

The politics

It's much easier writing for the *New Republic* if you're a liberal than if you're a conservative. If the publication has a different political bent than you, you might not be comfortable writing for it. Does the publication present its articles as if they're the definitive word on a subject or an exploration of the question? You might not be comfortable writing a dogmatic piece.

Presentation of evidence

Does the publication argue a point the way that you argue? Or does it rely on personal experience instead of heavy-duty research?

Credentials

Are others of your rank and status published in the magazine or do you have to have a "name" to appear in it?

Format and graphics

Are the articles in the magazine written as an ongoing narrative, or are they broken up with subheads and bullet points? Do the articles have charts and graphs? If so, your article might also be expected to contain this material.

Name association

Is this a publication you want to be associated with? It might not help your career to be published in a left-wing or right-wing magazine.

After you have analyzed the magazine, you have to come up with a topic to write about. If the magazine's last issue contained an article on the balance between family and work responsibilities, maybe they won't be doing another article on that topic for several months. You want your article to be timely. And remember, articles may appear three or four months after they're accepted. Find out the magazine's protocol and deadlines. Do its editors want you to submit your idea in a query letter or as a complete manuscript? Should you call or e-mail? It's important to approach editors in the ways they specify they want to be approached. If you have a question, call the magazine. Usually an assistant editor will answer your question.

If you send a query letter, remember that like a book proposal, it is a marketing tool. Your emphasis should be on how this article will benefit the audience. The second most important point is why are *you* qualified to write this article. If you've already published several articles on career development, attach copies to your query letter. Nothing gets you published like having been published.

Should you mention your position as the vice president of marketing at Colgate-Palmolive? If you want complete freedom to publish your article as is, then you would *not* identify the organization you're associated with. You would simply be identified as "Joe Smith, vice president of marketing for a Fortune 500 company," or as "Joe Smith, who spent twenty years in marketing." However, if you want to be associated with your organization, you would be identified as "Joe Smith, vice president of marketing for Colgate-Palmolive," and you would have your copy approved by your organization before you submit it to the magazine.

The editor might ask you for revisions. Editors' suggestions are usually on target. But if you have strong objections, you can bring your article to another publication.

After the article appears, send reprints of it to just about anyone you're trying to influence. Then immediately begin to think about the next article. Now that you've been published, you'll be taken more seriously by other publications. It's easier to get published the second and the third time.

Opinion-Editorials

Not enough people take advantage of the opinion-editorial (op-ed) section of the newspaper to market themselves and their points of view. A young man in real estate came to me and asked how he could get name recognition in Stamford, Connecticut. I suggested that he write an op-ed on a timely issue, such as rent control in Manhattan and how it could affect Stamford for the *Stamford Advocate*. He would get his name in print. He would be perceived as concerned with a community issue. He might receive invitations to speak on the issue at community groups. He would probably get calls for business. And he could mail out reprints to prospective clients.

A surprising number of people read op-eds. When I had an op-ed piece on the office grapevine published in the Sunday *New York Times*, I received a barrage of phone calls and letters from people I knew and from strangers, too. People are usually attracted by the idea that someone has expressed a strong point of view in print.

The easiest way to get an op-ed published is to be timely. If re-engineering is a hot topic, then you might express your opinion about it. Better yet, if you're opposed to the popular point of view, you can write a contrary piece, which has a good chance of getting selected for publication. How about a bill coming up for a vote in Congress, or the anniversary of a popular invention?

Another strategy for getting into print is to discuss a subject that doesn't receive much coverage, such as alcoholism among those over eighty years of age. You can explain to the editor that this important subject receives little attention and that it would be a public service to print your piece.

A third common strategy for an op-ed is to take an Andy Rooney–type stance and discuss a pet peeve. One young woman got three op-eds printed in *The Wall Street Journal* by discussing how much she disliked greeting cards, man-tailored outfits on women, and discussing business at lunch in the company cafeteria.

A fourth strategy is to take on a taboo. In 1981, a young woman published an op-ed in *The New York Times* in which she brought "pet grief" out of the closet. At that time, grieving for a pet was a subject still not much discussed. A number of other papers picked up the op-ed.

A fifth strategy is to release new information. Maybe your organization has just done some research and you've found some interesting results. You might release that information as an exclusive to a certain newspaper.

Study the op-eds. Ask yourself:

- What tone is taken? Is it passionate or well reasoned?

- What kinds of evidence are used to prove a point? How

much do the op-eds rely on statistics, expert opinion, or personal experience?

- Are only experts published, or can a layperson comment on education or health care?

- About how long is the piece? Usually op-eds run seven hundred to fifteen hundred words.

- Which op-eds elicited the most reader response in terms of letters to the editor? Those are the kinds of op-eds editors like to print.

The editor might ask you to revise the op-ed. It's worth the extra work. Frequently, writers present a problem but don't offer a solution. The editor will usually ask you for some way to resolve the problem you describe. Or the editor might ask you to change the tone of your piece. One man wrote a very angry piece about student interns at his company. The editor thought the writer had made a good point, but had made it too stridently. In addition, op-eds frequently don't have enough documentation to support their point. The editor might ask you to do more research.

Sometimes op-eds cause such a stir that they can become the idea for a book. A woman in Hartford, Connecticut, published an op-ed in the *Hartford Courant* on her experience with mental illness. Many other papers picked it up, and she received letters and phone calls about what she had written. She presented the op-ed along with the letters to an agent and asked if he thought she had a book. The agent did. I often advise a client to test out an idea for a book in the form of an op-ed. Test marketing in that way saves a lot of time.

After the op-ed appears ask the newspaper for the right to reprint it. That makes for an ideal mailer to everyone—from clients to government representatives.

Letters to the Editor

The Wall Street Journal ran a short article on executive development. In response, a consultant who ran an executive-development firm in

Westport, Connecticut, wrote a letter to the editor. In his letter he shared some of his own experiences. The letter was printed and he received eleven calls, some of them inquiring about his services.

Quite a few letters to the editor in a newspaper or magazine are from consultants. They know that writing letters to the editor is a wonderful way to get free publicity. It's also a gold mine for nonprofit organizations and organizations trying to reach target audiences.

The people who are most successful at getting letters published take a proactive approach. They scan publications with the idea in mind that they want to respond to *some* issue. In their letters they bring added value, such as statistics that aren't widely known or a unique experience. They also act quickly; they write the letter right away and send it by FedEx, e-mail, or fax.

This strategy can be overdone. You don't want to be known as someone who constantly writes to the editor.

Newsletters

Today, says newsletter expert Roy Sidewitz, there are more than ten thousand newsletters. In the early nineties there were about fifteen hundred newsletters. More and more ambitious people are creating their own newsletters both for free and for a fee. The impact can be enormous. Here are some examples of how professionals are using newsletters:

- A public relations person in Pittsburgh keeps in touch with the national market by sending a free newsletter giving suggestions on how executives can improve their presentations. He also mentions recent work he has been doing around the country. His newsletter demonstrates that he has a national clientele and that his business isn't restricted to Pittsburgh.

- A dentist in Troy, Michigan, didn't want to join a group practice. One way he's been able to remain independent is by sending a free newsletter to the city's Somerset apartment complex, which houses many transients with children. His newsletter contains special sections preventing tooth problems in children.

- The Sisters of Charity, based in Greensburg, Pennsylvania, prefers to use a soft sell in its fundraising. It sends out a free quarterly newsletter informing readers of all the good works it is doing. The newsletter is effective in getting people to contribute.

- In the fields of investment advice, medicine, career development, and public relations there is a growing number of newsletters that charge a subscription fee.

One of the precursors of all this newsletter activity was *The Contest Newsletter*. In the seventies an enterprising couple kept track of all the contests and sweepstakes occurring around the country and then compiled the information in a newsletter, charging about twelve dollars a year for a subscription. The readers could probably have come across most of this information on their own, but *The Contest Newsletter* packaged it in one easy format. It had a folksy tone and contained information about the winners. The upshot? The couple became millionaires.

The career-development department of a financial institution became a profit center by issuing a subscription-fee newsletter. During the early eighties Chrysler's internal communications department became a profit center by selling ads for the company newsletter. Since the ad salespeople worked on straight commission, this became a lucrative venture.

Benefits to the Publisher and Reader

Whether a newsletter is distributed free or by paid subscription, it offers distinct benefits to both the publisher and reader. The benefits for the publisher are:

- You have complete control over tone and content. If you want to make irreverent commentary on doings in the nation's capital, that's up to you. This is your forum.

- You can address a very narrow subject, as does *The Speechwriter's Newsletter.* Your newsletter can be about Victorian houses or no-load mutual funds.

- You can enhance your image as an expert in a certain field.

- You can target the precise audiences you want. You may want to send the newsletters only to CEOs of Fortune 100 companies or to speechwriters at Fortune 500 companies.

- You can determine how often the newsletter will go out.

- You can use it as a sales tool to let new prospects know that you'll be calling them or to describe new services and products.

- You can sell advertising if you want to break even or make a profit. You can also provide the newsletter by paid subscription only.

The benefits for readers include:

- You receive specialized information that might not be readily accessible elsewhere.

- You feel like an insider or a member of a select group.

- You can easily contact the publisher to express a point of view.

- You can receive the newsletter in a timely fashion.

Getting Started

Analyze many different types of newsletters. You probably already receive some of them in the mail. For others, check with your local library. What you need to determine from studying these samples is:

- Which graphic format is right for you? How should the newsletter be laid out? You might find a model that is just right for you. Will you use desktop publishing to produce the newsletter, or will you bring it to a full-service printer?

- How many pages should your newsletter be? How often will it come out?

- How do you want to organize content? Do you want to lead with a serious article or some bit of oddball news? Should the articles consist of straight facts or contain interviews? Do you want reader participation in the form of letters to the editor or bylined articles?

- Do you want to charge a subscription fee? If so, how much? Do you want to carry advertising? Will you need a sales staff to get those ads for you?

- What will it take to produce the first issue? You might contact the publishers of the newsletters you're studying and ask them what their start-up budget was.

- Which target audiences do you want to reach? Will you need to purchase mailing lists? Add that to your other start-up costs.

- How are you letting the world know that you exist? Try to think back to when you received pitch letters in the mail asking you to subscribe to someone else's newsletter. What was most effective in those letters? What wasn't? Which kind of reply mechanism did they provide? Were you able to put the cost on your credit card, or did they require a check?

- How will you conduct ongoing marketing? Many newsletters use paid advertising to make themselves known. Some publishers take out small classified ads in the back of suitable magazines.

Keeping It Going

The best way to build reader loyalty is to include readers in the newsletter's coverage. Interview them about an issue such as rent control. Have them contribute articles. Have pictures of them. Announce milestones in their lives.

Don't change your format unless there is a good reason for doing so. Maybe readers want larger type or more case studies. These are appropriate reasons to revise what you're doing. But if you change just to provide a fresh look, you'll lose readers.

Let the media know about your newsletter. The media can use you as a source of information on a specialized topic or as fillers. You might want to put media on your regular mailing list.

Keep canvassing for new readers. Some will inevitably drop out.

Publishing on the Internet

At a conference I attended, a former reporter for *Newsday* described what it was like writing copy for the Internet. As a reporter she was used to compressing the text. But that was nothing compared to the word-chopping she was expected to do when writing for the Internet.

When putting text on the Internet, you have to continually monitor which concepts and words are absolutely necessary. As the *Newsday* reporter learned, you can't write an article for the Internet the way you write for *The New York Times*. In the *Times* there might be a catchy lead—a "teaser"—to entice the audience to go on with the story. On the Internet the approach is more direct.

For example, in starting out his article "How to Achieve Success with Your Own Money-Making Newsletter," Roy Sidewitz gets right to the point. His first sentence reads, "Writing and publishing a successful newsletter is perhaps the most competitive of all the different areas of mail order and direct marketing." If he were writing a newspaper or magazine article, he might begin with a teaser like "You can make millions of dollars."

When writing for the Internet you also have to consider simplifying the text for readers. This might mean the use of short paragraphs, bullets, and other graphic markers. Although Internet authors don't often cite precise sources for information and statistics, they do provide facts and numbers (of course, there's no guarantee those facts and numbers are accurate!). Readers expect you to have done your homework and provide them with appropriate data and statistics.

If you want to do a homepage, shop around for the best cost. The most promising vendors have come through word of mouth, so if you're considering developing an Internet site, ask colleagues for recommendations; check out the vendor's work on the Internet; and study plenty of homepages so you can figure out which format you want.

Before posting anything on the Internet, review the material. Look at how you can make the text—both graphics and language—more accessible to the reader.

Things to Remember

- Print is far from dead. Opinion leaders, government representatives, the media, and most white-collar professionals all read.

- You can enhance your image, credibility, and marketability by having your name in print.

- The book business is now purely a business.

- Self-publishing is an alternative option to the agent/publisher route.

- Bylined articles and opinion-editorials (op-eds) are frequently overlooked ways to get your name in print.

- Your letters to the editor will get noticed.

- Newsletters give you total control.

- On the Internet your text should be immediately accessible. If it isn't, simplify it.

Notes

1. Business Wire, June 25, 1997.
2. Associated Press, June 27, 1997.
3. Jeff Herman, *Insider's Guide to Book Editors, Publishers, and Literary Agents, 1996–1997* (Rocklin, California: Prima Publishing, 1996), 569–73.

Chapter 9

Positioning and Repositioning

In an overcommunicated environment, people are selective as to the information they'll accept. . . . It's a self-defense mechanism against sheer volume.

—Jack Trout, marketing expert
and author of *The New Positioning*

In 1997, Woolworth's announced that it was closing down its remaining four hundred stores. You might say that Woolworth's five-and-dime stores, once a great institution in America, died because of overcommunication, or clutter in the marketplace.

At one time Woolworth's was as much a part of Americana as Coca-Cola and Ivory Soap. But other discount establishments, such as Kmart and Wal-Mart, came on the scene, offering customers prices as low as or lower than Woolworth's, more variety, better-looking stores, and, most important, a clear identity. Woolworth's competition told the marketplace who they were and who they weren't. In essence, they "positioned" themselves. They gave shoppers a reason to think of *them* first when it came time to go shopping. Woolworth's faded identity got lost in the clutter of other stores. Woolworth's didn't have a chance.

"Positioning," write Al Ries and Jack Trout in their landmark book, *Positioning*, "is an organized system for finding a window in the mind."[1] In other words, it's a way of getting past the clutter and making an impression on the customer's mind. For decades, McDonald's was so well positioned that customers ignored advertisements for all the other restaurants.

In today's volatile global marketplace, many companies around the world have repositioned themselves, changing the way customers see them. You've probably read about the fall from grace of Volkswagen and IBM and their slow climb back.

In this chapter I discuss how you can position or reposition your company. Instead of presenting an interview on the subject, I discuss aspects of a proposal by The Dilenschneider Group to reposition an old-line company.

Positioning Is Nothing New

As a concept positioning is nothing new. More than two decades ago marketing expert Jack Trout wrote an article for *Industrial Marketing* magazine titled "Positioning Is a Game People Play in Today's Me-Too Marketplace,"[2] in which he discussed the importance of the customer's perception. He explained that how the customer sees you *is* who you are—at least in the marketplace. You may be a great company with a great product, but if the customer perceives you as a company that shouldn't be taken seriously, you'll flounder. In the early eighties, not very many customers took Xerox seriously as a computer company. But Xerox marketed the prototype to the icon approach of the Apple computer. Xerox was ignored. Folks just didn't perceive Xerox as a designer and manufacturer of computers. The computer died.

After announcing his "communications gospel according to positioning," Trout joined forces with another marketing expert, Al Ries. Together they educated people around the world about the importance of positioning. The lessons they taught sunk in. Now positioning is a widely accepted concept. Every day the business media reports on companies that are positioning or repositioning themselves.

Clutter

What is new about positioning is the increased mental clutter in our lives and in the marketplace, which makes it more difficult for companies to get across their messages. If we want to get the attention of the marketplace, we have to do a much better job of positioning.

Clutter in Our Personal Lives

There's a lot on our minds today. I'm expected to give more attention to my family than my father gave to his. I have to watch my cholesterol. I have to exercise. I have to check out what people are saying in online chat rooms. There's more competition in my field. I have to think about opening a branch office in China. That's plenty to think about. Much of the time, most of us are preoccupied.

Clutter in the Marketplace

There are many more products and services in the marketplace than there were even ten years ago. Remember when there were only two computer companies—Apple and IBM—at least in our minds? Now there are many. How am I supposed to read all the product information for all those companies' laptops before I buy one? Ivory Soap, the mainstay when I was growing up, now has lots of competition on store shelves. There's also a glut in just about every profession, from doctors and lawyers to professors and management consultants. Many of these professionals can't make a living today unless they know how to position themselves.

Commercial Clutter

This brings me to the third type of clutter, the clutter of commercial messages. Open the Yellow Pages, look at your T-shirt, drink from your coffee mug, sit on a Manhattan subway, do a search on the Internet, read your church bulletin, go to your kid's Little League game—there are tons of commercial messages, everything from advice about plastic surgery to a message that Guy's Meat Store is sponsoring the Little Leaguers. You can take in only so many of those messages before you're saturated.

All this makes it difficult for companies to communicate with customers and the other groups it needs to reach—employees, shareholders, government officials, suppliers—making positioning all the more challenging. The road to commercial failure is paved with products and services that were positioned ineptly, such as McDonald's lean burger.

Amid all this clutter it is hard simply to focus, never mind choose a product or service. After a tough day in the office, the last thing I want to do is decide between a Hoover and a Panasonic vacuum cleaner. What I want is some way to make my choices *easier*. Smart companies, through their positioning, help me make that choice. They simplify the ways customers think about their products and services. They have you thinking in headlines, such as WHEN YOU CARE ENOUGH TO SEND THE VERY BEST or JUST DO IT or WE BRING GOOD THINGS TO LIFE.

Keep It Simple

At its core, positioning is a process of simplification: Companies telescope what they do into a simple, clear message. There are thousands of different operations at Ford Motor Company, but Ford simplifies it all as QUALITY IS JOB ONE. Xerox is the document company. FedEx means reliability. Wendy's means variety in fast-food service. Disney means fun for the family.

Customers also can think of your company in terms of headlines: ARCHIE'S REPAIR—FAIR DEAL; SATURN MOTORS—NO HASSLE; L.L. BEAN—QUALITY AND RELIABILITY; STARBUCKS—GREAT COFFEE, GREAT AMBIANCE.

There is also, of course, negative positioning. A medical doctor might be known as Mack the Knife; a restaurant as the Roach Palace; a university as Playpen for Pre-adolescents. Positive or negative, positioning is powerful.

Substance

Even clear, simple messages will get noticed only once unless there is substance in the product or service to back it up. Suppose you go to the card rack for Global Greetings, whose message is "If you're just sending one card, send Global Greetings." You're excited about finding a unique card to send to someone for a birthday, but at the rack you see only me-too-type cards. You won't look for Global Greetings again.

Advertising agencies, public relations firms, and media companies have brilliantly positioned products and services only to see them die because they didn't meet consumer expectations. Coca-Cola's positioning of New Coke in 1995 is an example. Many focus groups were held to find out which kind of taste consumers wanted in a cola. The best minds in the business worked on creating, naming, and promoting New Coke, and yet New Coke failed. It wasn't what people expected from Coca-Cola. IBM's copier division also failed because it wasn't perceived to be as good a value as the competition's. Even the powerful IBM brand name couldn't make it a go. Many mediocre colleges get millions of dollars from their alumni to position the college to high-school seniors. But if the college is nothing special, enrollment remains flat.

To succeed, a product and service need both positioning and substance. Successful companies—Nabisco, American Express Financial Advisors, Nike, Hallmark—have both.

Creating Your Positioning Statement

In his book *Selling the Invisible*, advertising and marketing expert Harry Beckwith writes about the importance of positioning. He's not alone, of course. It's hard to find a book dealing with communications today that doesn't discuss positioning.

Beckwith gives step-by-step instructions on how to go about writing a positioning statement. A positioning statement indicates how you *want* to be perceived, but it doesn't in any way guarantee that you *will* be perceived that way.[3]

We'll go through Beckwith's steps. Next we'll look at how customers perceive you. After that, we'll discuss how you can bridge the gap between how you want to be perceived, and how the customer already sees you.

Who Are You?

Beckwith advises you to ask yourself these questions about your enterprise[4]:

- Who are you?

- What business are you in?

- Whom do you serve?

- What are the special needs of the people you serve?

- Who is your competition?

- What differentiates you from your competitors?

- What unique benefits do your clients or customers derive from your services?

Let's apply this grid to a company we'll call Global Public Relations.

Who are you?
Global Public Relations is a five-hundred-million dollar full-service public relations firm that exclusively serves CEOs around the world. That means it considers itself a "white-shoe," or elite, firm.

What business are you in?
The firm helps CEOs get appropriate publicity anywhere in the world.

Whom do you serve?
CEOs who want to develop or change their image in the international media.

What are the special needs of the people you serve?

The typical client has an urgent need to have a broader, more positive image in the international media.

Who is your competition?

Just about any public relations agency around the world that handles international public relations.

What differentiates you from your competitors and what unique benefits do your clients derive from your services?

Global Public Relations has long-term relationships with international media, government organizations, and opinion leaders. As a result, clients get unique access to those who can give them exposure. Results come quickly.

The positioning Global Public Relations wants is: The firm that gets results around the world for CEOs.

OK, that's how the executives of Global Public Relations see themselves. Now we'll look at how clients and prospective clients see them.

How Customers Perceive You

Sometimes all you need to do in order to find out how clients and prospects see you is to ask them. The best way to do that is in a relaxed fashion—in person, by telephone, or e-mail. Ask your staff to do this also. Find out what clients thought about a project or what prospective clients think they can expect from your agency. Don't ask too many questions, though. You'll get the most feedback by letting them ramble in a free-flowing fashion.

Ask enough people and you'll begin to hear such themes as "When the project arrives it's very good, but why does it take so long to do it?" Or, "The account executive took too much of our time. Much of the information he asked us for he could have found in databases. He should have done a literature check. Also, he just couldn't get into our rhythm. He was too slow." Or, "You were much faster than International Publicity."

I find that clients are happy to get a chance to say what's on their mind about the service. In fact, they'll perceive you more positively because you *asked* them for their feedback. It's also not a bad idea to contact a prospective client who chose to do business with another agency. Ask them why they didn't choose you. I learn a lot that way, particularly that our agency can't be all things to all people and that we'll only remain successful sticking to what we do best.

You can also get quite a bit of information indirectly. If clients and prospective clients recommend you to others, they're sending a message. If they never return, they're sending you a message. If they're uncomfortable in your presence, you might have to figure out what their body language is saying. You may be a bad fit for that particular type of client.

Another way to find out how you're perceived is to read what the media and security analysts are writing about you and analyze how you're being treated in the community and halls of government. Not that you have to accept everything you find out. But if the majority of those commenting about you say that your firm has become ruthless, you might take that under consideration. Then you have to decide if you should reposition yourself.

You can also conduct focus groups and formal surveys. These can be designed to get exactly the information you want. Suppose you're a candy company and you want to find out how you and your product are perceived compared to your three top competitors. If you're just starting out, focus groups are useful in getting information about what you *should* be doing. If you want to be the premier daycare center in Pittsburgh, you can run a focus groups for parents there. Ask them what they'd expect from such a service and how much they would be willing to pay. You might find out that what Pittsburgh needs more than a daycare center for children is a daycare center for the elderly.

The advantage of focus groups conducted correctly is that they're open ended. Participants have the opportunity to comment on things you haven't directly asked them. That's how some companies get new ideas for products or input on product features they might never have considered.

Bridging the Gap

By talking with prospective clients or holding focus groups, you may learn that you should switch gears. If, for example, you discover that there's no perceived demand for a premier daycare center in Pittsburgh for children under five years of age, you may choose to drop the premier positioning and simply offer a very good center with certain strengths, such as a low caretaker-to-child ratio. That would create a niche for you. Alternatively, you can retain your premier positioning and seek to educate the parents of Pittsburgh about the advantages of a premier center. The makers of fax machines *created* a market for their product; consumers didn't tell the industry, "Hey, we want a fax machine." Or, you can start out as a nonpremier center and plan to reposition your service slowly (positioning, like establishing a brand name, is a long-term process). Or you can start a premier daycare center in Pittsburgh for the elderly.

There are also many tools available to you that will influence the customer's perception of you or your daycare center. I discuss these later. The goal in applying such tools is to bridge the gap between how you want to be perceived and how the customer actually perceives you. That doesn't always happen. In an attempt to seem hip, McDonald's made a variety of changes to its menu, adding pizza and other items. However, the company didn't get the expected result. Instead, its clear positioning became blurred. There's a gold mine of information in analyzing companies that are well positioned, such as Starbucks, and those that have had trouble successfully repositioning themselves, such as AT&T.

Do It Right the First Time

Positioning and repositioning is a lot like quality: You should do it right the first time. You rarely get a second chance, and further changes only tend to confuse consumers. In addition to adding novel items to its menu, McDonald's tried to discount the price of its burgers. When the 55-cent burger pricing strategy didn't work, the company tried to return to its original positioning. However, by that time a lot of people in America had lost their clear idea about who McDonald's was.

PepsiCo changed its image from that of a beverage company to a beverage and restaurant company. That repositioning didn't prove to be as profitable as the company anticipated. After spinning off most of its food business, PepsiCo faced the challenge of returning to its roots in the beverage industry.

On just about every street in Manhattan there's a restaurant without any business; usually it got into that fix by changing its positioning too often. It might have started out as a vegetarian restaurant. Perhaps there wasn't enough business, so the owners added diet foods. Later they decided they were a budget family restaurant. Eventually, customers gave up trying to figure out what the restaurant was all about and ate at restaurants with clearer identities. Another example of having too many identities is the craft shop that starts selling just about anything that's cute—even though it's not a craft. Shoppers don't have a definite reason for going into that shop.

Do It on Time

Timing counts in positioning. Several years ago, CIGNA, which offered life insurance, annuities, and health insurance, positioned itself as "the company that cares." In terms of health insurance, you might assume that the company would go out of its way to provide excellent coverage for medical treatment. But when it came to life insurance and annuities, you'd be more concerned about your return on investment than whether the company cares. The caring positioning probably worked against CIGNA in the life insurance and annuities sectors; in time the company announced that it had sold those businesses. Now it *can* appropriately be in the business of caring. Had CIGNA not introduced its caring motif so early in the game, it might have been more strongly positioned while it ran multiple services.

Tools for Positioning and Repositioning

For some businesses, certain positioning and repositioning strategies are more important than others. For public companies, for example, any strategies dealing with shareholders and the financial community are extremely significant. For private companies that aren't planning to go public, these strategies would be inappropriate.

The following positioning/repositioning stategies are helpful:

Align Your Substance or Content with Your Positioning

If you're a bakery and you claim that your products are wholesome, the ingredients for those products had better conform with what's considered wholesome. If you're a computer company and you position yourself as leading edge, your product line had better reflect that. If you're CIGNA and you position yourself as caring, your healthcare insurance policies should reflect a deep commitment to excellence in patient care.

If your substance and positioning are not in sync, you'll eventually go out of business or you'll have to change your content, positioning, or both. In the late eighties, IBM didn't align the product lines it was offering with its positioning as the number one computer company in the world. Eventually, the company suffered losses in market share and earnings. Now it has repositioned itself as a leading-edge company.

Know Who You Are

A firm consisting of internationally known writers didn't recognize its position as being in the upper 10 percent of communications companies in terms of its talent, clients, and revenues. Therefore it didn't know that it should accept only prestigious assignments, such as speeches for CEOs, instead of simple newsletters and boilerplate ads. When the company's clients found out that it was doing such mundane work, they began to doubt its credibility. To solve the problem, the company agreed to take on projects only at the high end. Should it want to take on simpler projects, it would start a subsidiary under a different name.

Know Where You're Going

Did CIGNA know where it was going when it adopted its caring positioning? What kind of entity is McDonald's becoming and do its executives know? In repositioning itself after the alleged kickbacks scandal in the seventies, the former Gulf Oil knew that it wanted to become a company of integrity. That was its number one mission. So it put in place a veritable Mr. Clean as its CEO. After its brush with bankruptcy,

Chrysler wanted to convince the financial community that it was financially solvent. That became its priority mission, since only in that way could it borrow funds again at reasonable rates in the private markets.

Mission statements have become very popular because most companies recognize that they have to know where they're going. If Avis didn't recognize that it was never going to be the next Hertz, it wouldn't have been able to position itself so brilliantly as Number Two. As the underdog, Avis captured the hearts of America.

Play to the Emotions

Your positioning should appeal to the heart, not just the head or the pocketbook. As Alan Webber points out in *Fast Company* concerning the connection between great companies and their recognition, "Emotion drives most, if not all, of our decisions." He adds that the emotional connection a company makes with a consumer should transcend the product.[5]

Disney makes an emotional connection with us. We feel good in its theme parks. We feel good about bringing our family to a Disney movie. We feel that it's worth spending fifteen dollars for a replica of the Lion King. So strong is the emotional connection between Disney and consumers that when Disney departed from wholesome family entertainment, some people become outraged. Owning the TV network that aired a show starring a lesbian wasn't well received by some consumers. It wasn't the way Disney was classically positioned.

Weight Watchers, which positioned itself as the company that treats the overweight with respect, also has a powerful emotional connection with its clients. People who join the program believe in Weight Watchers and, even if they gain back the weight, they still return to the program.

Find Your Unique Place among Your Competition

It's usually a mistake to go head-to-head with the competition. If Microsoft had done that with IBM during IBM's heyday, it would have looked just like an IBM wanna-be. Instead, Microsoft cultivated a maverick positioning unlike that of IBM or Apple. It was a unique entity, and still is. Most companies that are brilliantly positioned—Intel, Nike, Philip Morris—have a unique place in the customer's mind. If a company is going through hard times, it probably means that the company has lost its unique positioning.

Take Advantage of Strong Leaders

A significant amount of the positioning at Microsoft had to do with its brilliant chairman and former CEO Bill Gates. Ever since Frank Perdue appeared on TV hawking his Perdue stuffers, companies have recognized that a charismatic or atypical CEO can be an asset in establishing an image. In the case of Lee Iacocca, Jack Welch, and Warren Buffett, the personality at the top has been used to personify a company. On the other hand, a weak leader can hurt a company's positioning. Weak leaders increasingly are being removed by boards of directors.

Target Those Whom You Want to Reach

The concept of mass marketing no longer works. To influence people now, you have to figure out which specific groups you want to reach. Then you must create a message for them. Which groups does GE need to reach to sell all the services it now provides? No doubt those target groups will be very different from those the company used to reach when it was primarily an industrial company.

Many companies now are trying to reach a younger consumer group. They're discovering that their average customer is near fifty or older and that eventually that customer is going to die. To get younger customers these companies will have to alter their positioning. Imagine a company called Global Readers whose demographics profile is getting older. Its current positioning, "Feeding of the Mind," will have to be changed to attract a younger audience.

Remember how Global Public Relations served only CEOs? However, it also needed to take into consideration all those who have influence on CEOs, from administrative assistants and spouses to top-tier executives and members of their boards of directors. Targeting is key in positioning anything.

Word-of-Mouth Promotions

Frequently, the most credible endorsements for a company, product, or service comes through word of mouth. You can start the ball rolling by educating your key constituencies—employees, retirees, suppliers, customers—as to what your positioning is and *why* it is that way. Unofficial ambassadors for the company are your best public relations representatives.

Financial Positioning

If you're a public company, you might have to separate financial positioning from the rest of your positioning efforts. Tailor your financial positioning to the groups that matter the most in the financial community. They may be institutional investors rather than individual shareholders, or a handful of money managers. Your positioning might be, "We've always met your expectations."

Your financial positioning may differ from your positioning with other constituencies. But what interests the handful of money managers may be irrelevant to your customers.

Focus on the Media That Works for You

Not all print and electronic media will reach your target groups. One of my clients wanted to be interviewed by *The New York Times*. But that interview wouldn't have been very helpful to him or to his business. He needed to be interviewed by his local New York and New England media and trade magazines. His product wasn't ready to go national; in fact, his positioning was something like, "Best Polish Sausage on the East Coast." He believed that an interview with *The New York Times* would create a national demand for his product. But this rationale was premature.

There are countless other anecdotes of companies that knocked on the wrong media doors. A Pennsylvania college that recruited primarily from Pennsylvania and Ohio was mentioned in an Associated Press story. The exposure had little impact on requests for information about the college; apparently, that media outlet didn't target parents and prospective students in Pennsylvania and Ohio. A much better source would have been the *Pittsburgh Post-Gazzette* or the *Philadelphia Inquirer.*

Companies that do best in getting appropriate media coverage are organized and helpful to the media. Before they approach the media they have figured out an angle on the story that would make it marketable. For example, instead of putting forward something general like, "We have this great new class of antidepressant called Prozac," a company might say to one outlet, "It's a modem for the human mind; the depressed and the nondepressed can connect better." To another they might try the angle, "Prozac is the antidepressant without the weight gain." They have done the work to position the story with as many outlets as possible.

The company's media relations reps would also do the type of research that would interest a media person: the facts about depression and antidepressants, famous people who suffered from depression, mental illness in general, the impact of the Americans with Disabilities Act on mental illness, and the stigma surrounding mental illness. They would give this package to the media along with a pre-approved list of other sources, such as the chief of psychiatry at a local hospital or other individuals involved with depression.

Media relations reps who have a good track record are helpful to reporters and producers in other ways. They might tip off reporters about a story at another company, or make them feel welcome to contact experts at their own company about matters not directly related to the business. (For example, a reporter might call the vice president of marketing to find out why so many organizations are sponsoring so many special events.)

Successful media relations reps are also grateful. If the reporter or producer has done a good job, they let them know. Company executives might also thank them. I know a number of CEOs who send handwritten thank-you notes to the media.

Visual Frame of Reference

Since we live in a visual society, it pays to construct a visual frame of reference. That includes everything from your annual report to your Website. Visual impact is so important to Nike that it has 350 in-house designers.[6] First think visually, then add the words. How you look will have a lot to do with how people perceive you. More and more of our projects related to positioning will be designer driven. When people think of Coca-Cola, they think about a bottle of Coca-Cola—a picture. When people think of L.L. Bean, they think in terms of a picture of the catalogue or a certain product. What picture or pictures come to mind when people think of your company?

When explaining your philosophy of business, speak in terms of visual images. For example, discuss how you're not like the characters portrayed in the movie *Wall Street*. If you want to discuss a tradition in your company that is being discontinued—even though no one likes to see it disappear—you can talk about it in terms of the final episode of a popular TV show. If you're launching a product globally, you can explain that it will become as ubiquitous as Coca-Cola's red logo. The trick is to make sure that your target audiences recognize the image.

A teacher of eighteen-to-thirty-five-year-olds was surprised that few in the group picked up her allusion to a scene in *Gone with the Wind*. You might have to test market such a reference with the appropriate age group before you use it. There's a widening gap in the common experiences of baby boomers and Generation X'ers.

Repetition

Hammer the point home and keep on hammering that same point. This seems counterintuitive to many creative people who think that they should always come up with a new theme. Wrong. Points sink in—finally—only through repetition. That's why it's a waste of money to run an ad just once. The ad must be repeated a number of times.

Ford doesn't change its positioning every year. If it did, we all wouldn't know Ford as the quality company. Through most of Lee Iacocca's tenure at Chrysler the positioning was, "We may not be the biggest, but we're the best in our class." If Woolworth's had created a positioning, such as "A bit of small-town America," and kept repeating that positioning, it could have turned a negative into an asset. That's exactly what Volkswagen did with the Beetle. (Incidentally, when VW switched from the Beetle to more upscale, prettier cars, it got into trouble.)

Hammer the point home in an integrated way. In media interviews, op-eds, brochures, phone calls, one-on-one discussions with executives, the annual report, newsletters, e-mail, speeches, videos, the Website, your point should be made directly or indirectly. In this way the theme becomes a pull force.

"Media Around the World"

The Dilenschneider Group was called in to assess a company we'll call Media Around the World and recommend how to enhance its positioning in the global marketplace. A solid, old-line company, Media Around the World produces magazines, books, videos, and compact discs. Although it's been around for three-quarters of a century and has a respected, well-known brand name, it was receiving negative comments from the media and members of the financial community. The thrust of these criticisms was:

- The company's demographics were heavily weighted to the fifty-plus age group.

- The company's diversification from magazines to other media was not very successful.

- The company relied too much on direct mail as a marketing technique. New marketing approaches, such as the Internet, did not pay off as expected.

- A broad range of constituencies, including advertisers, the media, the financial community, and other important publics, perceived the management and the products of Media Around the World as dated.

- The company's revenues were flat. Shareholders were becoming impatient.

Internally, some employees responded to these negative comments by losing their vision of Media Around the World as a great company. Confidence needed to be restored in some quarters.

As a result of these external and internal perceptions, Media Around the World recognized that, after seventy-five years, it needed to be repositioned and its brand name rejuvenated.

Our Overview of Media Around the World

Here was a great company with deep historic roots. Over the years it became as much a part of Americana and foreign cultures as Coca-Cola. Its brand name carried clout. Like Disney, it was known for its good taste and mainstream morality and was a comfortable fit with many middle-class consumers worldwide.

Now, however, the company was in transition. It was evaluating its fundamentals in order to increase efficiency and was exploring strategic alliances to diversify its product base and marketing approaches. These changes would not happen overnight. It took IBM a few years to achieve its new positioning. But management did not need to hurry. It had two advantages. One was the size of its profit base; it had the reserves to ride out the period of change. The other was its temporary insulation from shareholder impatience provided by the large block of voting stock held by the founder's family. The family was willing to give management time.

Yes, there was a perception out there that the company's management and products are dated. Although we didn't think that perception was accurate, it had to be addressed.

Positioning

The Dilenschneider Group made the following observations and recommendations:

Getting the message out

Externally and internally, Media Around the World has to get the message out that it will take time to get its house in order. There should be no expectations in the financial community or media for a rapid turnaround. If there were such an expectation and it wasn't met, there could be even more criticism from the media and financial community.

Demographics

The assumption that the fifty-plus age category was a liability proved false. At this point in history, fifty isn't "old." Today's fifty-plus group includes many baby boomers who are still working and still spending a lot of money. This is a good market to have.

In order to attract simultaneously a younger market, the magazines should provide better graphics, provocative articles, and some investigative journalism. The company also should target more international markets for its magazines. In other words, increase its market base for magazines.

Diversification

The book, video, and compact disc businesses are strong; that fact should be celebrated. About 75 percent of the company's revenues come from these categories because of the boom in the home-entertainment market. Here the company should continue its emphasis on family entertainment and add new titles to the product line. The story of this successful diversification should be told to the media and financial community.

Marketing

As for using direct mail, the company's database of one hundred million names of those who have bought its products over the years is a tremendous asset. Expertise in direct mail should continue to be used; however, it should be supplemented with other marketing approaches, from a "gee-whiz" Website to exciting special events.

Theme

Overall, the attempt to retain current customers, attract younger customers, and increase the total number of customers should be formalized as a program. That program should be given a name. This will give people inside and outside the company a focus on the customer campaign.

Efficiency

Internal restructuring should reflect a move to become more efficient. This includes cutting costs.

The overall positioning will build on the company's legacy but focus on the future. It could be labeled "The Cutting Edge—The Next 75 Years."

Strategies for Implementing Positioning

The Dilenschneider Group identified the following positioning strategies:

Balance Media Around the World's rich legacy with an attempt to convey a hipper image

Yes, the brand name Media Around the World should be retained. It's still powerful. But the company shouldn't be constrained by the policies of the past. It might start a subsidiary with a different name, much like Disney's Touchstone. In that subsidiary there could be a bolder line of products packaged for a younger age group.

Fix or divest parts of the business that continue to lose money

For the company to appear dynamic, all its businesses must be successful.

Do not solicit widespread media attention at this time

Any media that approaches the company should be handled on a case-by-case basis. From recent coverage, it appears that most of the media have a negative view of the company and its products. Media Around the World can begin to solicit media as soon as its turnaround is under way.

Focus on the future

In positioning, the focus should not be on the company per se, but on the resources of the company to shape its future for the next seventy-five years. Its major executives, who are among its key resources, should be the major spokespeople and should make themselves available to the target groups. But there's no need for them to address everyone. There are about ten thousand opinion leaders, media, advertisers, and members of the financial community who must be reached in order to significantly change the perception of the company. The company first should tell its new story to these people.

Use a looser, more conversational way of talking and writing
The language and syntax used by the company should reflect the conversational style that is now common in mainstream society. Of course, this doesn't mean imitating the patterns of Generation X. But it does mean moving away from stilted, overly formal talking and writing.

Begin a search for appropriate strategic partners
By appropriate we mean companies that have a good track record in marketing to those under forty.

The Prognosis

Media Around the World has a good chance of entering a second golden age. Its executives are flexible and upbeat. It can attract strategic partners that will help update its image and products and can broaden its marketing techniques. Making necessary internal changes, such as cost-cutting, and getting its story out to its key constituents will be key factors in the company's repositioning success.

Things to Remember

- Positioning is a necessity in an overcommunicated, cluttered world.

- To position a company, extract its essence and put it in the form of a headline.

- Do your positioning right the first time. You may not get another chance soon.

- Don't release your positioning headline prematurely.

- Companies in trouble usually have inept positioning.

- Repositioning can save an old-line company. But it takes time.

- The success of a repositioning depends a great deal on internal improvements being made. These range from cost-cutting to an intensified customer focus.

Notes

1. Al Ries and Jack Trout, *Positioning* (New York: Warner Books, 1981), 19.
2. Jack Trout, *The New Positioning* (New York: McGraw-Hill, 1966), xi.
3. Harry Beckwith, *Selling the Invisible* (New York: Warner Books, 1997), 111–14.
4. Beckwith, 113.
5. Alan M. Webber, "What Great Brands Do," *Fast Company,* August–September 1997, 100.
6. Webber, 100.

Chapter 10

Small Business Communications

In a small business, unlike a large company, you have a limited budget for product advertising. You realize very quickly that public relations is a cost-effective way to get the word out about your products. Also, public relations is more credible since third-party endorsement from the media seems more objective to readers than advertising a company pays for. Through public relations you're able to reach all key constituencies in a targeted way. Based on my experience in both large and small organizations, public relations is more important to a small company than it is, for example, to a Coca-Cola or other large companies.

—Karen Hendricks,
chairman, CEO, and president,
Baldwin Piano & Organ

Smart entrepreneurs know that public relations gives them the biggest bang for their promotional buck. Suppose the *Cleveland Plain Dealer* carries an interview with a real estate agent who specializes in finding condos for senior citizens. This could have more impact on her business than a year's worth of full-page ads in that same newspaper. Should a bank in Chicago that wants to be known as the community bank run catchy ads with that message, or should it sponsor ethnic festivals throughout the Windy City's neighborhoods? The festivals would probably make more of a lasting impression, especially if the bank served authentic ethnic dishes. When lawyers from a small law firm in New Haven, Connecticut, ran free seminars and delivered free speeches on how to protect yourself from lawsuits, they saw their business grow.

In this chapter I show how a small business can use the tools of public relations to get the right kind of attention. For a small business, public relations can't be a function off to the side; it has to be integrated into the business. An Initial Public Offering (IPO) will go more smoothly if the company has a good feel for what public relations is all about. And so will a lot else.

Why We Loved Apple Computer

In the seventies and early eighties, Apple Computer, then a small company, was a master of public relations. It brilliantly used just about every PR tool there is. These are some of them:

- It cultivated the "bad-boy," or renegade, image. Apple was no IBM, and a big part of its image was the David-and-Goliath juxtaposition. In America, we tend to root for the little guy.

- The company, as its former CEO John Sculley pointed out, had a clear vision and mission: It was going to start a revolution by mainstreaming the computer.[1]

- The company resurrected the importance of personal performance on the job. This was well timed. As foreign competition began to eat America's lunch, investors were becoming disillusioned with how traditional companies operated.

- Everyone at Apple was an ambassador for the company's message. More a cult than a typical organization, employees became spokespersons for the Apple revolution—an informal type of speaker's bureau.

• The company understood positioning and repositioning. When Sculley ousted founder Steve Jobs, Apple repositioned itself from a maverick to an established company with traditional policies and procedures.[2] (Ironically, in the nineties, Steve Jobs took the helm again, repositioned Apple a second time, and led the company to unprecedented heights.)

Small Margin of Error

Not every small company is as lucky as Apple. The most common public relations mistake in a small business is to adopt PR strategies and tactics without first asking: Will this work for us at this phase of development in my business?

Small firms have a much smaller margin of error than large firms like Colgate-Palmolive. A large firm, for example, can run a speaker's bureau, and if the bureau is not successfully influencing public opinion, can eliminate it in a few years. A small firm can't squander its resources that way; it has to figure out quickly what works and what doesn't at each point in the firm's growth.

One small business that made rapid progress on the learning curve was Baldwin Piano & Organ, maker of America's best-selling pianos. The company has five manufacturing plants and more than 1,400 employees in North America. Its chairman, CEO, and president, Karen Hendricks, had come to Baldwin in 1994 after spending her formative career years in large companies. She quickly learned that the way public relations works for a smaller organization could be very different from how it works at a multinational giant.

Interview with Karen Hendricks:
An Overview of Small Business
Communications

Karen Hendricks sits on the board of directors of A. C. Nielsen Corporation and is on the Business Trustees at the Ohio State University. Prior to joining Baldwin, she was executive vice president and general manager of the Skin Care Division at the Dial Corporation, with profit-and-loss responsibility for Dial's domestic bar and liquid soap and for their industrial products. Before Dial, Hendricks spent twenty-one years at Procter & Gamble; during her last two years there she was manager of worldwide strategic planning for its international haircare business.

RLD: How does public relations differ at, say, General Widget than at Baldwin Piano?

KH: There are two major differences. One is accountability. Usually the large organization has an internal public relations staff and an outside public relations agency. Internal staff, though it might have a lot to do, frequently functions as an intermediary to the outside agency. And if there is success or failure, it is the outside agency who gets the credit or blame. At Baldwin, yes, we have an outside agency—The Dilenschneider Group—but the buck stops with *us* inside the organization. We're the ones who are primarily accountable. In a small business you have to stay very close to what's going on in every facet of operations, including public relations.

The second difference is perceptual. When you're in a large organization there are so many layers of expertise that you tend to see the issues through some type of filter. In a smaller organization, you have a more direct grasp of the problem. There aren't as many intermediaries between you and the issue. So I'm convinced that in a small business you can see more clearly.

What's the same in large and smaller organizations is the issues. My primary responsibility in large and smaller companies was to understand all the constituencies, from news reporters to investors. I had to figure out what they wanted to know and how to get that information to them.

RLD: So far, what has been your biggest public relations challenge at Baldwin?

KH: My most formidable challenge was fighting off a takeover by a dissident shareholder. First I had to understand what I was up against and what resources I would need in order to do the best thing for the company. I tapped into the "old girls' network" and explained what I was facing. I asked if anyone had any suggestions. One woman recommended that I hire a seasoned public relations agency. The investor relations firm I was using at the time simply couldn't provide what I needed and the head of the firm even admitted to me that he was in over his head.

The firm that was recommended to me was your firm, Bob. When you and I met, you sized up the situation and advised me to move quickly. Here public relations functioned as the orchestra leader. We assembled a sort of SWAT team of legal counsel, public relations personnel, and financial experts. This multifaceted approach allowed me to deal with every aspect of the crisis—lawsuits, press, proxy fights. I began by introducing a poison pill. The poison pill was somewhat controversial. But I was able to refine and keep refining my message and get my side of the story out. What was key here was keeping the message concise and clear. I learned to measure my words.

RLD: How are you reaching your other constituencies, in addition to shareholders and the financial community?

KH: Each group of constituents has to be approached in a different way. For example, I wanted to build relationships with the artistic community—concert pianists. Well, I'm not from a music background, so I asked the head of our music area to be the liaison. That worked out fine. I also wanted to reach our four hundred dealers. Since I was an outsider, there was initial suspicion about me, but I joined music-related trade associations and people got to know me. Through all these efforts, I was able to build the image I wanted for the company. At the heart of that image was how Baldwin could add value to what customers and dealers needed.

RLD: What public relations advice would you give to someone starting a company?

KH: The first thing they need to find out is what their various constituencies know about the company and what negative or incorrect biases must be changed. You might be selling music equipment, but the public thinks you sell only compact discs. So the first priority is researching how all your constituencies perceive you. Next you have to develop a vision of what kind of company you want to create. Then comes the job of educating the publics about who you really are and what you have to offer them.

Also, you'll need a spokesperson, usually the CEO or CFO. Sometimes, though, even with training, these are not the best people to represent your company. They may not be able to present themselves well.

In addition, you have to decide on the format, tone, and content of *all* your communications vehicles, from the annual report to employee communications. There should be a central theme or a handful of themes. For example, in all employee communications you might want to talk about the core values of the company and how they influence daily operations.

RLD: In a small business, what's most important about the way the CEO communicates?

KH: In a small business, there can't be any disconnect or gap between what the CEO says and does. If CEOs say they support a balance between family and work, then they have to act accordingly. If an employee's child becomes very sick, the company has to be able to accommodate that employee's needs. When I first arrived at Baldwin I took down the values statement posted on the walls throughout the company because they were not commonly shared by employees or did not originate from the employees and management. It has taken a year to build a consensus about values just among the management team. Employees will recognize that I as the CEO and the top management team are serious about company values only when they see us "walk the walk."

Choosing Your Public Relations Tools

Few groups of people get more unsolicited advice about how to promote themselves than small-business people. In addition to being annoying, all that advice can be confusing and ultimately counterproductive. In the late eighties, a woman set up a writing service after she was downsized from a food company. Everyone advised her to start networking. Her gut told her not to network until she had a clearer idea of what services she was going to offer and at what fee. But she caved in to the pressure. She went to meetings of the International Association of Business Communicators, the Public Relations Society of America, the local chamber of commerce, rotary clubs, and women entrepreneurs. Because she wasn't focused, she didn't come across in her best light. From that disaster she has learned to trust her instincts. Not every promotional tool is a good fit for every small business at every phase of its development.

Entrepreneurs can also become confused about whether to go for quick results or build the business for the longer term. Actually, the two aren't mutually exclusive: You should be working to get immediate business *as well as* laying the groundwork for the future. I know some very bright, capable entrepreneurs who focus exclusively on one or the other. They should be doing both.

In reality, there often isn't a big difference between prospecting for short-term results and for longer-term ones. Take a direct mail campaign. You send it out and hope for immediate business. If you've managed the campaign well, you'll probably get some new business. Direct mail is a good tool because it can sit on someone's desk for months, and six months after the mailing, you just might hear from Merck or the United Way asking for your services. The speech that you deliver to the chamber of commerce on how to plan for retirement while paying for college tuition can get you immediate business as well as business two years later. A few years after I gave a speech on how to create an enduring image, an executive from a small company who had been in the audience needed help with investor relations. He remembered my name and I got the business.

Let's now look at the tools of public relations. You decide which ones are a good fit for your business right now.

Direct Mail

Direct mail has gotten a very bad rap in terms of its effectiveness as a marketing tool. As a result, some entrepreneurs aren't using this tool extensively and are therefore putting their business at a competitive disadvantage.

Direct mail can work well if you do it right. Whether or not you fail to elicit a response will depend on your database, the format and content of the mailing, your "call to action," and your follow-up.

How you target—what databases or mailing lists you use

Every entrepreneur should be building a database of names of clients and of prospects. If you do this, you may not have to buy mail lists. The names in your database should come from all over. Maybe a man came up to you after you gave a free seminar, told you how useful the information was, and handed you his card. That name should be in the database. Maybe you read in the business media about an executive who believes in change as a way to keep an organization on its toes and you fully agree with this executive's philosophy of management. That name should be in your database. You probably have plenty of satisfied customers whose names also should be in your database. You taught a course in financial accounting as an adjunct professor at New York University. Have you kept the names of your colleagues, superiors, and students? It could be lucrative to keep them posted about what you're doing. Or you might run an ad providing information about dos and don'ts when contacting the media. Anyone who requests the information from you should be listed in your database.

Also, ask people whom you contact for possible business. Everyone has a few names. Those names can pay off.

As your business or the marketplace changes, so might your target markets. Because of your success in selling real estate to the fifty-plus crowd, you might choose to specialize in services to the mature consumer. Your database would therefore reflect this new focus. You would have a mailing list of homeowners fifty or older, heads of senior citizen organizations, experts in gerontology, and those who have parents over fifty years old. A changing database is a sign of a dynamic business.

The format and content of the mailing

If you send a three-page letter in which you talk nonstop about your services and not how those services will help solve customers' problems, your direct mail will probably fail. But if you put together the right package, you could get new business, enhance relationships with current clients, and get potential clients thinking about you.

There is no one right approach to direct mail. In *Marketing Magic*, a book targeted at small business, entrepreneur Don Debelak writes that the copy for direct mail "needs to be clear and snappy, and full of word pictures."[3] That might hold true for copy from Time Warner about buying some special-edition books or for copy about workout equipment. But that isn't how I package my messages to clients. The tone and language I use are somewhat formal. And, I don't create word pictures. If you analyze the letters you receive from providers of services, I bet that the tone of most of them is old-fashioned and statesmanlike.

You'll figure out the best approach for yourself if you obtain and study your competitors' material. Each field has a certain voice, certain word choices, and certain formats. A top-tier management consulting firm will probably have a tone of self-assurance and eagerness to serve others. It will use terms like "accountability," "results," "long-term relationships with clients." The letter and envelope will be high-quality bond with or without a visual logo. There won't be any visual gimmicks, such as a thumbs-up or a thumbs-down on the envelope. The address on the envelope will look as if it had been typed separately. There probably won't be paste-on computer labels.

Suppose you're a management consultant. By analyzing the material from four or five of your competitors, you'll be able to ferret out what's effective in that category. For your first few mailings you'll stick pretty close to the formula that the established firms are using. Direct mail doesn't always have to be original or attention-getting to be effective.

But suppose you're a veterinarian and you want to remind clients that it's time to bring their pets in for an examination. Since you're dealing with the "warm and fuzzies"—people love their pets—instead of a formal communications, you might send a cute postcard.

If you're a retail establishment and you want to announce a sale, you could also send a postcard. If you deal in fashion, the graphics could make some type of fashion statement. Here, you *would* use snappy language.

Suppose you're a new car-repair shop and you want to send out a mailing to introduce yourself. You have a number of choices: You can send a packet containing a tiny car part to each household; you can point out that the parts you use are of higher quality than those of other repair shops, cost less, and are guaranteed; or you can send a folksy letter in which you talk, one human being to another, about how difficult it is to get a car repaired and explain in an earnest tone and with simple language how you can simplify the process, at no extra cost.

You'll fail in your direct mail effort if you don't concisely tell the reader who you are and don't spell out the benefit or added value to the customer.

In direct mail, a corporate writer who works primarily for senior executives might describe herself as a business writer serving senior management. She might also give other types of information about her services that would be helpful to those receiving her letter. If her clients allow her to use their names, she might say that they range from Merck and IBM to a small industrial company and a mom-and-pop deli in Manhattan. If her clients don't allow her to use their names, she can say, more generally, that they range from Fortune 100 companies to a mom-and-pop deli. What other information about herself or her services might be useful? She has to put herself in the shoes of the reader and determine what the reader wants to know about her or her services. If she thinks there's nothing else to say at this point, she leaves this part of the letter as is. However, there might be an accomplishment she is especially proud of. She might say she wrote speeches for President Clinton's 1996 re-election campaign or that she won four awards for financial writing, including the IABC Gold Quill Award.

The benefit or added value of your service should be boiled down to a simple statement such as, "We help companies remain independent" or "We help companies become more innovative." Then you would provide evidence of how you accomplish that—how you provide added value—for those companies. If these companies give permission, you can use their names; otherwise, refer to them generically as a two-billion-dollar food company or a start-up computer company.

To support your assertion that you helped companies become more innovative, you might cite such evidence as:

- By a change in the corporate culture at a billion-dollar chemical company, the company was able to increase new product introduction by 36 percent.

- Through the installation of new technology a five-hundred-million-dollar food-processing company was able to add value to 80 percent of its products, increasing profits by 23 percent.

- By implementing new financial systems, a company freed up two billion dollars for new product development.

Provide enough data to show that you have a strong track record—but not so much material that you appear insecure. In giving evidence to a sophisticated audience, less is often more.

Your "call to action"

Tell customers to call you for a free consultation. Ask them to take ten minutes to talk to you, free of charge, about their problem. Give them a fax number to request more information. Ask them to: do a literature search about your company so they can see for themselves that you're a true partner to corporate America; invite you to their office for a fifteen-minute chat about their business; read the attached article on innovation that you published in the *Harvard Business Review*. If you don't ask the customer to do something, you are letting them off the hook. The purpose of direct mail is to involve the customer in a process.

Follow-up

Follow-up takes all forms. You may say in your letter or postcard that you'll be calling them in a week; then you call, just as you said you would. You can send a letter explaining what you've recently done for clients or inviting them to read an article you just published in *American Banker*. You can send a complimentary copy of your newsletter. You also can follow up with a copy of a brochure that describes your services in more detail.

Often it takes several contacts to make an impression on a potential customer. Direct mail is a lot like advertising in that frequency can get better results. However, you have to be careful not to make a pest of yourself. If you contact the prospect by mail every few weeks, the odds are that the prospect will cease opening your mail.

Newsletters

Some people consider newsletters a form of direct mail. They may be right. However, newsletters are becoming so sophisticated and are delivering so much added value that they may belong in a different category. Some organizations have even made newsletters profit centers by charging a subscription price.

Your newsletter must fill a certain niche; you have to have expertise that few others have. If you're a small food company, your newsletter could contain recipes that show an ingenious use of spices or that give the history of spices. You could run a *Crossfire*-type column offering contrasting viewpoints about nutrition. You could also add value with a futuristic column about what eating might be like in the year 2050.

Some organizations put a price on their newsletter so that those who receive it free will think they're getting a bonus. But most people see through that strategy and are offended by the gimmick.

It's important that your newsletter be regularly scheduled. If you can't meet those deadlines, don't start a newsletter. An erratic schedule for your newsletter can hurt your image.

Special Events

As every retailer knows, marketing is theater. The great department stores such as Bloomingdale's and Macy's have been masters of special events. Just think of the vampish models parading around Bloomingdale's with a new makeup, or Macy's Thanksgiving Day Parade. No business is too small for a special event. If you don't have room at your facilities, you can always rent a room in a local hotel.

More and more of the marketing dollar is going into special events. That's because special events are "feel-good" experiences that create memorable impressions—and frequently provide opportunities for customers to take home material from the event.

You might be wondering how you could possibly sponsor a special event. Well, there are all kinds of ways. One small business, a new age bookstore, sponsored an "Evening of Witchcraft." There were motifs from witchlore, and witches were on hand to give readings or tell people about their lives and futures. A lot of books were sold that evening.

Customers who ordinarily wouldn't have entered a new age bookstore left with a good introduction to this philosophy.

One discount women's clothing store hosted a "Petite Sunday." It stocked more than the usual amount of petite sizes. It hired a stylist on hand to help short women look their best. It mounted a photo essay, "Petite Women in History," on the wall. And, of course, it served low-calorie food.

The key to a well-received special event is a good idea that is well executed. A subsidiary of a medium-size company that produced a low-calorie cooking spray sponsored a special event at a spa. Chefs from famous restaurants cooked gourmet recipes using the spray. Participants ranged from nutrition experts to food editors. Invitations in the form of small shopping bags full of gourmet foods were sent out. The speakers were experts whose names were well known. A series of press releases was issued to maximize coverage. Names of the participants were put in a database. Judging by the media coverage, the event was a success. It was a good idea, well executed.

If your event is imaginative or serves a good purpose, such as raising money for a cause, you are likely to receive good press pickup. Think up different angles for different press releases. If you want TV coverage, schedule activities that will make for good visuals.

Media Relations

You can also use media relations to get attention for your company and its products and services. You can issue press releases; call press conferences; tell the business editor of the local paper that there's no longer a "season" in real estate, and explain why the public and business community might be interested in a story on this. The editor might bite, and your real estate firm might be prominently featured in that article. You can also write articles, op-eds, and letters to the editor for newspapers and magazines. You can make pitch calls to producers of talk shows on radio and TV, telling them why you'd make a good guest.

If you want the media to pick up on what you have to say, be prepared to present your story in an attractive package. That package should contain a good idea; an explanation of why readers or viewers would be interested; background material on the subject; the names and phone numbers of other sources to interview; and any relevant visuals. Media coverage, when it is positive, is free advertising. Use it.

Seminars

If you read the community calendar in the local newspaper or the listing of events for the week in the business section, you'll see a variety of free seminars that are open to the public. Among the organizations offering these seminars are financial services firms, arbitration companies, real estate agencies, and cosmetics manufacturers. Usually the topic is sufficiently interesting to attract a crowd; some companies will sponsor drawings for TV or provide small free gifts to ensure that enough people show up.

Usually some immediate business and more names for the database can be gained from holding such a seminar. The people attending these seminars expect that there will be some type of sales pitch. They're probably already thinking about doing business with the firm and are going to the seminar to get a better feel for what the company is all about.

Club Membership

If you're a pizza company, you might want to start a "With or Without Club" (the name refers to the fact that pizza can be enjoyed with or without toppings). Patrons of your store can join the club free of charge. They will receive a membership card and a punch card to record each purchase. For every five pizzas purchased, club members get a free pizza, with or without. Their names are put in the database and they receive free newsletters describing ingenious ways to eat cold pizza and strategies to cut fat and calories.

Many dining establishments have clubs for regular customers. The membership benefits include better seating, discounts on food, and novelties to take home, such as a sample of a new dish. Club membership gives people a feeling of belonging, of being on the inside, of getting special consideration. More and more marketers are using club membership to develop loyalty among younger users of their services and products. As the old American Express commercial put it so well, "Membership has its privileges."

Community Service

Look around your city, town, or suburb. No matter where you live or work, there are probably plenty of small-business people who volunteer for community work. Public service has always been an excellent way to establish a presence in the community. The trick is to find an activity that you really care about and will stick with over the long term. It might be improving care for dogs at the pound or raising money for the local hospital. Unless you want to be controversial, choose a "safe" activity. If your name is frequently in the local press for supporting a shelter for the homeless in a posh neighborhood, that attention will distract from the product or service you're offering.

Some people are shy about receiving public recognition for what they've accomplished in the community. Big mistake. Public ceremonies honoring you give your business a much higher profile and are opportunities to network from a position of strength.

To get started you can call the volunteer office of a local organization, or—if you have a special skill, such as marketing or financial expertise—contact the appropriate person at the organization and explain what you have to offer. Often it's wise to apply directly to the department concerned; if you're a marketer, you would contact the organization's marketing staff rather than the executive director or the president. By introducing yourself to the organization by way of a department you run a lesser chance of ruffling any feathers. Many volunteers get purged from an organization because they went over someone's head or took on too much responsibility without proper approval.

Name Change

Small businesses change. Often the easiest way to signal that change is simply to change the name of the organization. A public relations person who broadened her services from just writing to media relations changed the name of her business from Miller's Writing Services to Miller's Communications.

As Roberta Maynard points out, any name change has to be carefully planned and executed. Maynard recommends analyzing your identity and determining whether a name change will do more harm than good for your business. She suggests you talk to others who have changed their company name and explore legal issues, such as conducting a trademark check on the name.[4]

In dealing with clients who are considering a name change, I impress on them that they had better do it right the first time. A company can't keep changing its name; that's lethal for its identity in the marketplace. My test about name changes is the "rule of benefit": Will a name change help your business more than it will hurt it? Sometimes it's worth the investment to consult a name-change expert. Your local public relations can give you referrals.

Things to Remember

- Public relations is a cost-effective, credible way to get attention for your business.

- Handling public relations for a small business can be different than for a large business.

- Not every public relations tool is a good fit for every small business.

- You can pursue "quick hits" and longer-term forms of business simultaneously.

- Direct mail can still be effective if you know what you're doing.

- Special events, media relations, and seminars are ways to get attention for your business and build up your database.

- People love to belong to clubs.

- Volunteering usually pays off for small business if you don't put anyone's nose out of joint.

- Don't change the name of your business without giving it plenty of thought.

Notes

1. John Sculley, *Odyssey* (New York: Harper & Row, 1987).
2. Sculley, passim.
3. Don Debelak, *Marketing Magic* (Holbrook, Massachusetts: Adams Media Corp., 1994).
4. Roberta Maynard, "Should You Change Your Company's Name?" *Nation's Business,* April 1997, 13.

Chapter 11

Keeping
Communications Young

"So magical, so modern, so adventurous. So hip, so new. So de la Renta," said Jane O'Connor, director general worldwide of Oscar de la Renta Parfums.[1]

—Louise Farr,
Women's Wear Daily

There are all sorts of code words for "young." They include: magical, modern, adventurous, hip, new, contemporary, edgy, fun, innovative. All of them mean one thing: marketability.

What's youthful is perceived as saleable. You might be pitching cars, a message to employees, or an idea for a sitcom. No matter what it is, you'll probably receive a better reception—and make that sale faster—if your approach is youthful. Imagine trying to pitch an idea at a meeting by referring to it as old or mature. No way. As members of Generation X would say, "Not cool." As a nation we're all trying—or ought to be trying—to think, act, and look more youthful. (In a study by Combe Inc. cited in *Business Week,* many people rate individuals with gray in their hair as "less energetic, less capable, and even less broad-minded."[2])

Every week in my office in Manhattan I receive numerous calls from CEOs, marketing executives, and public relations vice presidents seeking to update their communications. Here are some of their concerns:

- "Our annual report wins awards, but we come across as a company that is a little too comfortable."

- "Our employees don't believe a word we say. What have we been doing wrong?"

- From the CEO: "During the last speech I gave on our environmental policy, I saw a sea of bored faces in front of me."

- "The president of our subsidiary did what we thought was a great video on contributing to the United Way. But we didn't raise as much as last year—when the president was out sick and didn't even address this issue."

- "From the new enrollments, it looks like nobody bothered to read our brochure on therapy for eating disorders. Yet we have one of the most advanced therapeutic programs in the world."

- "I don't know what kind of message we're giving off, but we're not attracting MBAs from the top schools."

In this chapter, I show how to make communications more youthful and therefore more effective. Youth counts not because of youth itself but from the perception in the marketplace that youth is a good thing. Coca-Cola, one of the most successful companies in the world, has some of the most youthful communications.

Taking Your Cue from the Media

To learn how to get your communications ahead of the curve, work in a public relations agency for a few years, get a master's degree in communications from a top school, or make it a habit to study media produced by the powers-that-be—such as Ted Turner—and those produced by organizations trying to put across a point of view. If you analyze what's going on in media, you will get a handle on which modes of communication are effective and which seem to belong to your parents' generation. As media expert Karen Ritchie points out, young people are 100 percent media savvy. Many of them who were "latchkey kids" spent hours home alone watching TV. During that time, they learned to analyze everything, from the formula of a sitcom to the assumptions made in advertising.[3] The values, sense of time, sense of humor, and marketing preferences of today's youth have been shaped largely by the media. I would even go so far as to say that "young" is synonymous with "media." In one of his poems, William Butler Yeats observed that you can't separate the dancer from the dance. Likewise, you can't separate what's youthful from what's cutting-edge media.

Anyone who truly understands how the media works has a youthful mind-set. Disney's CEO Michael Eisner is past fifty years of age, but he has unique insights about how media operates. No one would call Eisner old, over the hill, or long in the tooth. The late Princess Diana instinctively understood media. And though she was moving toward forty years of age at the time of her death, she was perceived as young. On the other hand, I'm convinced that the British royal family did not understand the media when Princess Diana died. Otherwise they would have responded to the nation's grief immediately and in an appropriate way. Inept communications will label you out of touch faster than any outdated policies or actions.

Not Brain Surgery

You don't have to be a genius to understand media. There aren't a lot of geniuses around, yet plenty of people are conducting their communications effectively. Today's successful communicators—Bill Gates, Elizabeth Dole, Tina Brown—all have one thing in common: They have the media down cold.

What's Going on Here and Why?

When he was only nine, the late TV mover and shaker Brandon Tartikoff analyzed TV shows such as *Dennis the Menace* and figured out what was working, what wasn't, and why. His English professor at

Yale, the novelist Robert Penn Warren, advised him to enter the television industry. By the time Tartikoff was thirty-one, he was chief of NBC's entertainment division.[4] The late sixties radical Jerry Rubin, who helped change cultural values, understood how the media influences perception. It was Rubin who got credit for the concept "street theater"—doing whatever it took to get the media's attention. The actress Mia Farrow, who's from a media family, knew exactly which moves to make to discredit her former lover, Woody Allen.

If you know how the *Tonight* show differs from the *Late Show with David Letterman* and how those differences affect each show's target audiences, you have a good fix on communications. Do you understand why *Mary Tyler Moore Show* sitcoms are still popular today or what makes CNN's *Moneyline* work so well?

Whether we're a lawyer going into court, a medical doctor lobbying in Washington against mandatory restrictions on postoperative hospital stays, or a CEO requesting patience from the board of directors, the media gives us our marching orders for how we communicate. Johnnie Cochran helped in the successful defense of O. J. Simpson because he knew how to make a pitch in front of the cameras. And though he was an older man, his arguments seemed to come from a young, idealistic person. Cochran certainly recognized the advantages of sounding youthful.

Not Always Hip

When I was starting out in public relations in the sixties, the communications we turned out were not very hip. Oh, those folks in advertising could be iconoclasts (remember "A little dab'll do ya"?), but in public relations we were the guardians of so-called good taste. The image we usually tried to communicate for our clients was one of credibility. The texture and shade of the paper, the tone, the graphics, the words—they all reinforced the idea that an organization was a good citizen and should be trusted. We called that kind of approach to communications "statesmanlike."

Then there was a convergence of forces. Technology made the media ubiquitous. It sped up our sense of time. Fax machines sped up our ability to complete projects in a few hours rather than days. A global marketplace changed all the rules of business and volatility was the new norm. Ralph Nader started the consumer movement. Buyers wanted more from corporations than just a trustworthy image; they wanted a responsive human being there when they had a problem.

All these forces came together at Chrysler when Lee Iacocca was at the helm, and at Apple when Steve Jobs was first riding high. Communications became hip. It became the personalized statement—the trademark—of an organization. GE sounded different from GM, and GM sounded different from Ford. CEOs were expected to be as polished and cool as TV anchors. This led to the so-called CEO cult of personality. As media consultant Jack Hilton points out, most CEOs now understand that their major role is to be seen and heard—not just function as competent business people.[5]

The effect of all these changes was felt throughout the organizational world. Once-staid IBM instructed its corporate newsletter writers to follow the model of *USA Today* instead of its old model—what I call banker's prose. Now the stories were simplified, short, and graphics driven. Employees in corporate America watched President Clinton on TV conducting town meetings; soon management was conducting town meetings—in person—instead of sending around a video. Annual reports became entertaining. It was no longer OK just to provide the necessary information.

During this time of transition from statesmanlike to communications-as-real, the appearance of things became very important. Media—images and perceptions—now shaped our opinion of our leaders. Ronald Reagan and Bill Clinton are classic examples of this.

Thanks to the media, our perceptions of communications are also a moving target. You have to be up on the media to be up on communications. If you've never watched *Oprah*, listened to Imus or Howard Stern, watched the news on CNN, read *USA Today*, watched a video at home, or surfed the Internet, you're at a great disadvantage in communications.

Not a Spectator Sport

Understanding the media doesn't just mean consuming it. We have to analyze, analyze, analyze. What kind of ongoing changes is *The New*

York Times making to become more accessible to readers? These changes will influence everything, from our sentence structure in formal communications to what kinds of leads we use in our newsletters. Why is CNN's *Burden of Proof* so popular? Hey, even people who are not fascinated with legal issues watch it regularly.

If a certain form of communications is extremely popular with the target markets we're interested in reaching, it's up to us to analyze why and use that analysis to conceptualize, write, design, and promote our own communications. Here are some of the features of *Burden of Proof* that influence its audience and that can be applied to our own efforts:

Timeliness

Because it carries late-breaking news, it brings predictability to people's lives. If there are new findings in a highly publicized, ongoing murder investigation, you know that this will be discussed on the program. The show's fans will be anxious to see how *Burden of Proof* handles the findings. Shouldn't a seminar we sponsor on child abuse be just as timely? If on the day of the seminar, a major article on child abuse comes out in *The New England Journal of Medicine*, we know it should be discussed at the seminar. Timing is everything; the power of media has forced us to be up to the minute.

Diverse points of view

This makes the discussion lively. There are two moderators on *Burden of Proof*, one male and one female, and often they disagree on issues. Experts are brought in whose opinions also differ. At our special events, we should have that same diversity; maybe we, too, should have two moderators.

A high level of expertise

This gives viewers assurance that they're getting a top-quality legal consultation. You always want those who participate in your own panels to be top-tier. If you can't attract brand names, don't have the event.

A fast pace

Unlike the legal system itself, *Burden of Proof* moves at a gallop. Viewers don't get bored. You might want to review the speeches and visuals for your own child-abuse seminar ahead of time to remove slow-moving passages and redundancies.

The Formula

As a culture, we pride ourselves on being creative. But beneath every creative success is a formula. Those who excel in our business know how to work with that formula. They add to it, detract from it, bend the rules. In studying the media, we have to ferret out the formula and learn how the media works with it. Then we apply these lessons to our own communications.

How, for example, did the creators of *All in the Family* add depth to the stereotype of the naive, passive housewife as personified by Edith Bunker? It was those variations on a theme that made her character so memorable. How did Archie and Edith influence communications in business back in the early seventies? What was the basic premise of the *Golden Girls* in the eighties or *NYPD Blue* in the nineties, and how did that influence business communications?

Here is an important challenge for you: How can you make the formulas used by these media useful to your business communications?

The news shows

Do the formulas of the morning and evening news programs on the same channel differ? What are they? Have they changed from, say, five years ago? Now look at newscasts on different channels. What's the formula for CNN? For ABC? What does CNN do with its formula? How can you apply this knowledge to your own presentations, newsletters, and employee videos?

For one thing, you'll make them more real. You'll probably follow CNN's formula rather than that of CBS News. For another thing, you'll distill concepts down to their simplest form and serve up information in manageable bites. GE's CEO

Jack Welch is a master of this. He reduces complex material to one sentence—as when he articulated the company's new business strategy by saying that it would be number one or number two in every field it stayed in or entered.

Crime-oriented programs

Why are crime shows so popular? What's the formula? These shows have clear, unambiguous notions of right and wrong. This makes viewers feel secure. There's suspense and an acceptable resolution at the end. How can this affect your communications? For one thing, although you might discuss various sides of an issue, you, too, should have a clear, unambiguous position about where you stand. This gives the audience something solid to relate to. They can agree or disagree with you. Cast the issue in the form of a story. We never outgrow our love for stories.

Print publications

Why do certain magazines sell while others struggle? Why is *People* a much better seller than *Mirabella*? Why is the *Globe* more popular than *Harper's*? How can *Scientific American*, which has a niche audience, stay in business? For your commute home on the train, do you choose to read *Fortune* or the *Harvard Business Review*?

Ask yourself: Why should anyone pick up and read what *I* write? What formula am I using, and how am I putting my individual stamp on it? It isn't effective just to imitate Berkshire Hathaway's annual report. You have to put your own stamp on what you communicate. There is one Berkshire Hathaway annual report. The world doesn't need a second one.

Music and talk shows

Why are music and talk shows so effective on radio and the Internet? How can this knowledge reshape how you present your material? At the next seminar you sponsor, should there be chat rooms during the breaks? Should there be more panel discussions?

Keeping Up

You can't analyze the latest media unless you know it exists, what influence it has, and how it's changing. Some of my colleagues still haven't taken the time to investigate the magazine *Wired*, music videos, or stand-up club comedy. But it really doesn't take that much time to keep up.

Today, keeping up with media is imperative. Not keeping up is like going to the workplace without your laptop.

Ask

One way of finding out what's going on in media—especially new media—is simply to ask. At Xionics Document Technologies in Burlington, Massachusetts, CEO Robert Gilkes, 58, asked Omar Green, 27, just about everything. Green is the point man for the CEO.[6]

One of the biggest askers at The Dilenschneider Group is Richard Kosmicki, who handles media for our clients. In every job Richard has had, he's attracted young people into his circle of friends. Although he's past fifty, he's a completely open system. He has absolutely no trouble soliciting and taking in new information. As a result he'll always be able to produce an interesting angle for positioning a media story. If you keep up with media, your well won't run dry.

On the way up to the office in the elevator I ask young people what they think of popular TV shows. Once we build up a rapport, they'll volunteer what they thought of the president's address or a current business disaster. They know I'm interested. Anyone can have young scouts out there sizing up what's happening in the media.

Be Hands-On

With so much to read, see, and listen to, we might have gotten into the habit of reading about new and changing media and discussing them without actually experiencing them. A man in my building reads a number of reviews of a film and vigorously debates their merits, their cultural implications, and their influence on other films, but he never sees them. Not surprisingly, he sounds foolish and out of touch. Some of my colleagues have very strong opinions about the Internet, but they've never gone online. How can they really understand how the Internet is reshaping our consciousness? A CEO confided to me that he thinks Howard Stern is destroying the moral fiber of the nation. However, he has never watched or listened to Stern. This pontificator sounds stupid. He's clueless as to why Howard Stern attracts people.

I have to admit that I have a hard time reading *Wired*, watching MTV, or tracking down information on the Internet. But I do it. I ask myself what kind of read *Wired* is and which aspects of its style and content are applicable to the communications I handle. Communications is one game you can't fake. It's experiential.

Perhaps the best way to get hands-on experience is to actually work in the media. There are plenty of low-budget operations that advertise for part-time help. As an insider you would have access to the whys and wherefores of the publication or local-access cable channel. This training is equivalent to working on the campus newspaper in college. Remember what an eye-opener that experience was? But here, of course, you have to watch out for a conflict of interest. You don't want your extracurricular activities to conflict with the interests of your day job.

You can also get on the board of a media outlet where you'll find out how economics drives strategies. I would love to be on the board of the magazine *US*. Why, for example, does one publication do investigative reporting while another sticks to pleasant stories?

Research

A talk show like *Charlie Rose* gives some brilliant insights about the role of media. Or at least they *seem* brilliant. Often, in fact, they're clichés. A little research can give us access to the best thinking about media. In a bookstore, look for Kathleen Hall Jamieson's *Packaging the Presidency* and *Eloquence in an Electronic Age*; Ian Mitroff and Warren Bennis's *The Unreality Industry*; and W. Russell Neuman's *The Future of the Mass Audience*. There are also numerous courses on all aspects of the media in all types of settings, such as YMCAs and college and university continuing education programs. Search engines on the Internet can lead you to a wealth of material. You can also conduct your own research online. For example, you could survey people over fifty about their preceptions of how the media treats them.

Becoming an Opinion Leader

It's fun to wrestle with ideas and you learn a tremendous amount. Some years ago I was convinced that the op-ed was a dying source of influence. I studied op-eds in newspapers and magazines. I asked a researcher in my office to retrieve information about trends in op-eds. I started publishing a broad variety of op-eds in all sorts of publications. Within a few months I realized that my hypothesis was wrong. The op-ed *was* thriving, partly because opinion, intuition, and personal experience are now very important. You don't have to have a Ph.D. in media to voice your opinion and be taken seriously.

Trust Your Instincts

Around 1994 a speechwriter told me that speechwriting was a dying art in business and that executives increasingly will create their talk around visuals produced by software, such as Microsoft's PowerPoint. Instead of a full-text speech, executives would want point outlines; rather than wordsmiths, speechwriters would be think tanks who would research the topics for executives and come up with fresh points of view. But this woman didn't heed her instincts. What she predicted did occur in many corporations and her workload diminished. She should have been honing her research skills and discovering the best electronic sources. She didn't, and her earnings took a hit.

Many things unfold in the media that you probably sense but can't fully articulate. Trust your instincts. Explore the topic further by engaging in conversations with colleagues, spending time in electronic chat rooms, and publishing an op-ed on the subject. Kathleen Hall Jamieson became a formidable presence in media scholarship because she trusted her instincts. She noticed many of the same things that we noticed about TV and politics, but she looked into their implications and had her say.

The Chuckles Test

When I begin thinking about how I will deliver an address I first think of the nineteen-year-old intern in our office. If I speak about the importance of excellence in today's society, I ask myself, would that intern laugh? If I sense he would, I change the direction of the communications I'm preparing.

When I'm clueless about a subject, I'll dig up an intern or another young person in the flesh and ask, "Off the record, do you think that if I wrote an article on credit-card debt for your friends in an it-could-happen-to-you tone, they would chuckle?" I call this the Chuckles Test.

Interview with Kristin Ausanka: An Overview of Keeping Communications Young

Kristin Ausanka, in her mid-twenties, is a public relations manager at the William Carter Company. She graduated from the University of Notre Dame. I asked her to let us peek into her head and heart.

RLD: We hear the word "old" a lot. What makes people seem old?

KA: The big tipoff is how they interact with others. Being old and thinking old are two different things. I know twenty-two-year-olds who think old simply because they don't want to experience new things or entertain different or unique ideas. I used to think it was inevitable that people would enter the working world and simultaneously become rigid and boring, never being able to go out and enjoy themselves in order to revitalize their spirits. What I have learned is that you control your own mind-set and actions. Seeming old has nothing to do with a person's age. It evolves from remaining too comfortable in your ways and ceasing to grow. Accept change and simply enjoy life.

RLD: How do people become stale?

KA: People become stale when they stop expanding their minds and yearning to grow. Stale people are disinterested in new technology and in general are hesitant to accept change. Because people are always changing, a good way not to become stale is to constantly be in tune with others' needs and desires. Researching your target market once a year isn't good enough anymore. It needs to be done more often because trends and technology—and thus people—are constantly changing. Thinking youthfully, wondering, reflecting, being creative, and exploring are ways to break out of the rut of stale thinking.

RLD: Suppose you were in charge of communications at Company X. What would you do to update its publications?

KA: First, I would identify the target markets and what they are interested in reading. I would use focus groups, surveys, and one-on-one interviews to get inside their heads. Generally speaking, though, I would utilize bold colors and reader-friendly layouts to attract the readers' eye. Special sections for current events and true-life stories are also appealing.

RLD: What's your take on the Internet?

KA: The Internet is a great new tool not only for businesses and advertisers but also for information seekers. I used it to prepare for job interviews by researching companies and as a source for researching college assignments. Also, one can learn a lot about various subjects by scanning the Net. If I want to find a friend's e-mail address or learn more about the pasteurization of apple juice—college term-paper research—it's all right at my fingertips.

RLD: As a young person, what do you think of the kinds of communications like the tabloids that cover celebrities?

KA: I think tabloid stories are out of control. I respect the theory that famous people put themselves in the limelight and, by being famous, have to expect pointed journalism. But I believe many have gone too far. There are no clear boundaries between public and private life anymore. Tabloids could be put out of business tomorrow if consumers stopped buying them. But we are a society consumed by celebrity watching. As long as consumers keep purchasing tabloids, they will continue to be produced.

RLD: Do you anticipate that you will get old?

KA: Physically yes, but mentally no. Old is a state of mind. There are many things in my life I have no control over, but my outlook on life is not one of them. My desire to keep experiencing new and creative things and my overall attitude will keep me exactly as young as I want to be.

I recently read a quote in the *New York Post* that immediately reminded me of this quest to remain mentally young. The quote was by Lou Holtz, former Notre Dame football coach. As you know, Holtz left Notre Dame and became a commentator for CBS Sports. When asked if he misses coaching the Fighting Irish, he said, "I miss dreaming. I miss getting a group of people to dream. That's what it's really all about. That's what keeps you young."

Great Makeovers

Xerox is one of those companies that was able to come back to life. After a big splash in the sixties, it became an out-of-touch, old-line company. It was a laggard in the marketplace. But it reinvented itself and is now the "dynamic document company." Other great makeovers occurred at IBM and Fleet Bank. John Travolta, Sean Penn, and Bob Dole have all been able to get a second wind. *Your* publications, videos, speeches, e-mail, lobbying materials, phone calls to opinion leaders, and media relations can also become more dynamic. Here are some suggestions:

Find out what people *really* think of what you're doing

You might find that when shareholders see the printed quarterly report in their mailbox, they think of your company as old-fashioned. Instead of mailing out the quarterly report, put it on the Internet and set up an 800-number to deliver highlights.

Find out what others are doing

There are plenty of good ideas out there and you can borrow most of them. In a dynamic environment, you're always borrowing from elsewhere. If you're not borrowing, you're a closed system.

If you think you're getting stale, you probably are

Hundreds of CEOs and vice presidents have expressed concern to me that they were slipping. They were. The best thing to do when you're losing touch is to stop. Have an outside vendor do that issue of the newsletter or that speech while you read Nelson DeMille novels or spend a week smelling the roses. Being stale is not an irreversible condition. The information age is an ongoing saga of comebacks.

Retire a good idea before you have to

If you're having a lot of success with an op-ed format for your annual report, try another format. Your readers will sense that you're staying ahead of the curve.

Things to Remember

- Youthfulness is a prized commodity in our civilization.

- If you understand the media, you can keep your communications hip.

- If you're avoiding the new media, you're on a suicide mission.

- Model your communications on what's effective in the media.

- We lose respect for people who let themselves get old.

- Being stale is never irreversible.

Notes

1. Louise Farr, "Oscar's New Ad: So Youth-Oriented," *Women's Wear Daily*, August 1, 1997, 5.
2. Lisa Sanders, "Get Out the Grecian Formula," *Business Week*, September 15, 1997, 8.
3. Karen Ritchie, *Marketing to Generation X* (New York: Lexington Books, 1995).
4. Thom Geier, "He Always Understood Television," *U.S. News & World Report*, September 8, 1997, 16.
5. G. Pascal Zachary, "CEOs Are Stars Now, But Why? And Would Alfred Sloan Approve?" *The Wall Street Journal*, September 3, 1997, A1.
6. Jonathan Kaufman, "How Omar Green, 27, Became the Point Man and Protégé for a CEO," *The Wall Street Journal*, July 22, 1997, A1.

Conclusion

I vividly remember Sister Mary Euphasia at Our Lady of Victory School telling our class about the explorer Ponce de León. He went in search of the fountain of youth, said Sister with a little disapproval, and instead found Florida. Sister wasn't high on Ponce because she believed that we weren't supposed to toy too much with nature. I still recall that day in class because, at eleven years of age, I was puzzled why anyone would have to go to a fountain of youth. *I* certainly didn't need it. Today, when I'm on the phone past midnight with a client emergency, I wistfully think about Mr. de Leon—and wish that he had been successful.

But the concept of Ponce de León is a public relations person's dream. There's substance there. The concept has legs. And as the baby boomers continue to age, the idea of a fountain of youth will be ever more enticing. Any shrewd marketing person can develop an almost infinite number of variations on the theme.

In this book, you've learned some strategies and tactics for getting your message across. More important, you've learned that your message must have substance. When it comes to depth, it has to be right up there with the fountain of youth. If brilliant strategies and tactics were enough to work on their own, then New Coke wouldn't have been a bust, Snapple wouldn't have fallen on hard times, and China wouldn't be having image problems.

A retired CEO consulted with me about finding work in the communications field. He was thinking of becoming a columnist, lecturer, or book author. At the time, he didn't have much to tell the world that it hadn't already heard. I advised the man to join volunteer organizations that counsel small business, thinking it would at least keep him busy. Well, it did more than that; it gave him a whole new mind-set for seeing the world. He began to look through the lens of small-business owners. All his life he had worked in large organizations and had never dreamed that any other world existed. Now he had something of substance to communicate. He chose to give motivational seminars. He's doing very well.

Most people, products, and services that seem to lack substance can be "beefed up." As a public relations person, you can expose clients to new experiences just as I did. Maybe they can teach a course on the stock market to an elementary school class, or spend a month in a developing country and analyze the changes taking place there, or work in a totally different job. And if a product or service isn't making a bang, sometimes we can find new uses for it. Kraft did this with Velveeta cheese, making the has-been consumer item into a wonderful dip for nachos. When the American Automobile Association was getting a little sleepy and irrelevant to the world, it developed new ways of serving customers. AAA now offers funeral services and nonautomobile travel.

Once you're dealing with substance, you can start applying what you've learned in this book to transmitting your message. Here they are, in no special order of importance:

- A worthy cause becomes a lot worthier when you have something to give to those who help out. The favor bank—the ability to reward those who give you their time, money, or support—is just as important to the nonprofit sector as to a for-profit business.

- It's irresponsible to go into a crisis unprepared. There now exists a whole body of knowledge and experience that will help you get ready for whatever can—and probably will—happen. Develop a crisis plan. Train your staff for the worst-case scenarios.

- Your way of communicating may seem old because you haven't aligned what you want to write or say with how the media currently operates. Your speeches, for instance, might use the style and word choice of Walter Cronkite rather than Geraldo Rivera.

- When promoting a small business, you can't get caught up in trends. If "everyone says" that direct mail doesn't work, try it anyway. Do a small mailing and study the results. As John Micklethwait and Adrian Wooldridge point out in their book *The Witch Doctors*, large organizations are easily hoodwinked by trendy ideas. Hey, they can afford to; they have deep pockets. But a small business, always short of resources, has to keep experimenting with whatever works. And that might include so-called outmoded ideas.

- Books can bring added credibility. Where would the management guru Peter Drucker be without his many books? Go into any corporation and you'll see his books on the shelves. The trick is coming up with a topic that puts you in a certain niche. For example, Martha Stewart has her niche—gracious living. Should your clients do books? Test that idea out by having them publish op-eds on the subject and see what kind of reaction they get.

- Leaks are a sign that you've made some poor management decisions. They usually happen because you've either hired the wrong people or have confided information too widely. On the other hand, if you *want* to leak to the media, you had better know what you're doing. Plan ahead—by cultivating those in the media whom you trust.

- Showmanship is power. Any retailer can tell you that. If you're communicating, find ways to be theatrical. Even Martin Luther King Jr. was theatrical: He preached but he also performed.

- Don't give employees a newsletter about your competition. Set up an experience in which they can get hands-on knowledge of the competition. When Rubbermaid held an employee fair in which their workforce got to study competitors' products, the company got the employees' attention.

- Reposition the client, product, or service you are representing *before* they actually get stale. In our youthful culture, stale is a death sentence. General Motors wouldn't have lost as much of its market share had it reinvented its lineup of cars sooner.

- Competition for capital is now worldwide. What does your company have to offer investors that an established company in France or a start-up firm in Russia doesn't? In addressing investors, security analysts, and the rest of the financial community, let them know a little about the present—and a lot about your company's future.

- Talking *always* has to be strategic. For example, the Darien, Connecticut, speech coach Granny Toogood advises employees to use wisely those ninety seconds on the elevator with the CEO. Instead of talking about last Sunday's football game, bring the CEO up to date about how the new product launch is going. Give up the pleasure of small talk—for talk that gets you where you want to go.

When I went to Ohio State for graduate work in communications, the professors impressed on us that we were going to have to acquire tools for our communications toolbox. I did get those tools. Now *you* also have them. How well you use them will depend primarily on how much courage you have in the face of uncertainty. As my colleague, presidential adviser Roger Ailes, points out in his book *You Are the Message*, "Courage isn't the absence of fear. It is action in the presence of fear."

What separates the pros from the amateurs in public relations is this: The pros are able to move ahead even though all the facts aren't in. If the client wants a press release in two hours about new eating trends, the pro will spend thirty minutes doing research and the rest of the time wrestling with the ideas and how to put them together. That's professional guts.

In the old days, I had the time to research a subject to death. I could spend days in the library and browse in the bookstores. I could call up experts to find out what they had to say. Then I could think for a few more days. Today, we have to do more with fewer resources in less time.

The sign of an amateur is the degree of complaining they do about not having enough of something—direction, time, resource, feedback from the client. There is no room for amateurs in these wild and crazy times.

Use the Chuckles Test to see if you're a pro or an amateur: Your client's CEO just resigned, one of its products is being recalled, and a road show is scheduled in two weeks. If you don't see a little bit of humor in this, you're not a pro.

Index